CAPTAIN AMERICA

THE MAN WITH NO FACE

WRITER: Ed Brubaker
PENCILER, ISSUES #43-45: Luke Ross
INKERS, ISSUES #43-45: Fabio Laguna, Rick Magyar, Mark Pennington & Butch Guice
ARTIST, ISSUE #46: Steve Epting
ARTIST, ISSUES #47-48: Butch Guice
with Luke Ross & Steve Epting
COLORIST: Frank D'Armata
LETTTERER: Virtual Calligraphy's Joe Caramagna
COVER ART: Steve Epting
ASSOCIATE EDITOR: Jeanine Schaefer
EDITOR: Tom Brevoort

Captain America created by Joe Simon & Jack Kirby

Collection Editor: Jennifer Grünwald
Editorial Assistant: Alex Starbuck
Assistant Editors: Cory Levine & John Denning
Editor, Special Projects: Mark D. Beazley
Senior Editor, Special Projects: Jeff Youngquist
Senior Vice President of Sales: David Gabriel

Editor in Chief: Joe Quesada
Publisher: Dan Buckley
Executive Producer: Alan Fine

CAPTAIN AMERICA: THE MAN WITH NO FACE. Contains material originally published in magazine form as CAPTAIN AMERICA #43-48. First printing 2009. Hardcover ISBN# 978-0-7851-3153-3. Softcover ISBN# 978-0-7851-3163-2. Published by MARVEL PUBLISHING, INC., a subsidiary of MARVEL ENTERTAINMENT, INC. OFFICE OF PUBLICATION: 417 5th Avenue, New York, NY 10016. Copyright © 2008 and 2009 Marvel Characters, Inc. All rights reserved. Hardcover: $19.99 per copy in the U.S. (GST #R127032852). Softcover: $15.99 per copy in the U.S. (GST #R127032852). Canadian Agreement #40668537. All characters featured in this issue and the distinctive names and likenesses thereof, and all related indicia are trademarks of Marvel Characters, Inc. No similarity between any of the names, characters, persons, and/or institutions in this magazine with those of any living or dead person or institution is intended, and any such similarity which may exist is purely coincidental. Printed in the U.S.A. ALAN FINE, CEO Marvel Publishing Division and EVP & CMO Marvel Characters B.V.; DAN BUCKLEY, President of Publishing - Print & Digital Media; JIM SOKOLOWSKI, Chief Operating Officer; DAVID GABRIEL, SVP of Publishing Sales & Circulation; DAVID BOGART, SVP of Business Affairs & Talent Management; MICHAEL PASCIULLO, VP Merchandising & Communications; JIM O'KEEFE, VP of Operations & Logistics; DAN CARR, Executive Director of Publishing Technology; JUSTIN F. GABRIE, Director of Publishing & Editorial Operations; SUSAN CRESPI, Editorial Operations Manager; ALEX MORALES, Publishing Operations Manager; STAN LEE, Chairman Emeritus. For information regarding advertising in Marvel Comics or on Marvel.com, please contact Mitch Dane, Advertising Director, at mdane@marvel.com. For Marvel subscription inquiries, please call 800-217-9158.

10 9 8 7 6 5 4 3 2 1

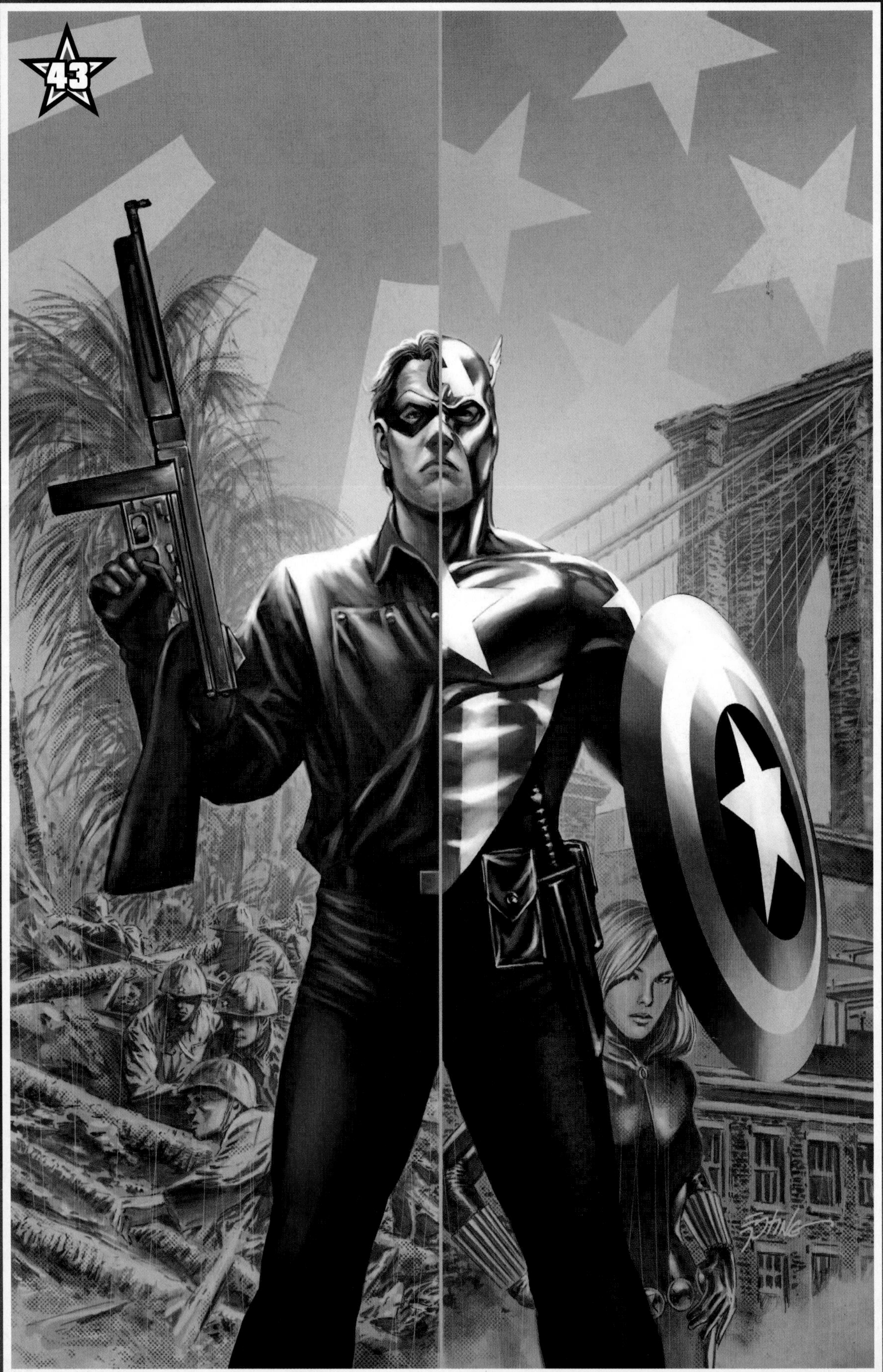
43

TIME'S ARROW PART ONE

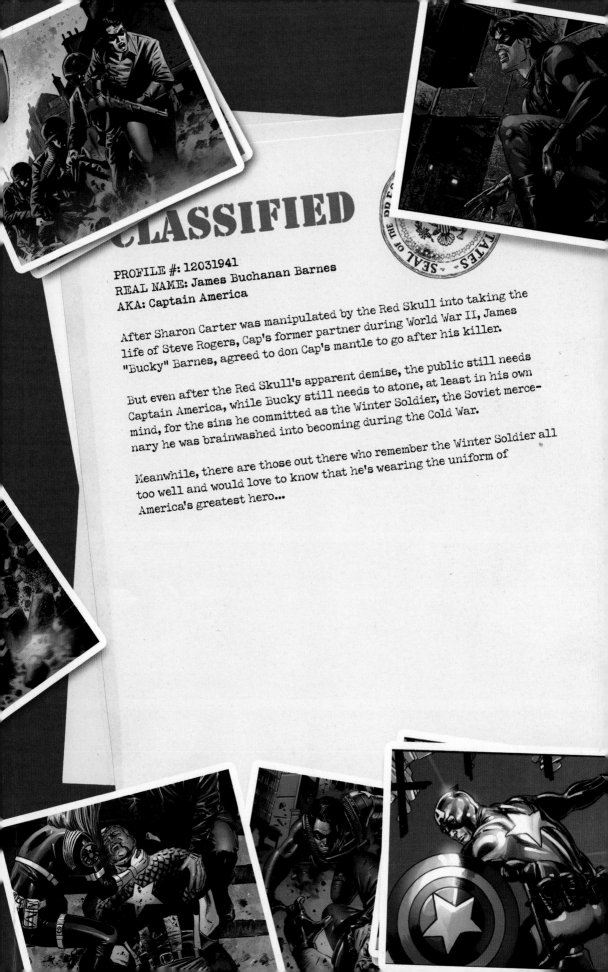

CLASSIFIED

PROFILE #: 12031941
REAL NAME: James Buchanan Barnes
AKA: Captain America

After Sharon Carter was manipulated by the Red Skull into taking the life of Steve Rogers, Cap's former partner during World War II, James "Bucky" Barnes, agreed to don Cap's mantle to go after his killer.

But even after the Red Skull's apparent demise, the public still needs Captain America, while Bucky still needs to atone, at least in his own mind, for the sins he committed as the Winter Soldier, the Soviet mercenary he was brainwashed into becoming during the Cold War.

Meanwhile, there are those out there who remember the Winter Soldier all too well and would love to know that he's wearing the uniform of America's greatest hero...

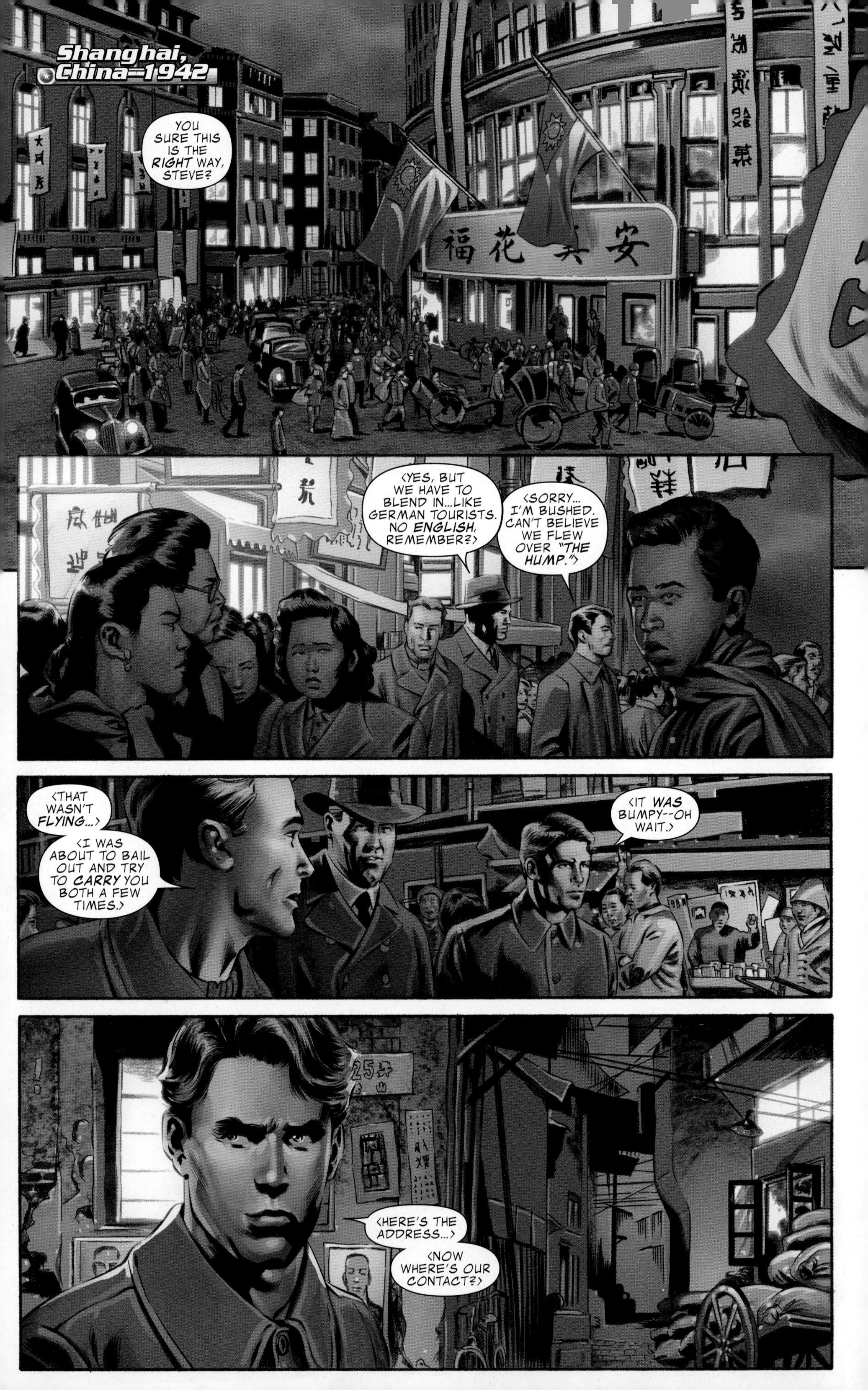

Shanghai, China–1942
YOU SURE THIS IS THE RIGHT WAY, STEVE?
‹YES, BUT WE HAVE TO BLEND IN...LIKE GERMAN TOURISTS. NO ENGLISH, REMEMBER?›
‹SORRY... I'M BUSHED. CAN'T BELIEVE WE FLEW OVER "THE HUMP."›
‹THAT WASN'T FLYING...›
‹I WAS ABOUT TO BAIL OUT AND TRY TO CARRY YOU BOTH A FEW TIMES.›
‹IT WAS BUMPY--OH WAIT.›
‹HERE'S THE ADDRESS...›
‹NOW WHERE'S OUR CONTACT?›

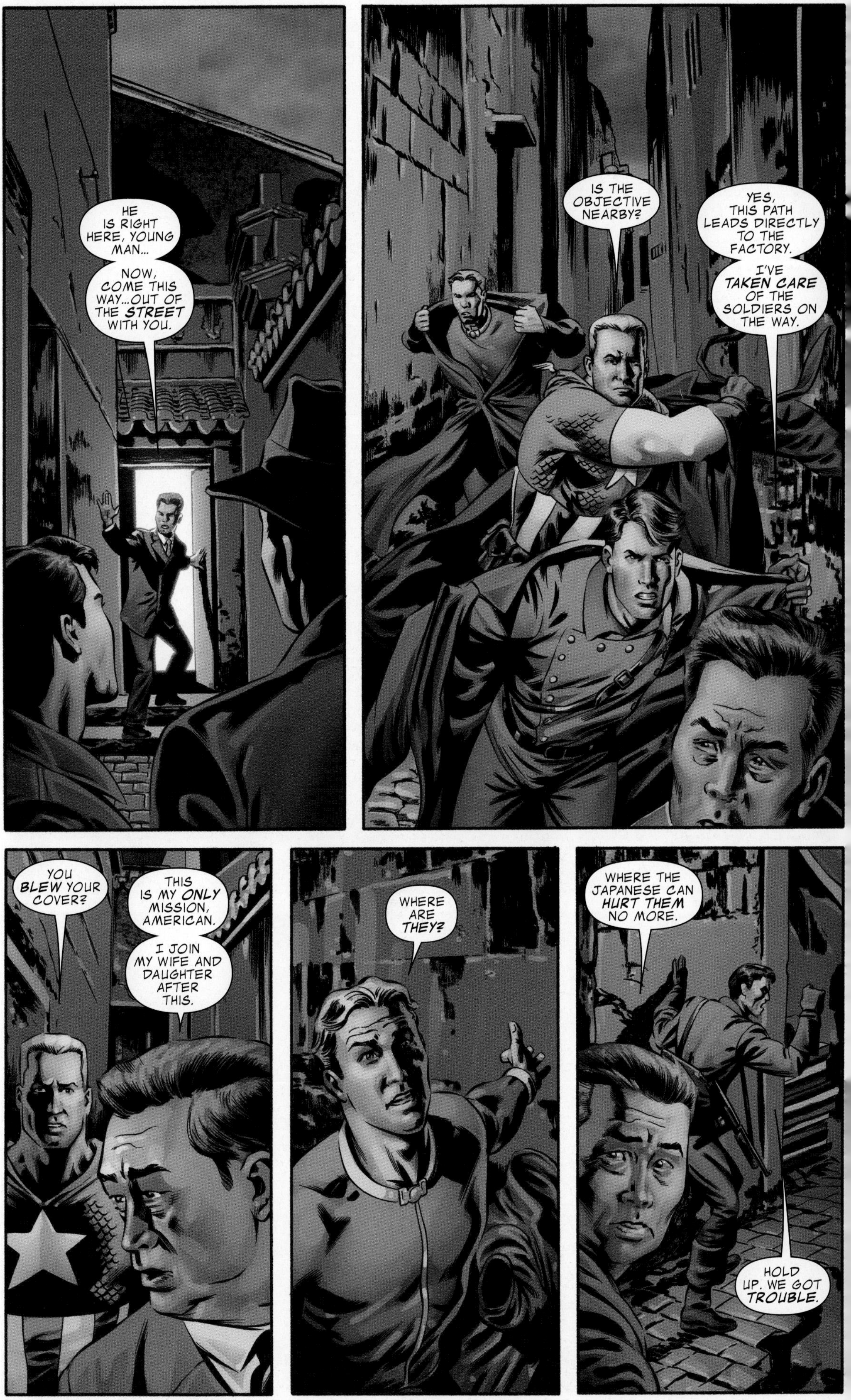
HE IS RIGHT HERE, YOUNG MAN...
NOW, COME THIS WAY...OUT OF THE STREET WITH YOU.
IS THE OBJECTIVE NEARBY?
YES, THIS PATH LEADS DIRECTLY TO THE FACTORY.
I'VE TAKEN CARE OF THE SOLDIERS ON THE WAY.
YOU BLEW YOUR COVER?
THIS IS MY ONLY MISSION, AMERICAN.
I JOIN MY WIFE AND DAUGHTER AFTER THIS.
WHERE ARE THEY?
WHERE THE JAPANESE CAN HURT THEM NO MORE.
HOLD UP. WE GOT TROUBLE.

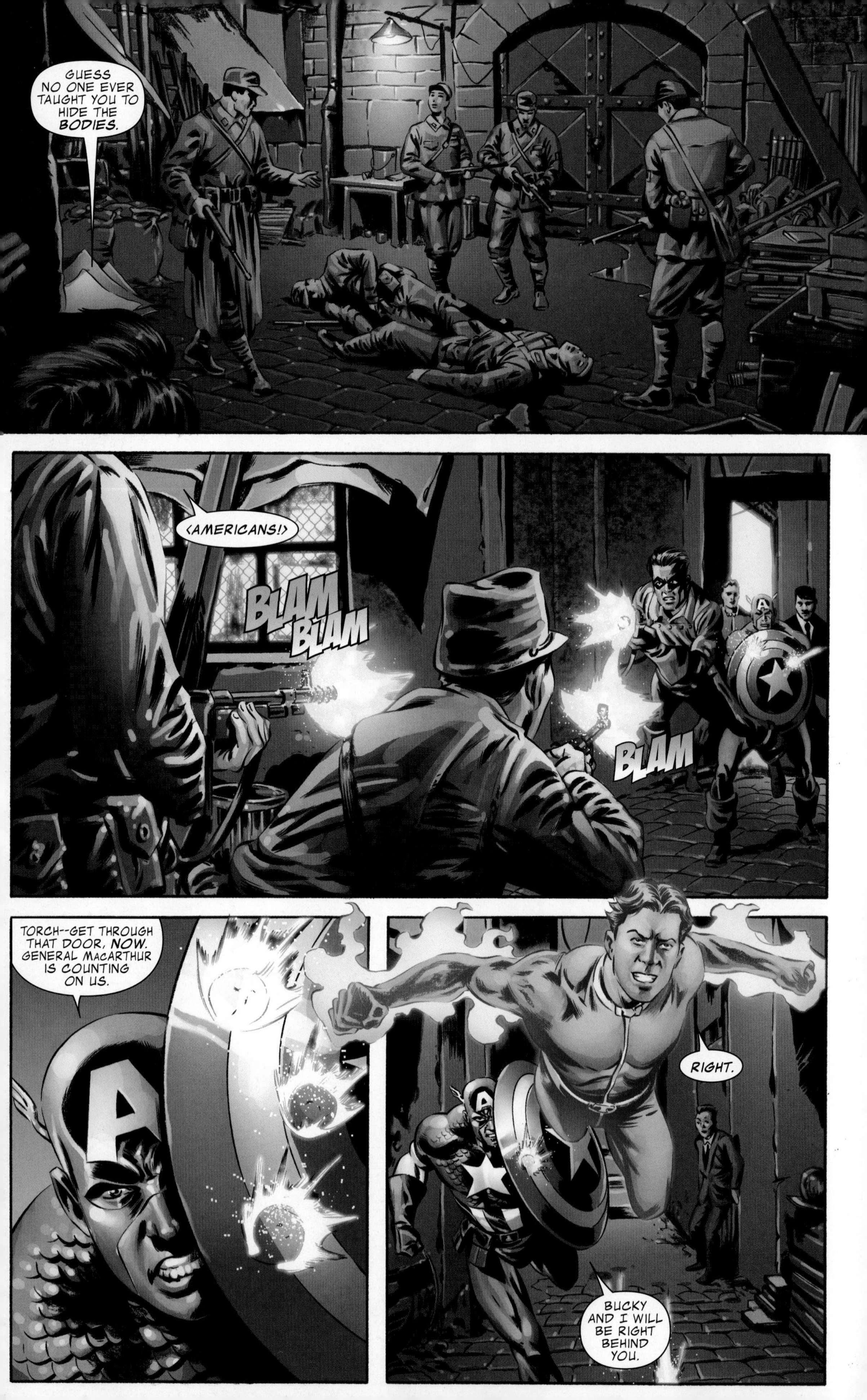
GUESS NO ONE EVER TAUGHT YOU TO HIDE THE BODIES.
<AMERICANS!>
BLAM BLAM
BLAM
TORCH--GET THROUGH THAT DOOR, NOW. GENERAL MacARTHUR IS COUNTING ON US.
RIGHT.
BUCKY AND I WILL BE RIGHT BEHIND YOU.

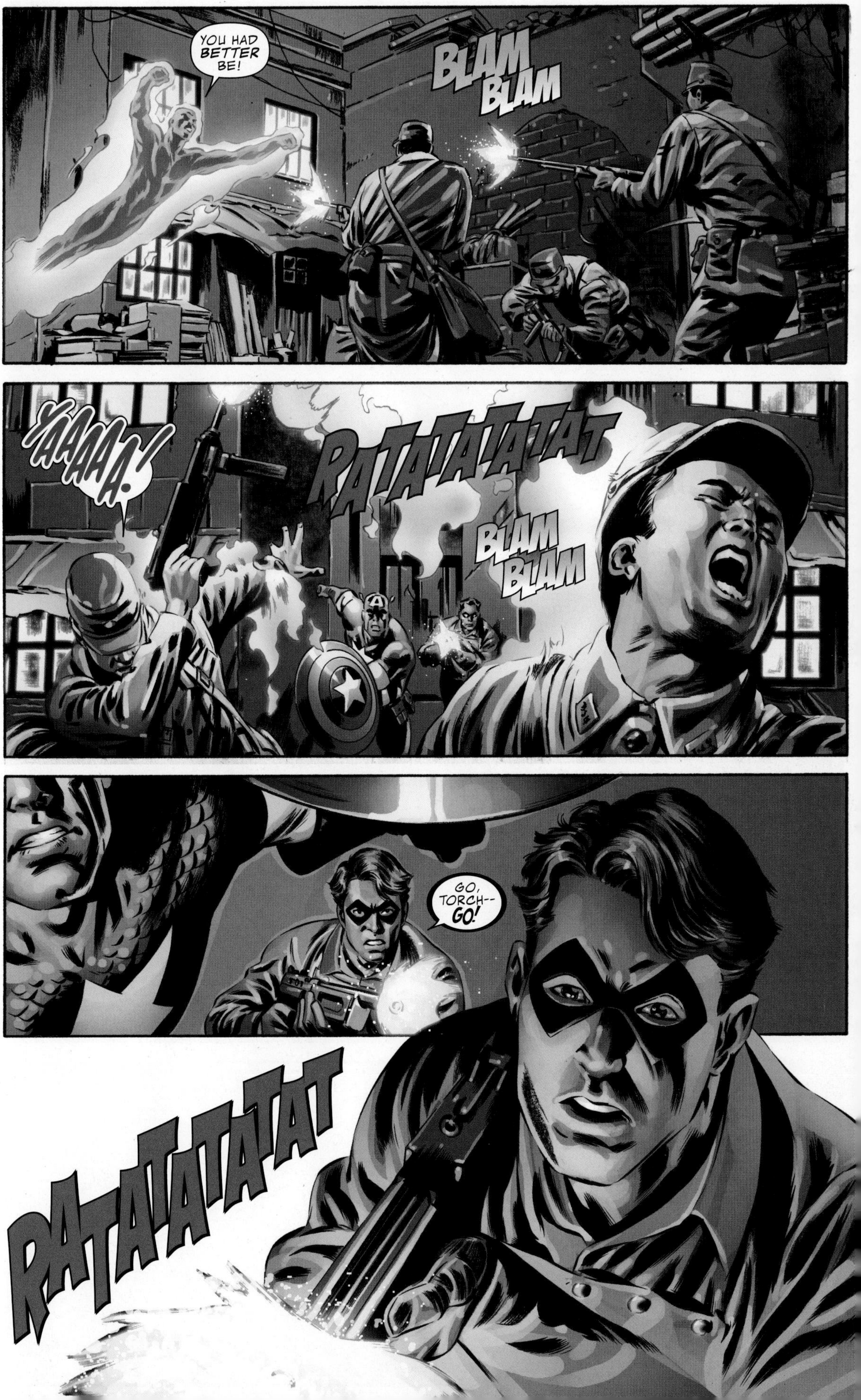
YOU HAD BETTER BE!
BLAM BLAM
YAAAAA!
RATATATATAT
BLAM BLAM
GO, TORCH-- GO!
RATATATATAT

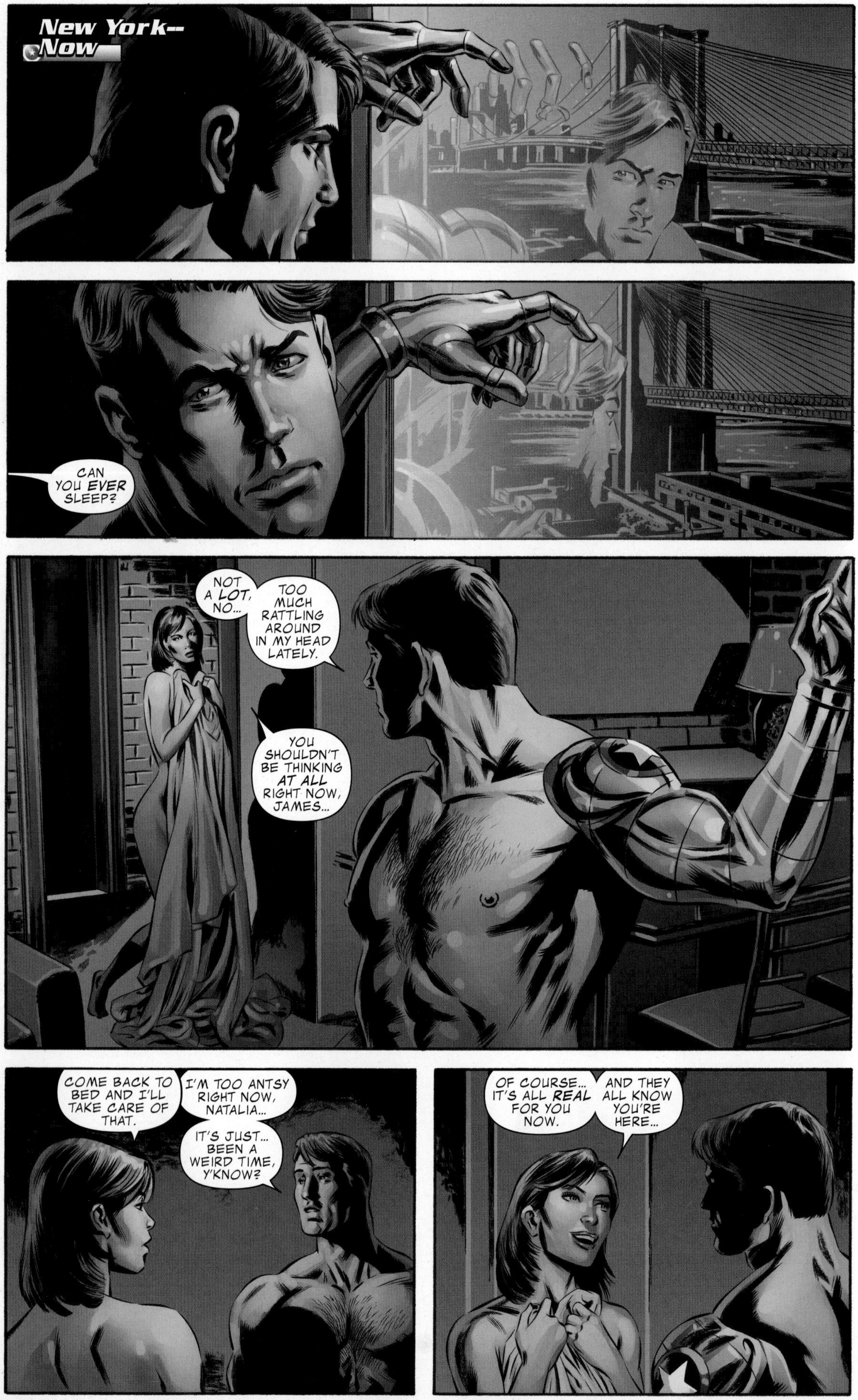
New York--
Now
CAN YOU EVER SLEEP?
NOT A LOT, NO...
TOO MUCH RATTLING AROUND IN MY HEAD LATELY.
YOU SHOULDN'T BE THINKING AT ALL RIGHT NOW, JAMES...
COME BACK TO BED AND I'LL TAKE CARE OF THAT.
I'M TOO ANTSY RIGHT NOW, NATALIA...
IT'S JUST... BEEN A WEIRD TIME, Y'KNOW?
OF COURSE... IT'S ALL REAL FOR YOU NOW.
AND THEY ALL KNOW YOU'RE HERE...

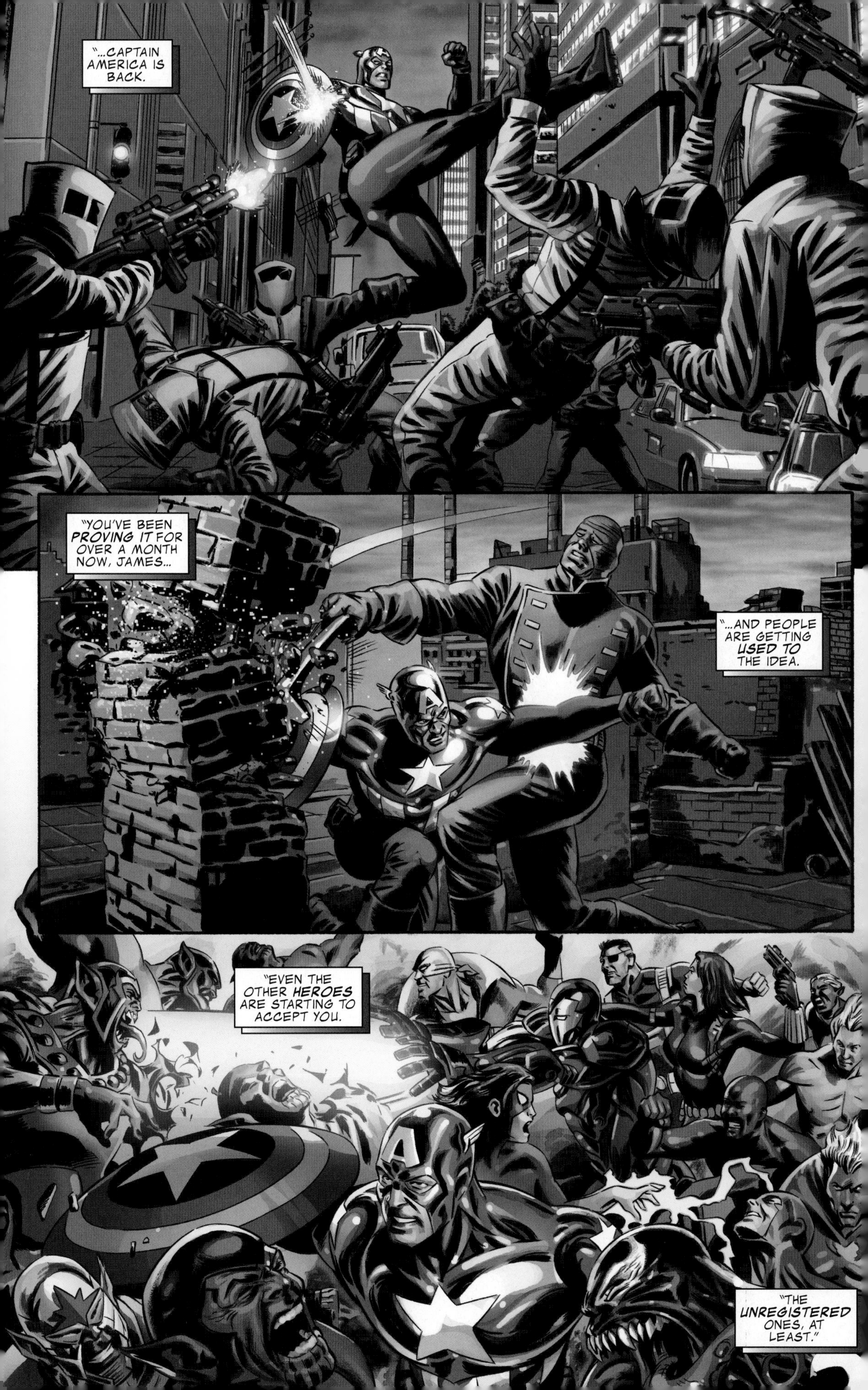
"...CAPTAIN AMERICA IS BACK.
"YOU'VE BEEN PROVING IT FOR OVER A MONTH NOW, JAMES...
"...AND PEOPLE ARE GETTING USED TO THE IDEA.
"EVEN THE OTHER HEROES ARE STARTING TO ACCEPT YOU.
"THE UNREGISTERED ONES, AT LEAST."

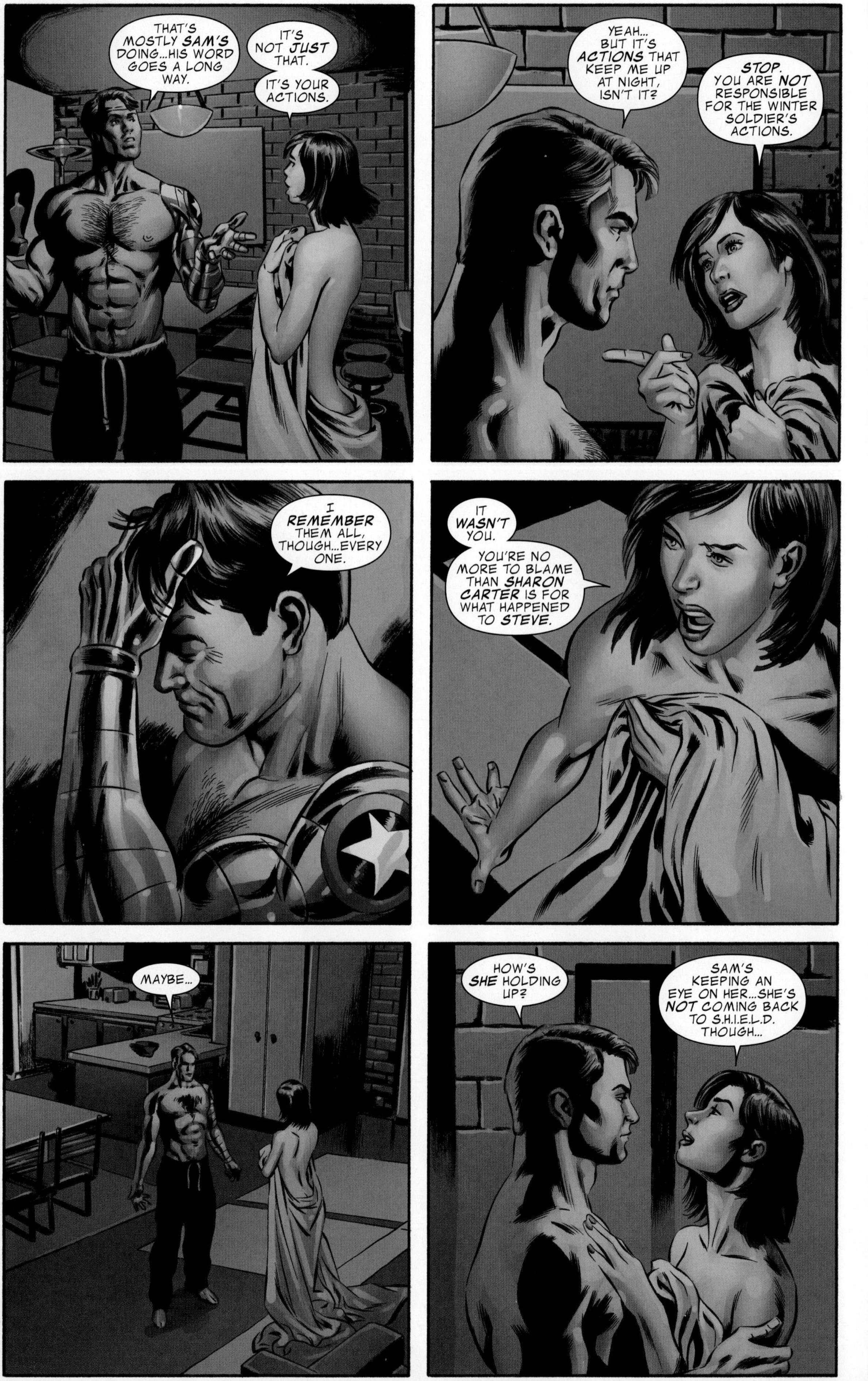
THAT'S MOSTLY SAM'S DOING...HIS WORD GOES A LONG WAY.
IT'S NOT JUST THAT.
IT'S YOUR ACTIONS.
YEAH... BUT IT'S ACTIONS THAT KEEP ME UP AT NIGHT, ISN'T IT?
STOP. YOU ARE NOT RESPONSIBLE FOR THE WINTER SOLDIER'S ACTIONS.
I REMEMBER THEM ALL, THOUGH...EVERY ONE.
IT WASN'T YOU.
YOU'RE NO MORE TO BLAME THAN SHARON CARTER IS FOR WHAT HAPPENED TO STEVE.
MAYBE...
HOW'S SHE HOLDING UP?
SAM'S KEEPING AN EYE ON HER...SHE'S NOT COMING BACK TO S.H.I.E.L.D. THOUGH...

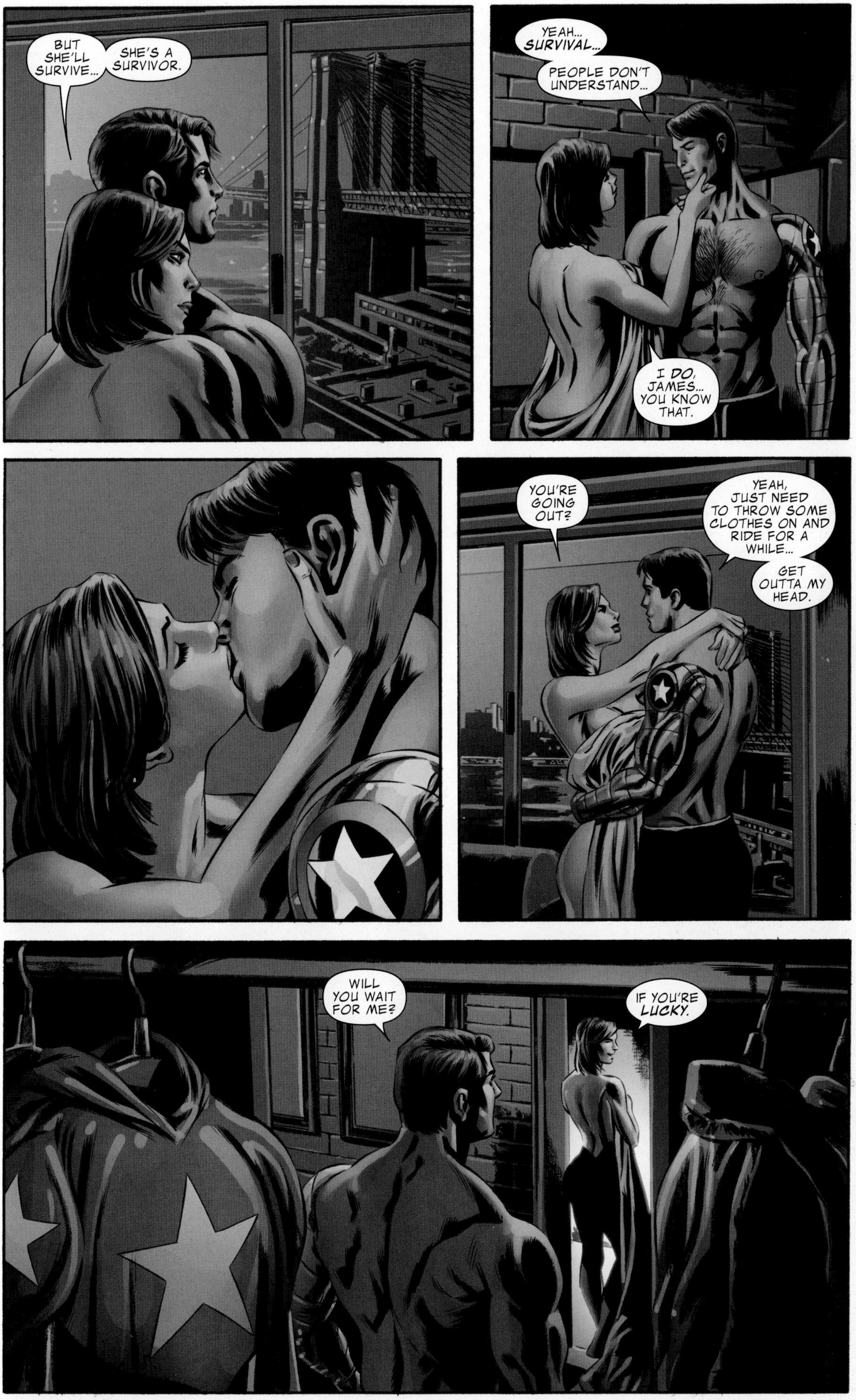

BUT SHE'LL SURVIVE...
SHE'S A SURVIVOR.
YEAH... SURVIVAL...
PEOPLE DON'T UNDERSTAND...
I DO, JAMES... YOU KNOW THAT.
YOU'RE GOING OUT?
YEAH, JUST NEED TO THROW SOME CLOTHES ON AND RIDE FOR A WHILE...
GET OUTTA MY HEAD.
WILL YOU WAIT FOR ME?
IF YOU'RE LUCKY.

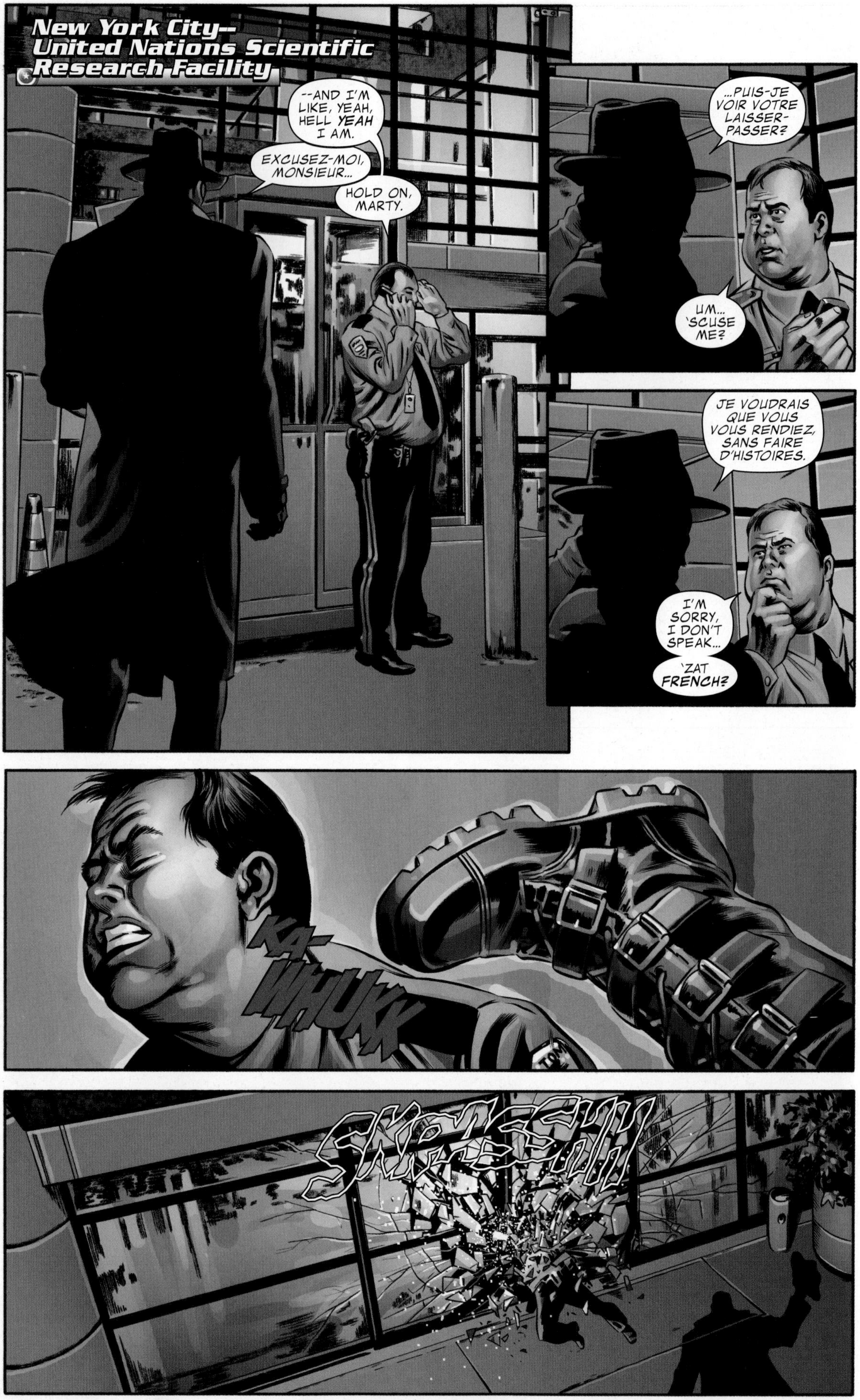
New York City— United Nations Scientific Research Facility
--AND I'M LIKE, YEAH, HELL YEAH I AM.
EXCUSEZ-MOI, MONSIEUR...
HOLD ON, MARTY.
...PUIS-JE VOIR VOTRE LAISSER-PASSER?
UM... 'SCUSE ME?
JE VOUDRAIS QUE VOUS VOUS RENDIEZ, SANS FAIRE D'HISTOIRES.
I'M SORRY, I DON'T SPEAK...
'ZAT FRENCH?
KA-WHUKK

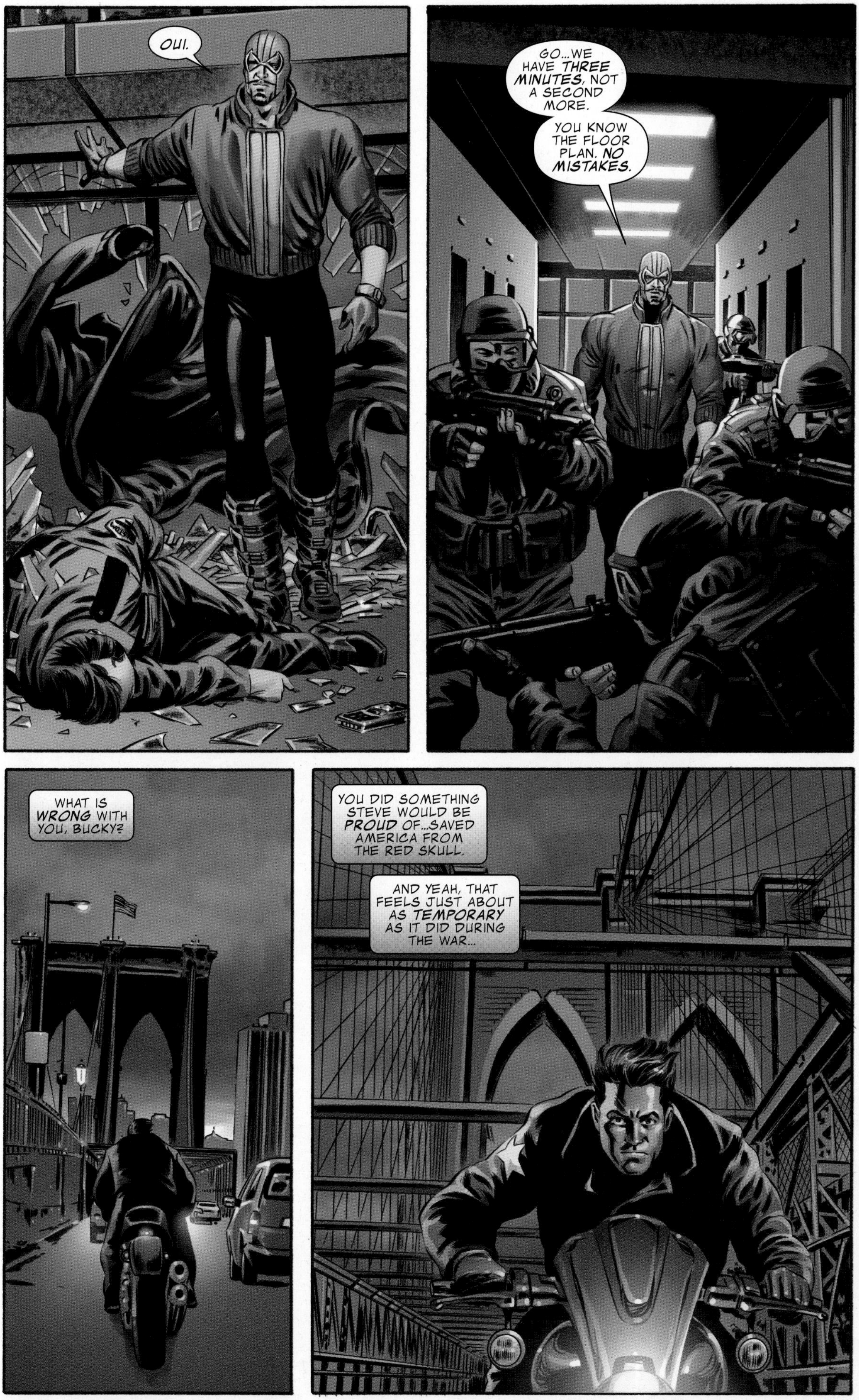
OUI.
GO...WE HAVE THREE MINUTES, NOT A SECOND MORE.
YOU KNOW THE FLOOR PLAN. NO MISTAKES.
WHAT IS WRONG WITH YOU, BUCKY?
YOU DID SOMETHING STEVE WOULD BE PROUD OF...SAVED AMERICA FROM THE RED SKULL.
AND YEAH, THAT FEELS JUST ABOUT AS TEMPORARY AS IT DID DURING THE WAR...

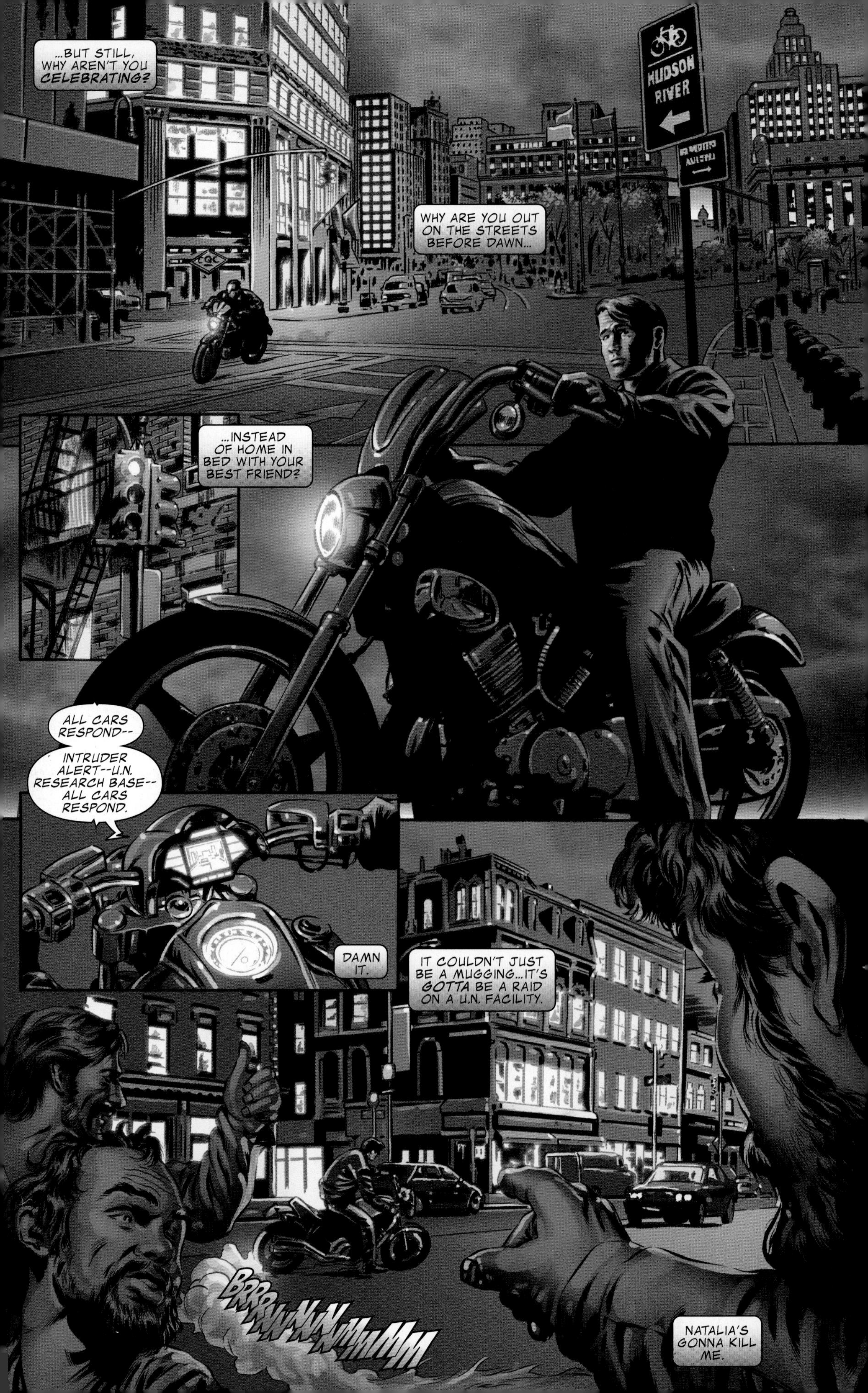
...BUT STILL, WHY AREN'T YOU CELEBRATING?
HUDSON RIVER
WHY ARE YOU OUT ON THE STREETS BEFORE DAWN...
...INSTEAD OF HOME IN BED WITH YOUR BEST FRIEND?
ALL CARS RESPOND--
INTRUDER ALERT--U.N. RESEARCH BASE--ALL CARS RESPOND.
DAMN IT.
IT COULDN'T JUST BE A MUGGING...IT'S GOTTA BE A RAID ON A U.N. FACILITY.
BRRRNNNNNMMMMM
NATALIA'S GONNA KILL ME.

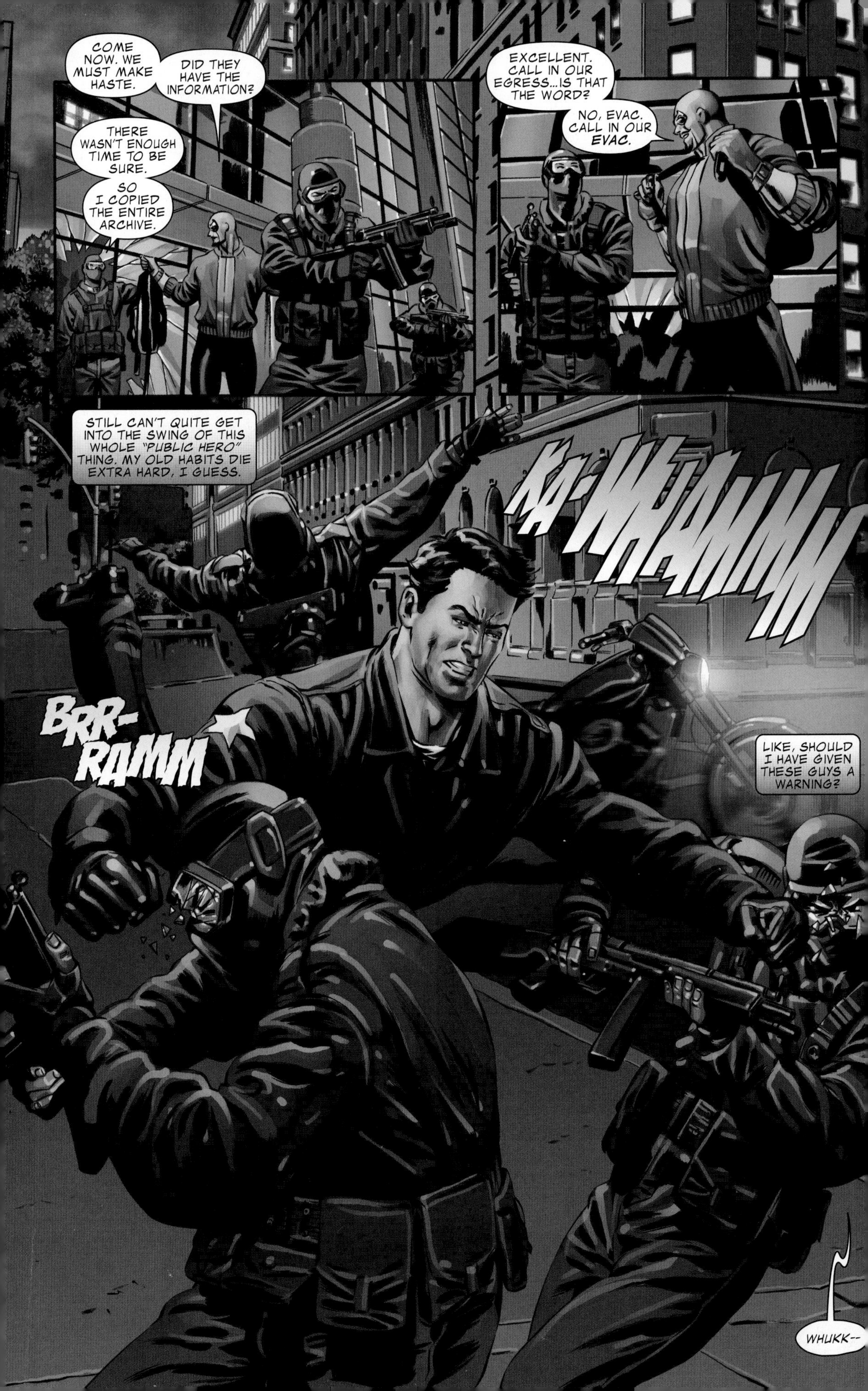
COME NOW. WE MUST MAKE HASTE.
DID THEY HAVE THE INFORMATION?
THERE WASN'T ENOUGH TIME TO BE SURE.
SO I COPIED THE ENTIRE ARCHIVE.
EXCELLENT. CALL IN OUR EGRESS...IS THAT THE WORD?
NO, EVAC. CALL IN OUR EVAC.
STILL CAN'T QUITE GET INTO THE SWING OF THIS WHOLE "PUBLIC HERO" THING. MY OLD HABITS DIE EXTRA HARD, I GUESS.
KA-WHAMMM
BRR-RAMM
LIKE, SHOULD I HAVE GIVEN THESE GUYS A WARNING?
WHUKK--

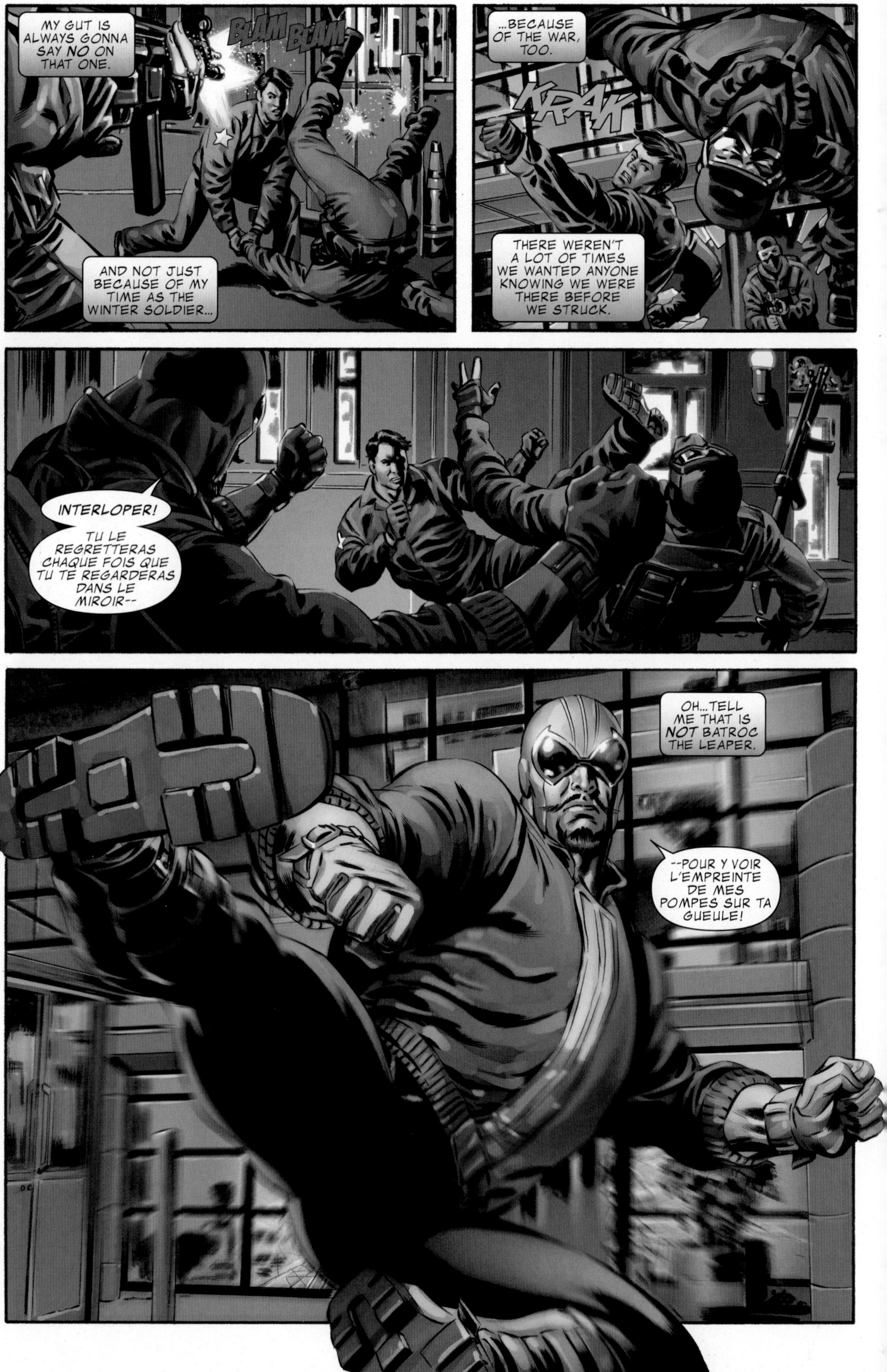
MY GUT IS ALWAYS GONNA SAY NO ON THAT ONE.
BLAM BLAM
AND NOT JUST BECAUSE OF MY TIME AS THE WINTER SOLDIER...
...BECAUSE OF THE WAR, TOO.
KRAK
THERE WEREN'T A LOT OF TIMES WE WANTED ANYONE KNOWING WE WERE THERE BEFORE WE STRUCK.
INTERLOPER!
TU LE REGRETTERAS CHAQUE FOIS QUE TU TE REGARDERAS DANS LE MIROIR--
OH...TELL ME THAT IS NOT BATROC THE LEAPER.
--POUR Y VOIR L'EMPREINTE DE MES POMPES SUR TA GUEULE!

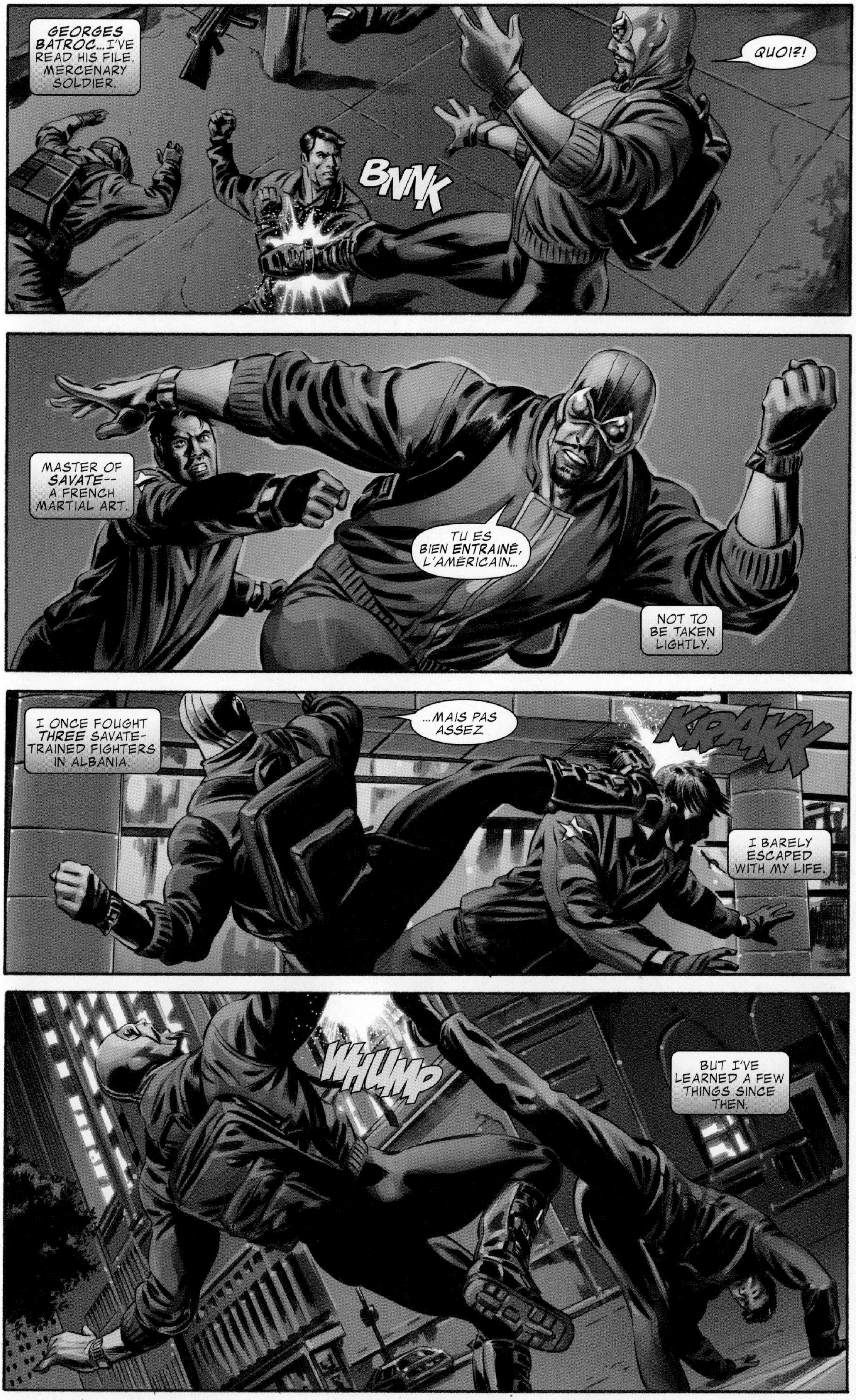
GEORGES BATROC...I'VE READ HIS FILE. MERCENARY SOLDIER.
QUOI?!
BNNK
MASTER OF SAVATE-- A FRENCH MARTIAL ART.
TU ES BIEN ENTRAINÉ, L'AMÉRICAIN...
NOT TO BE TAKEN LIGHTLY.
I ONCE FOUGHT THREE SAVATE-TRAINED FIGHTERS IN ALBANIA.
...MAIS PAS ASSEZ.
KRAKK
I BARELY ESCAPED WITH MY LIFE.
WHUMP
BUT I'VE LEARNED A FEW THINGS SINCE THEN.

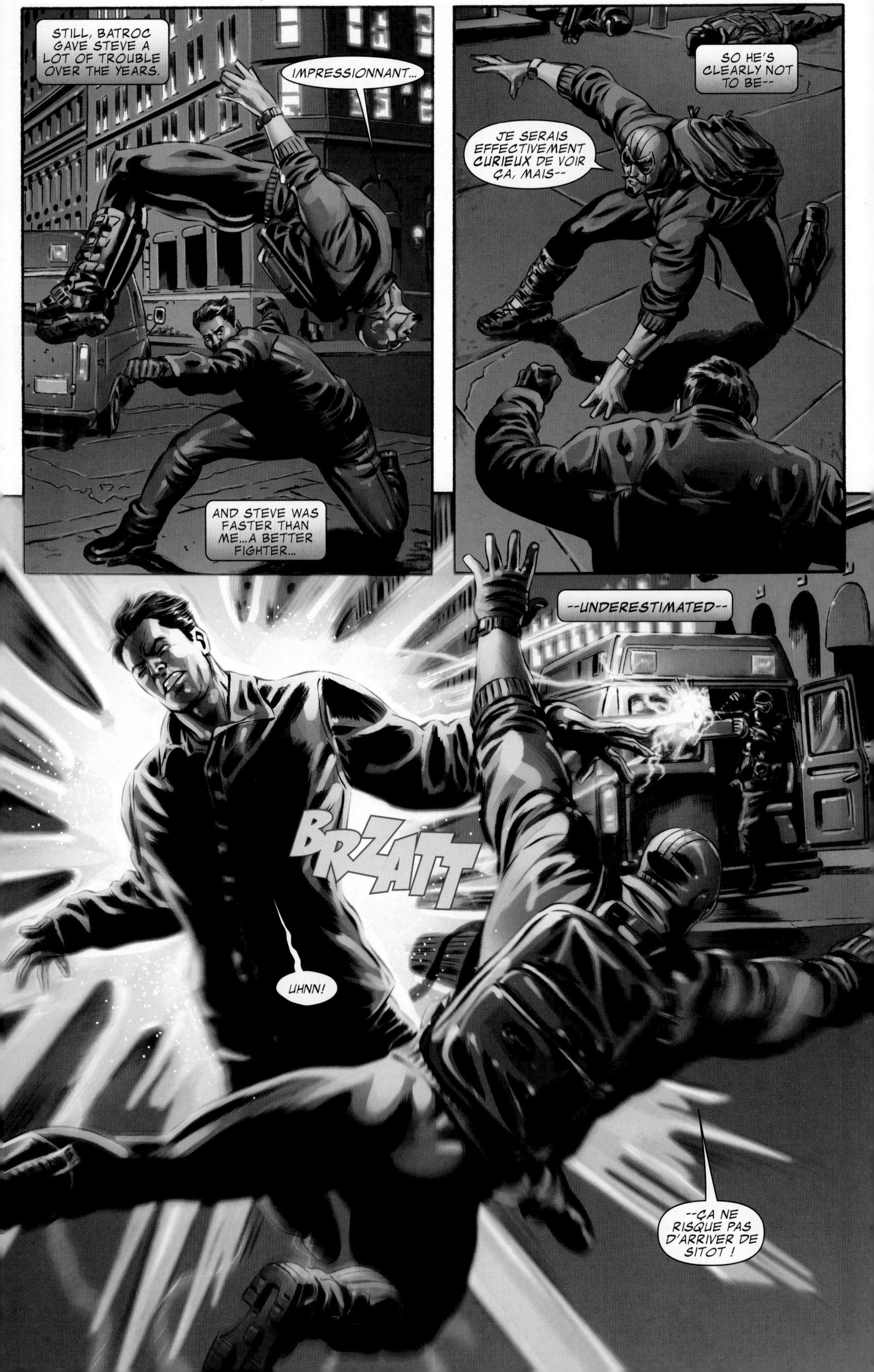
STILL, BATROC GAVE STEVE A LOT OF TROUBLE OVER THE YEARS.
IMPRESSIONNANT...
AND STEVE WAS FASTER THAN ME...A BETTER FIGHTER...
SO HE'S CLEARLY NOT TO BE--
JE SERAIS EFFECTIVEMENT CURIEUX DE VOIR ÇA, MAIS--
--UNDERESTIMATED--
BRZATT
UHNN!
--ÇA NE RISQUE PAS D'ARRIVER DE SITOT !

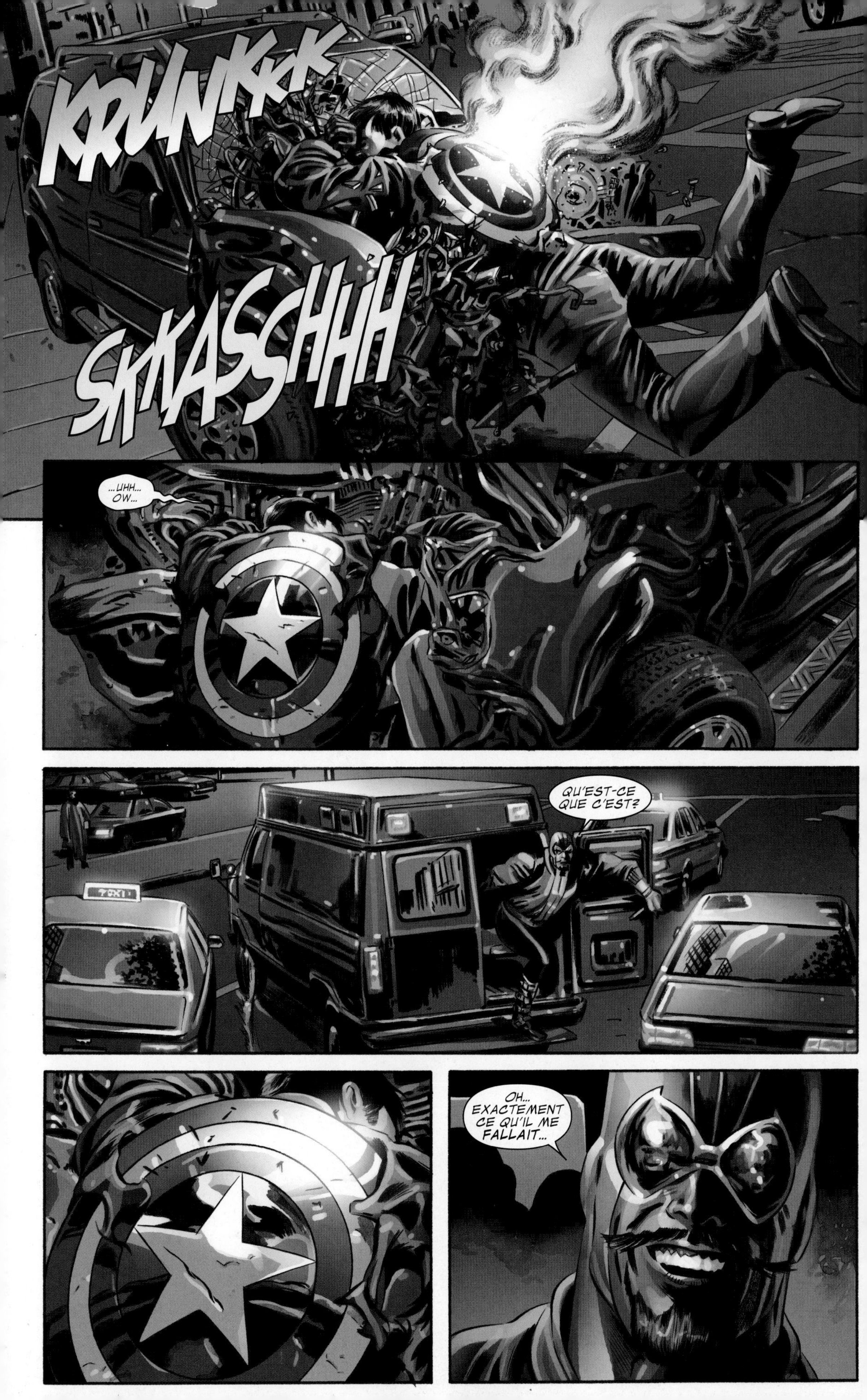
KRUNKKK
SKKASSHHH
...UHH... OW...
QU'EST-CE QUE C'EST?
OH... EXACTEMENT CE QU'IL ME FALLAIT...

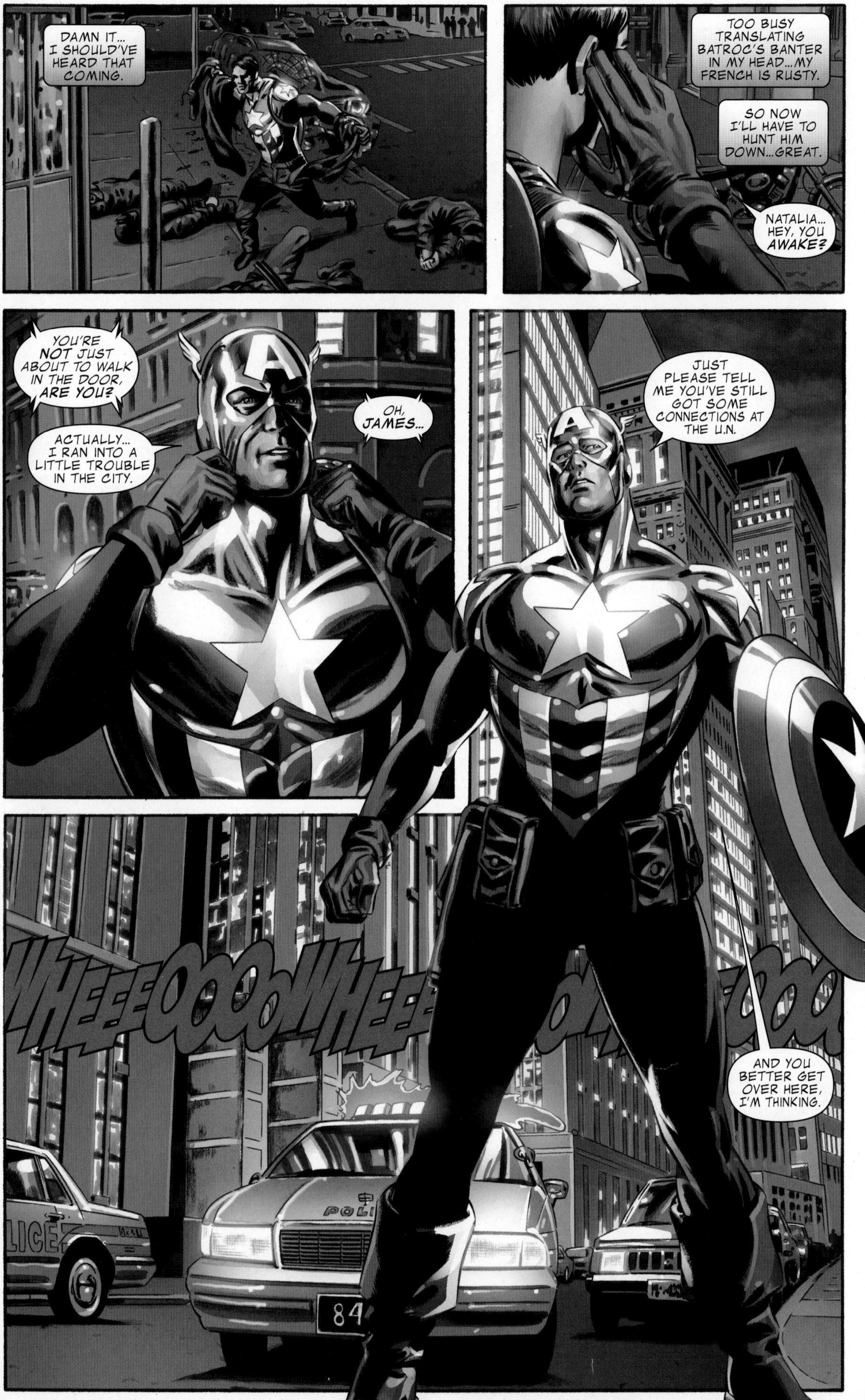

DAMN IT... I SHOULD'VE HEARD THAT COMING.
TOO BUSY TRANSLATING BATROC'S BANTER IN MY HEAD...MY FRENCH IS RUSTY.
SO NOW I'LL HAVE TO HUNT HIM DOWN...GREAT.
NATALIA... HEY, YOU AWAKE?
YOU'RE NOT JUST ABOUT TO WALK IN THE DOOR, ARE YOU?
ACTUALLY... I RAN INTO A LITTLE TROUBLE IN THE CITY.
OH, JAMES...
JUST PLEASE TELL ME YOU'VE STILL GOT SOME CONNECTIONS AT THE U.N.
AND YOU BETTER GET OVER HERE, I'M THINKING.

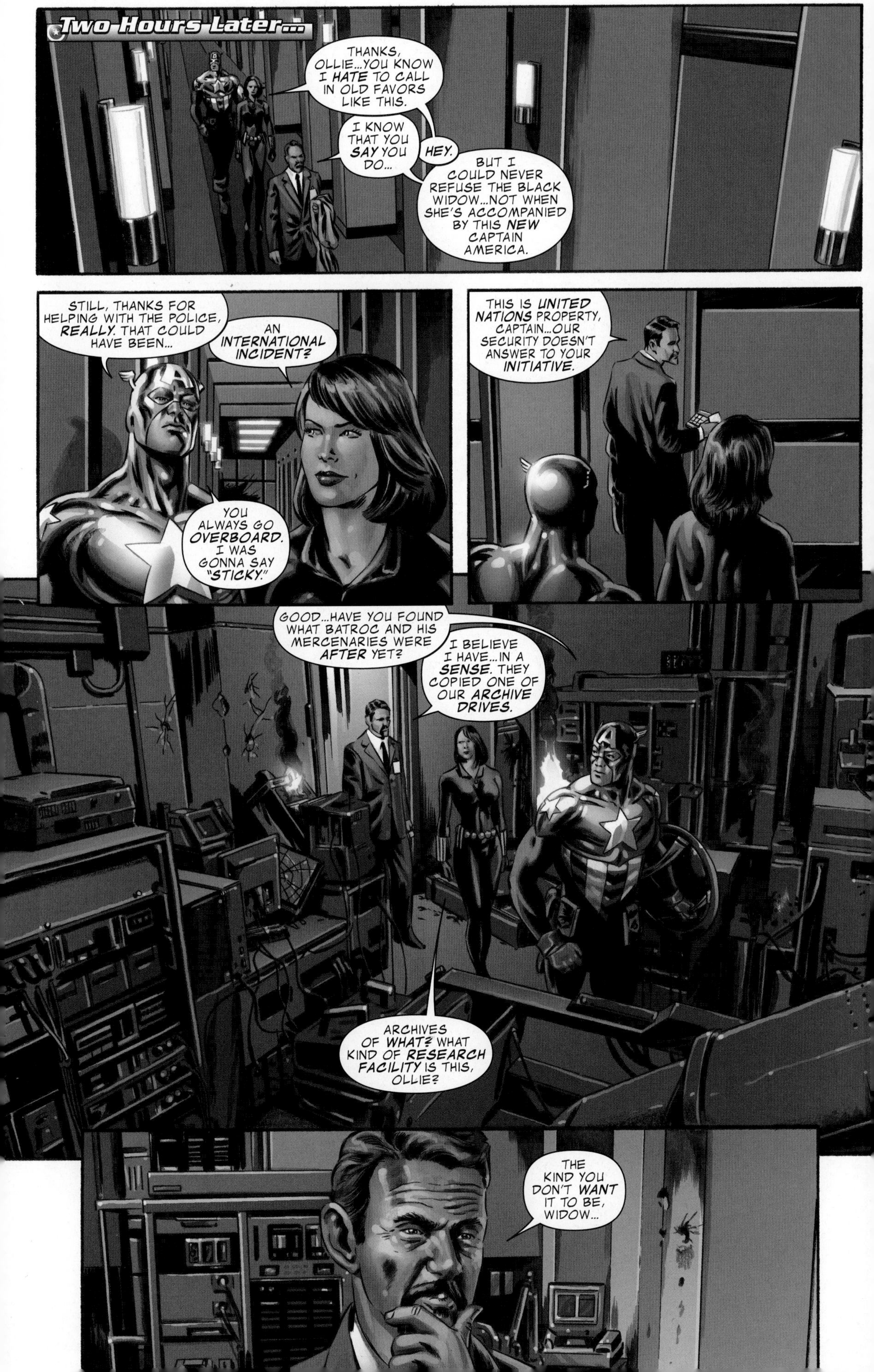

Two Hours Later...
THANKS, OLLIE...YOU KNOW I HATE TO CALL IN OLD FAVORS LIKE THIS.
I KNOW THAT YOU SAY YOU DO...
HEY.
BUT I COULD NEVER REFUSE THE BLACK WIDOW...NOT WHEN SHE'S ACCOMPANIED BY THIS NEW CAPTAIN AMERICA.
STILL, THANKS FOR HELPING WITH THE POLICE, REALLY. THAT COULD HAVE BEEN...
AN INTERNATIONAL INCIDENT?
YOU ALWAYS GO OVERBOARD. I WAS GONNA SAY "STICKY."
THIS IS UNITED NATIONS PROPERTY, CAPTAIN...OUR SECURITY DOESN'T ANSWER TO YOUR INITIATIVE.
GOOD...HAVE YOU FOUND WHAT BATROC AND HIS MERCENARIES WERE AFTER YET?
I BELIEVE I HAVE...IN A SENSE. THEY COPIED ONE OF OUR ARCHIVE DRIVES.
ARCHIVES OF WHAT? WHAT KIND OF RESEARCH FACILITY IS THIS, OLLIE?
THE KIND YOU DON'T WANT IT TO BE, WIDOW...

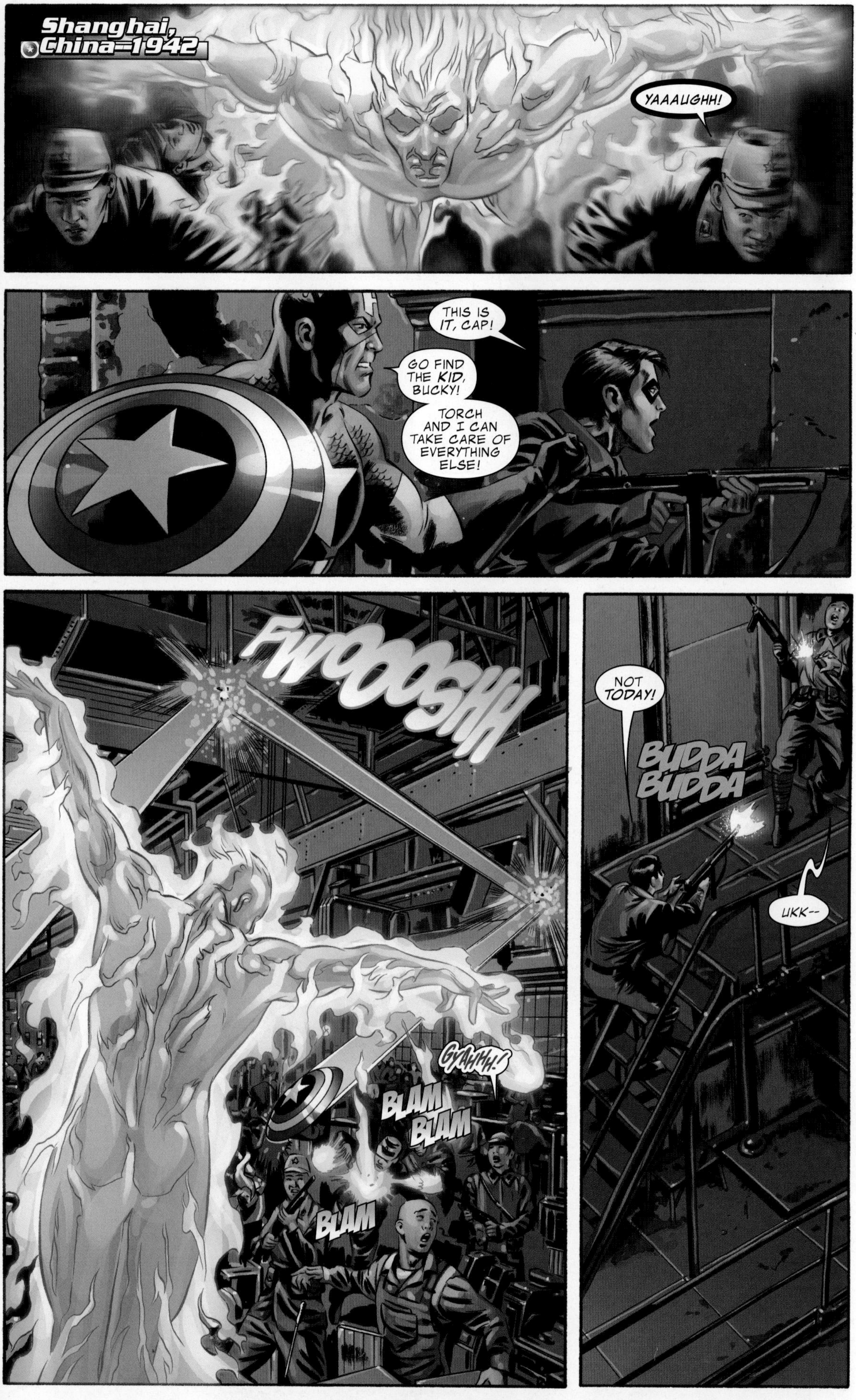
Shanghai, China—1942
YAAAUGHH!
THIS IS IT, CAP!
GO FIND THE KID, BUCKY!
TORCH AND I CAN TAKE CARE OF EVERYTHING ELSE!
FWOOOSHH
GYAHHH!
BLAM BLAM
BLAM
NOT TODAY!
BUDDA BUDDA
UKK--

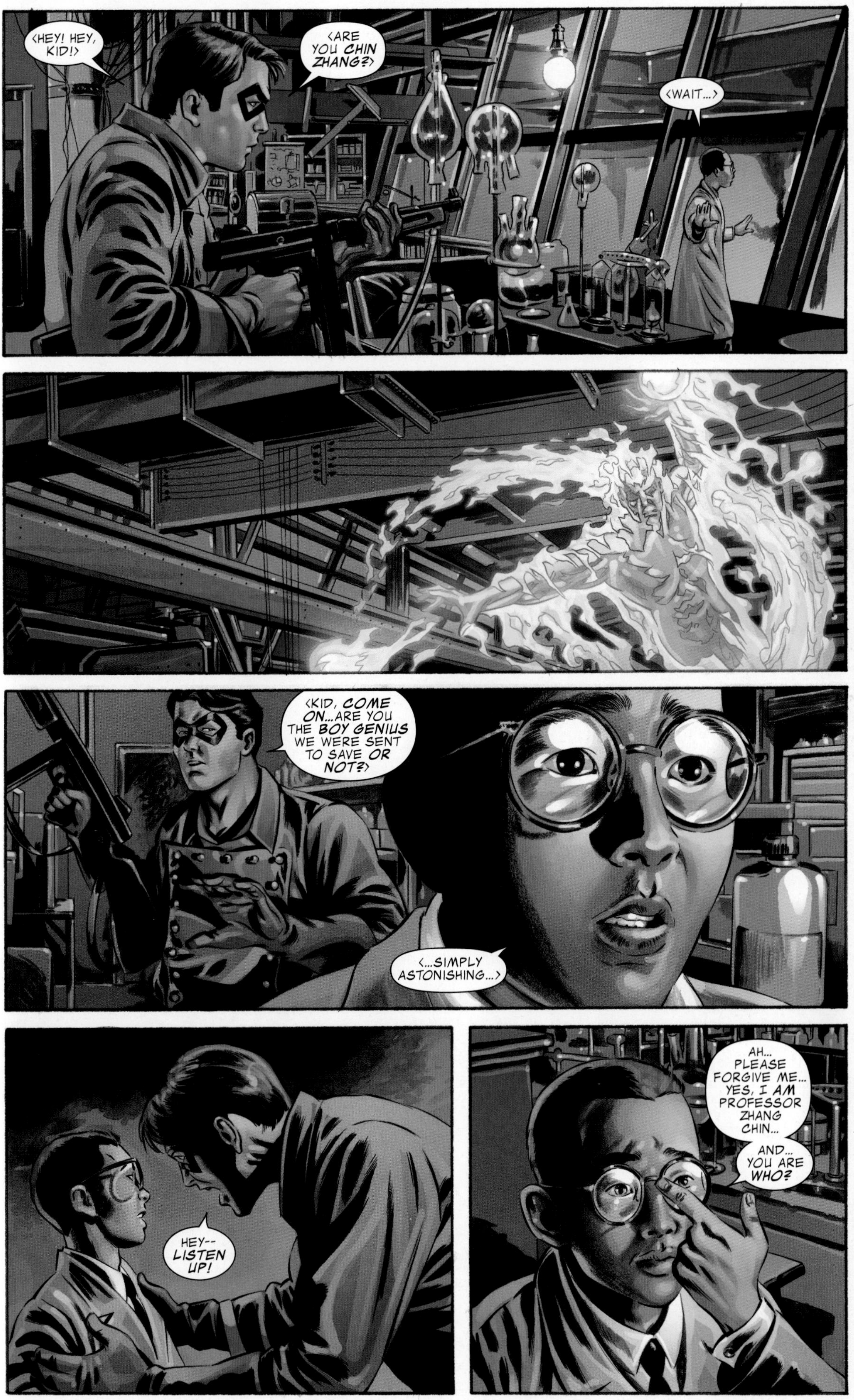
<HEY! HEY, KID!>
<ARE YOU CHIN ZHANG?>
<WAIT...>
<KID, COME ON...ARE YOU THE BOY GENIUS WE WERE SENT TO SAVE OR NOT?>
<...SIMPLY ASTONISHING...>
HEY-- LISTEN UP!
AH... PLEASE FORGIVE ME... YES, I AM PROFESSOR ZHANG CHIN...
AND... YOU ARE WHO?

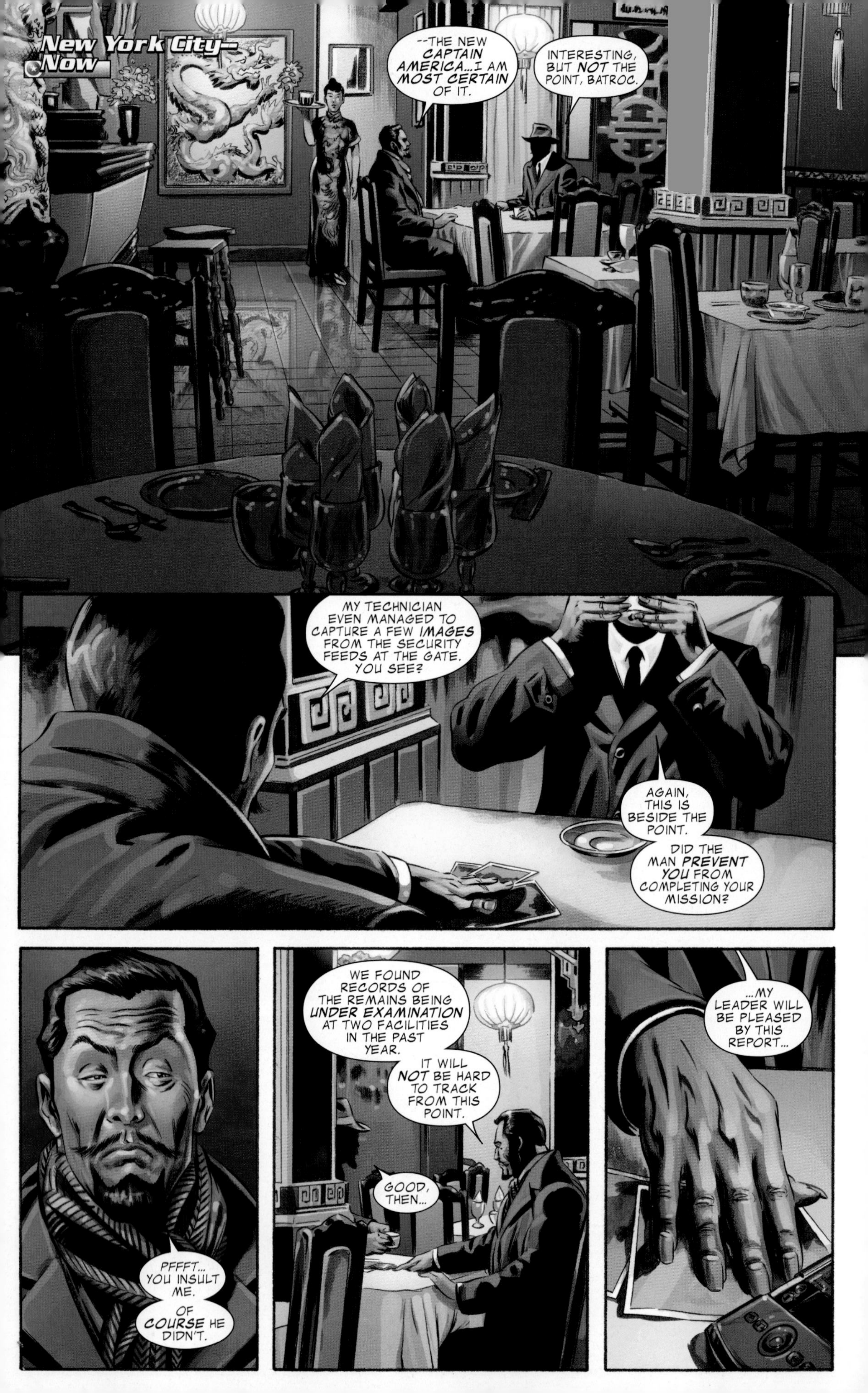
New York City— Now
--THE NEW CAPTAIN AMERICA...I AM MOST CERTAIN OF IT.
INTERESTING, BUT NOT THE POINT, BATROC.
MY TECHNICIAN EVEN MANAGED TO CAPTURE A FEW IMAGES FROM THE SECURITY FEEDS AT THE GATE. YOU SEE?
AGAIN, THIS IS BESIDE THE POINT.
DID THE MAN PREVENT YOU FROM COMPLETING YOUR MISSION?
PFFFT... YOU INSULT ME.
OF COURSE HE DIDN'T.
WE FOUND RECORDS OF THE REMAINS BEING UNDER EXAMINATION AT TWO FACILITIES IN THE PAST YEAR.
IT WILL NOT BE HARD TO TRACK FROM THIS POINT.
GOOD, THEN...
...MY LEADER WILL BE PLEASED BY THIS REPORT...

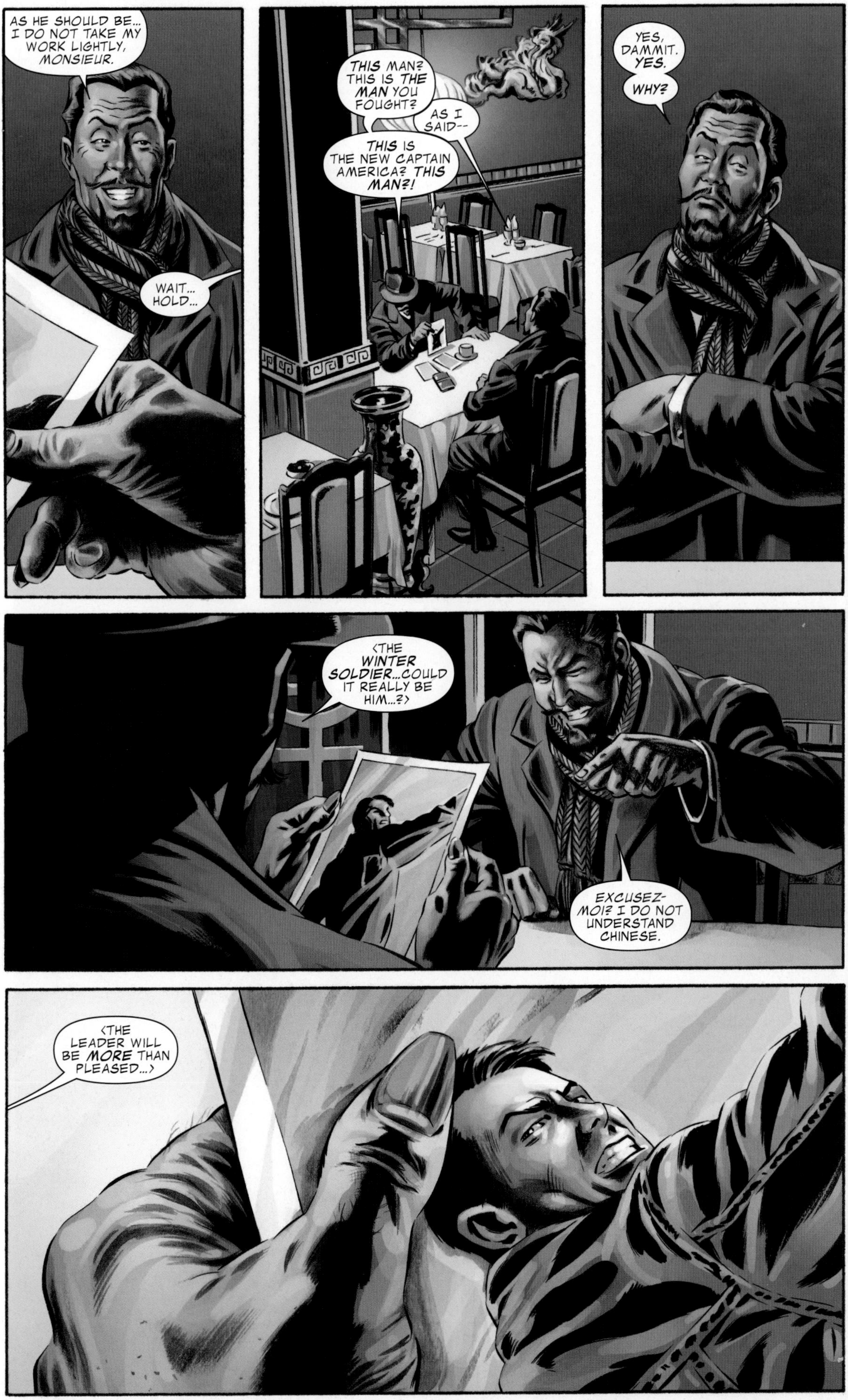
AS HE SHOULD BE... I DO NOT TAKE MY WORK LIGHTLY, MONSIEUR.
WAIT... HOLD...
THIS MAN? THIS IS THE MAN YOU FOUGHT?
AS I SAID--
THIS IS THE NEW CAPTAIN AMERICA? THIS MAN?!
YES, DAMMIT. YES.
WHY?
<THE WINTER SOLDIER...COULD IT REALLY BE HIM...?>
EXCUSEZ-MOI? I DO NOT UNDERSTAND CHINESE.
<THE LEADER WILL BE MORE THAN PLEASED...>

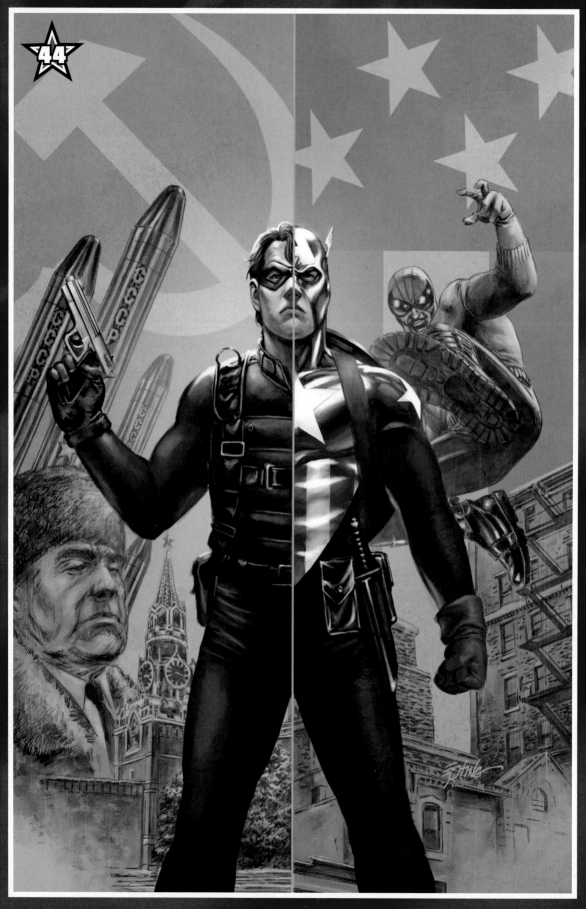

TIME'S ARROW PART TWO

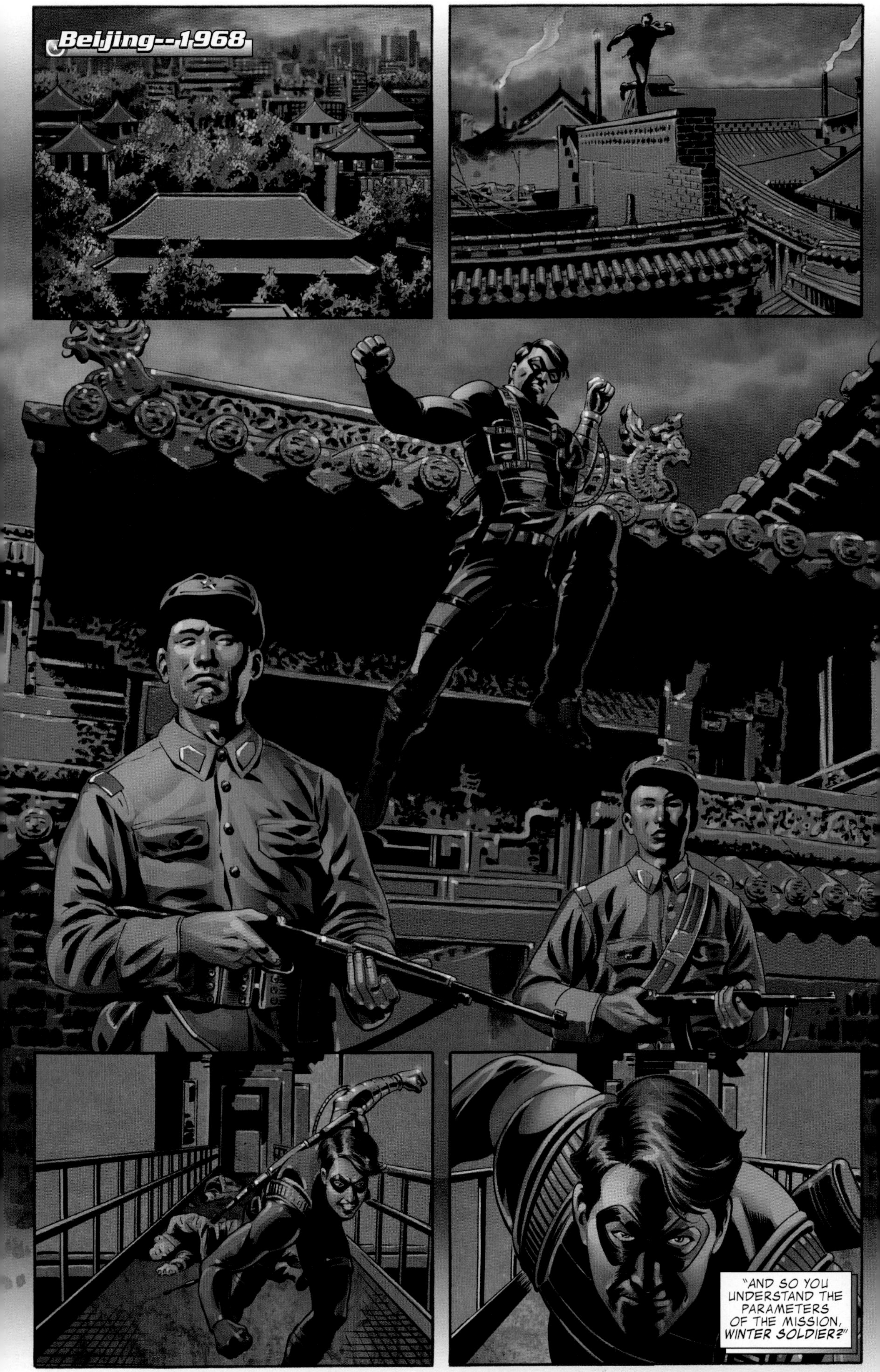
Beijing--1968
"AND SO YOU UNDERSTAND THE PARAMETERS OF THE MISSION, WINTER SOLDIER?"

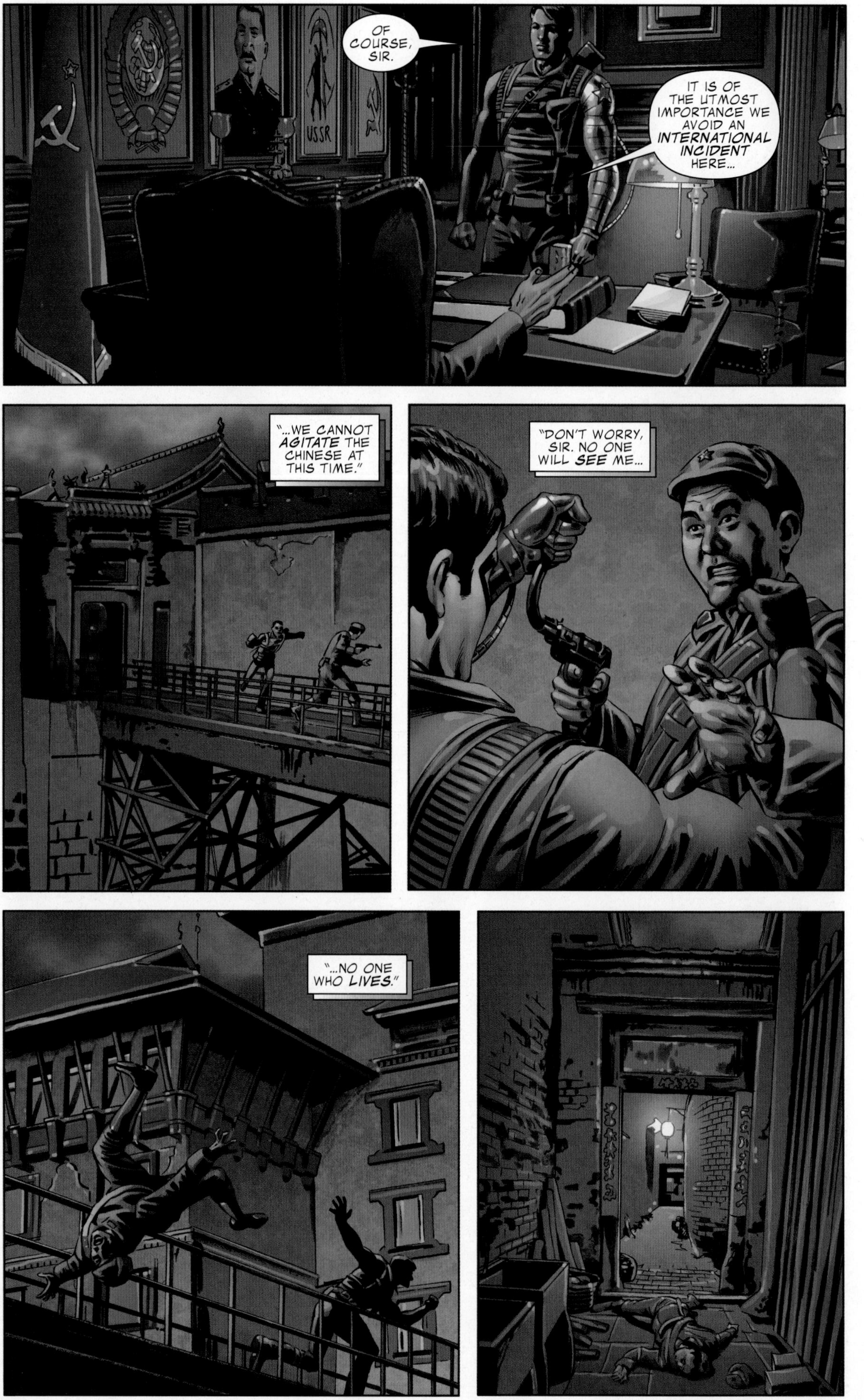
OF COURSE, SIR.
IT IS OF THE UTMOST IMPORTANCE WE AVOID AN INTERNATIONAL INCIDENT HERE...
"...WE CANNOT AGITATE THE CHINESE AT THIS TIME."
"DON'T WORRY, SIR. NO ONE WILL SEE ME...
"...NO ONE WHO LIVES."

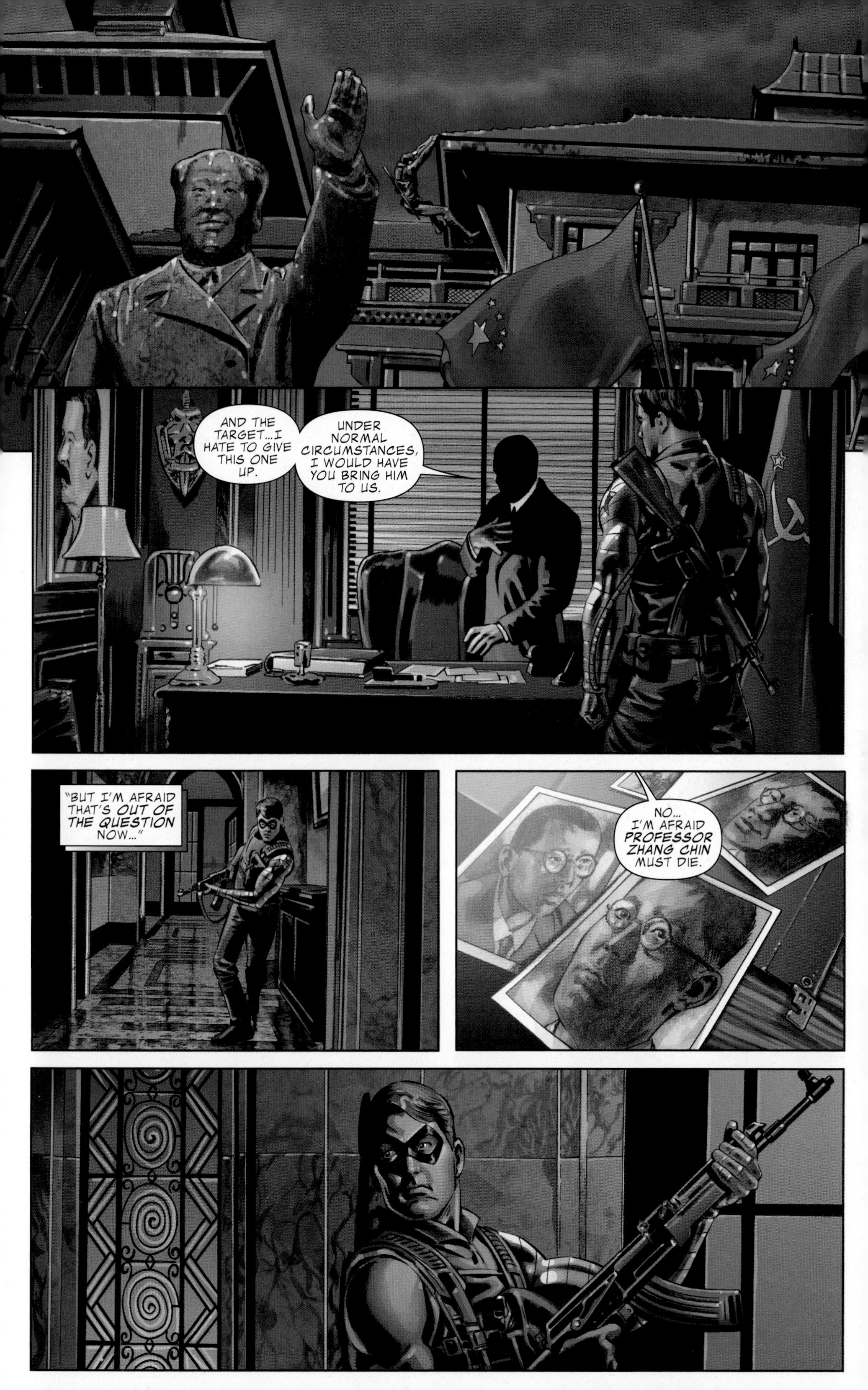
AND THE TARGET...I HATE TO GIVE THIS ONE UP.
UNDER NORMAL CIRCUMSTANCES, I WOULD HAVE YOU BRING HIM TO US.
"BUT I'M AFRAID THAT'S OUT OF THE QUESTION NOW..."
NO... I'M AFRAID PROFESSOR ZHANG CHIN MUST DIE.

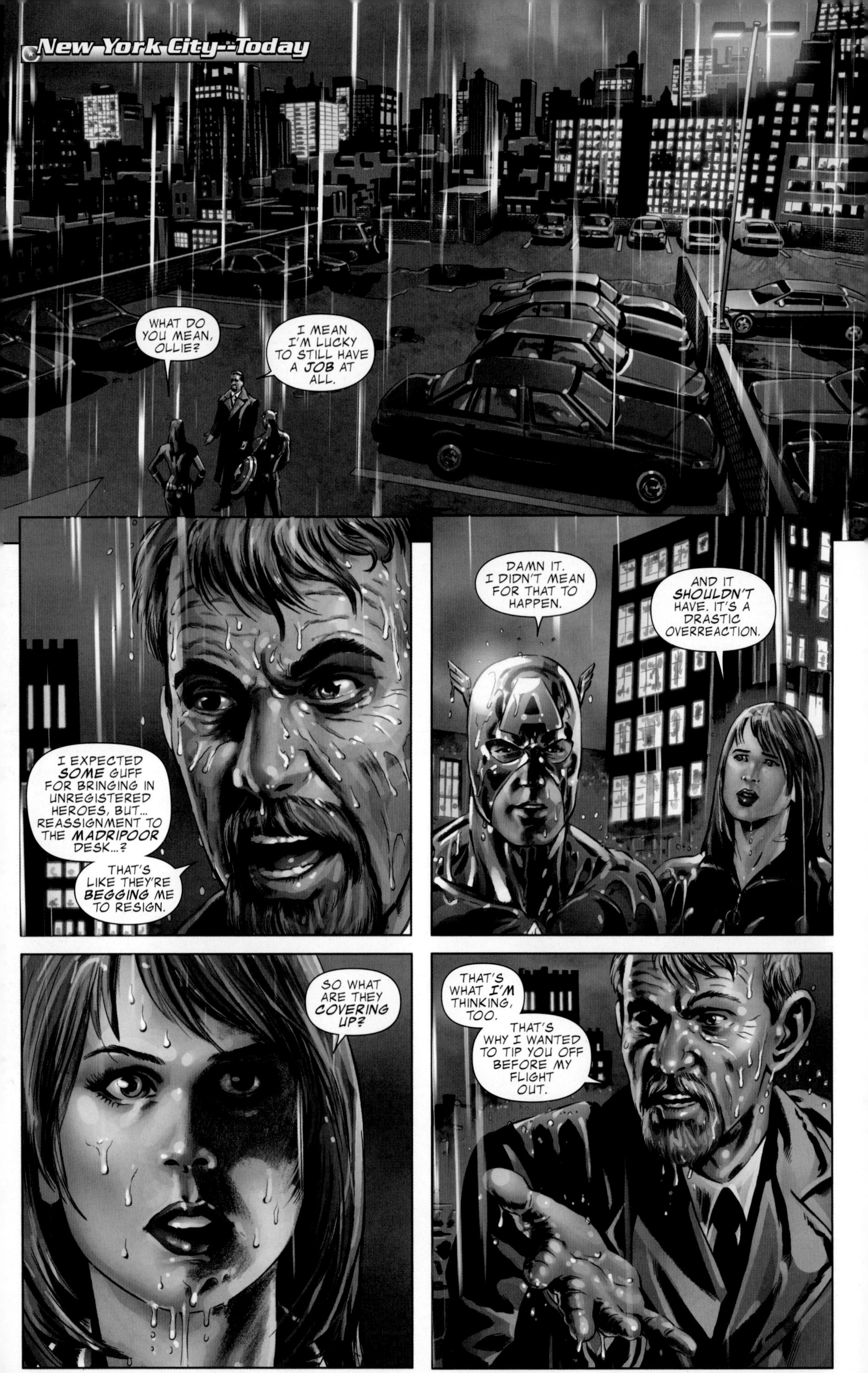
New York City--Today
WHAT DO YOU MEAN, OLLIE?
I MEAN I'M LUCKY TO STILL HAVE A JOB AT ALL.
I EXPECTED SOME GUFF FOR BRINGING IN UNREGISTERED HEROES, BUT... REASSIGNMENT TO THE MADRIPOOR DESK...?
THAT'S LIKE THEY'RE BEGGING ME TO RESIGN.
DAMN IT. I DIDN'T MEAN FOR THAT TO HAPPEN.
AND IT SHOULDN'T HAVE. IT'S A DRASTIC OVERREACTION.
SO WHAT ARE THEY COVERING UP?
THAT'S WHAT I'M THINKING, TOO.
THAT'S WHY I WANTED TO TIP YOU OFF BEFORE MY FLIGHT OUT.

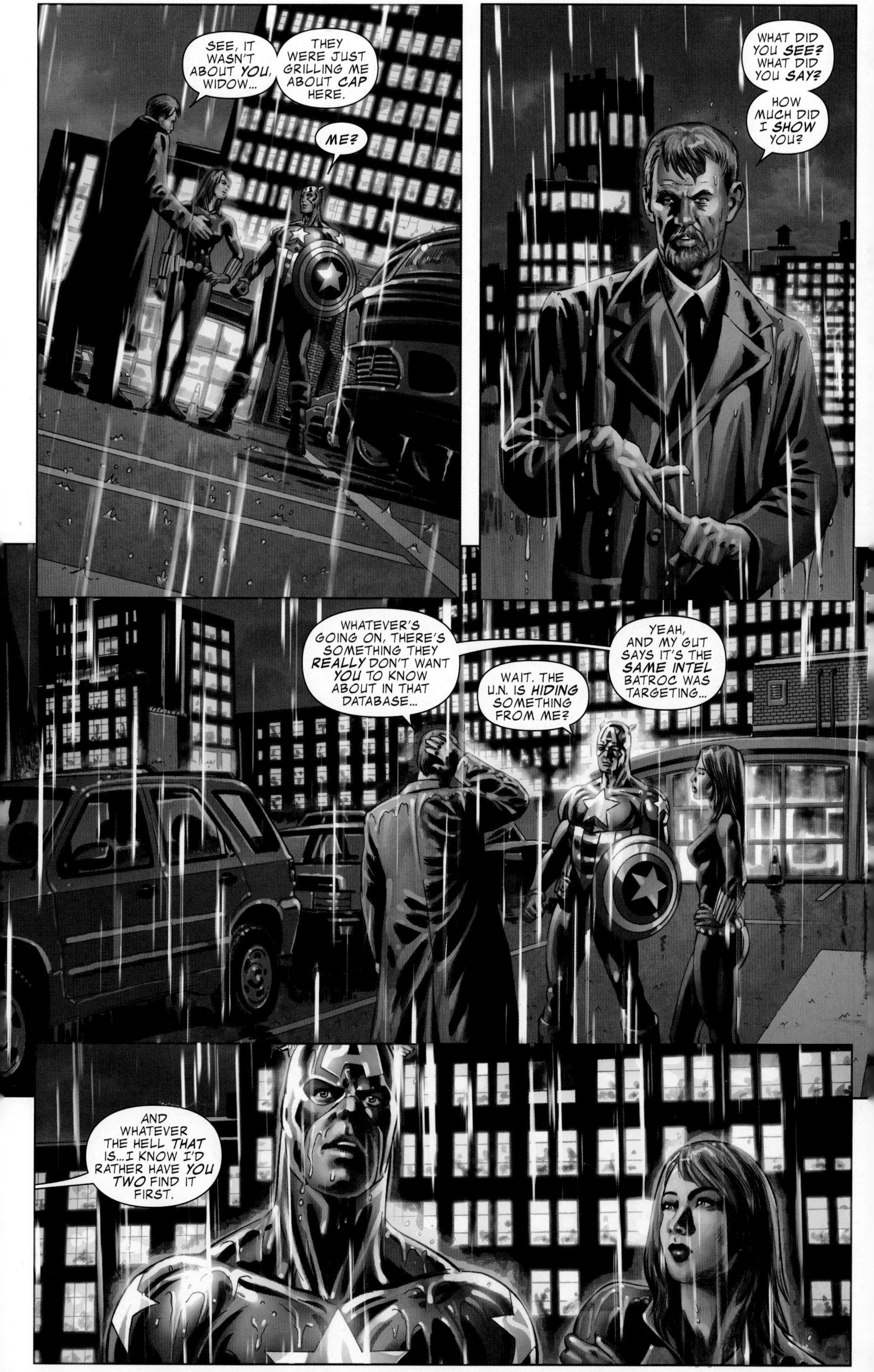
SEE, IT WASN'T ABOUT *YOU*, WIDOW...
THEY WERE JUST GRILLING ME ABOUT *CAP* HERE.
ME?
WHAT DID YOU *SEE?* WHAT DID YOU *SAY?*
HOW MUCH DID I *SHOW* YOU?
WHATEVER'S GOING ON, THERE'S SOMETHING THEY *REALLY* DON'T WANT *YOU* TO KNOW ABOUT IN THAT DATABASE...
WAIT. THE U.N. IS *HIDING* SOMETHING FROM ME?
YEAH, AND MY GUT SAYS IT'S THE *SAME INTEL* BATROC WAS TARGETING...
AND WHATEVER THE HELL *THAT* IS...I KNOW I'D RATHER HAVE *YOU TWO* FIND IT FIRST.

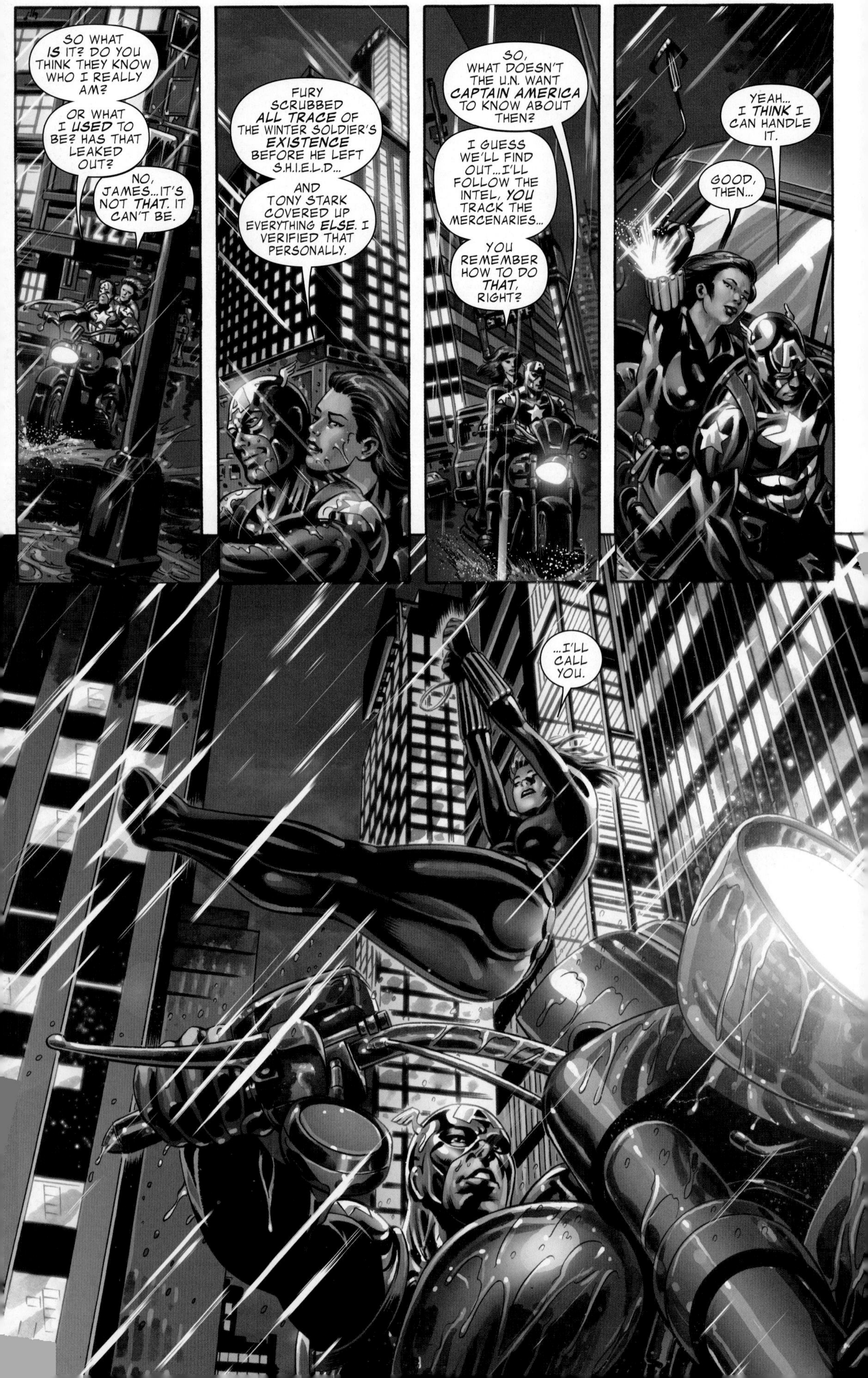

SO WHAT IS IT? DO YOU THINK THEY KNOW WHO I REALLY AM?
OR WHAT I USED TO BE? HAS THAT LEAKED OUT?
NO, JAMES...IT'S NOT THAT. IT CAN'T BE.
FURY SCRUBBED ALL TRACE OF THE WINTER SOLDIER'S EXISTENCE BEFORE HE LEFT S.H.I.E.L.D...
AND TONY STARK COVERED UP EVERYTHING ELSE. I VERIFIED THAT PERSONALLY.
SO, WHAT DOESN'T THE U.N. WANT CAPTAIN AMERICA TO KNOW ABOUT THEN?
I GUESS WE'LL FIND OUT...I'LL FOLLOW THE INTEL, YOU TRACK THE MERCENARIES...
YOU REMEMBER HOW TO DO THAT, RIGHT?
YEAH... I THINK I CAN HANDLE IT.
GOOD, THEN...
...I'LL CALL YOU.

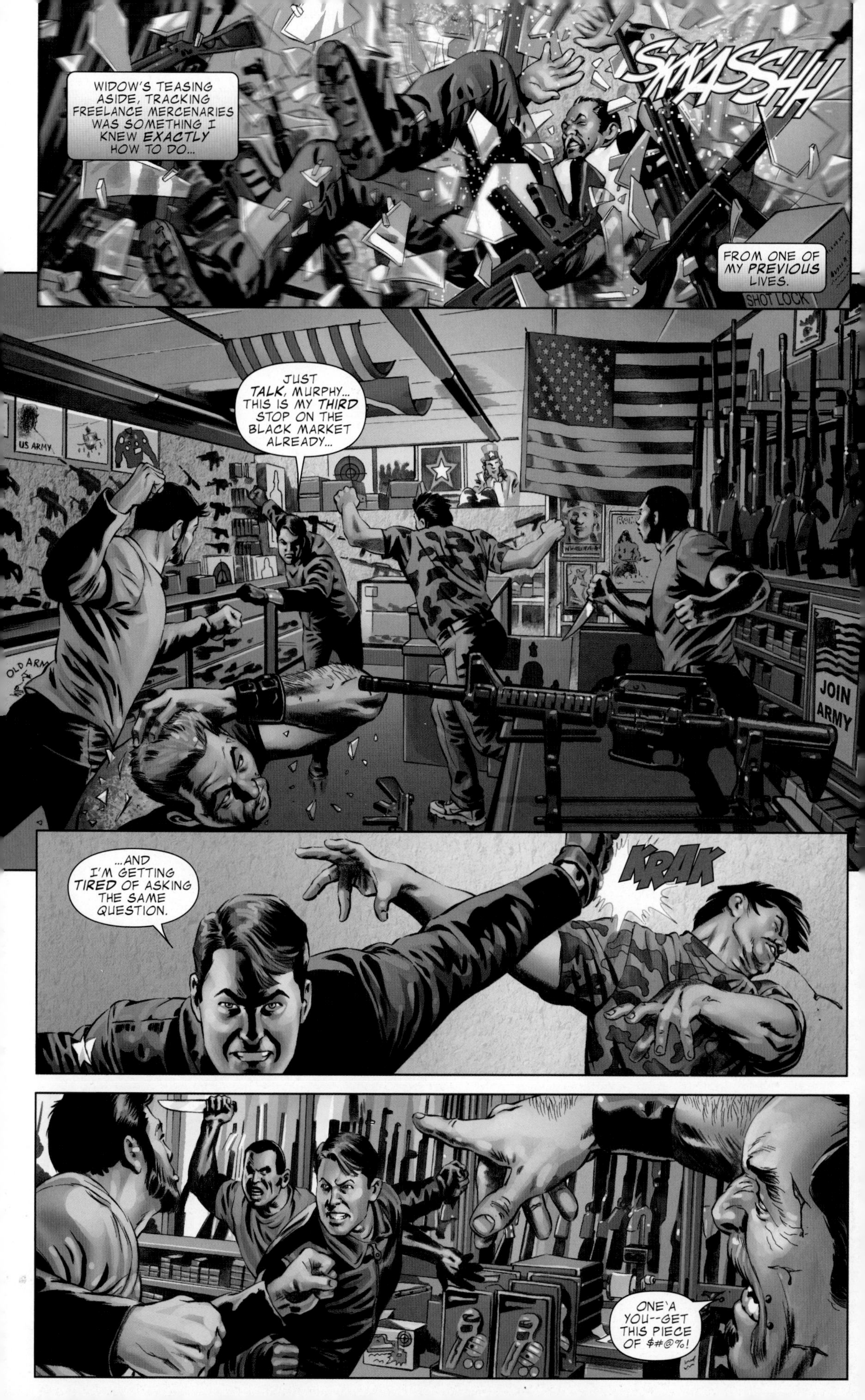
WIDOW'S TEASING ASIDE, TRACKING FREELANCE MERCENARIES WAS SOMETHING I KNEW EXACTLY HOW TO DO...
SKKASSHH
FROM ONE OF MY PREVIOUS LIVES.
SHOT LOCK
JUST TALK, MURPHY... THIS IS MY THIRD STOP ON THE BLACK MARKET ALREADY...
US ARMY
OLD ARMY
JOIN ARMY
...AND I'M GETTING TIRED OF ASKING THE SAME QUESTION.
KRAK
ONE'A YOU--GET THIS PIECE OF $#@%!

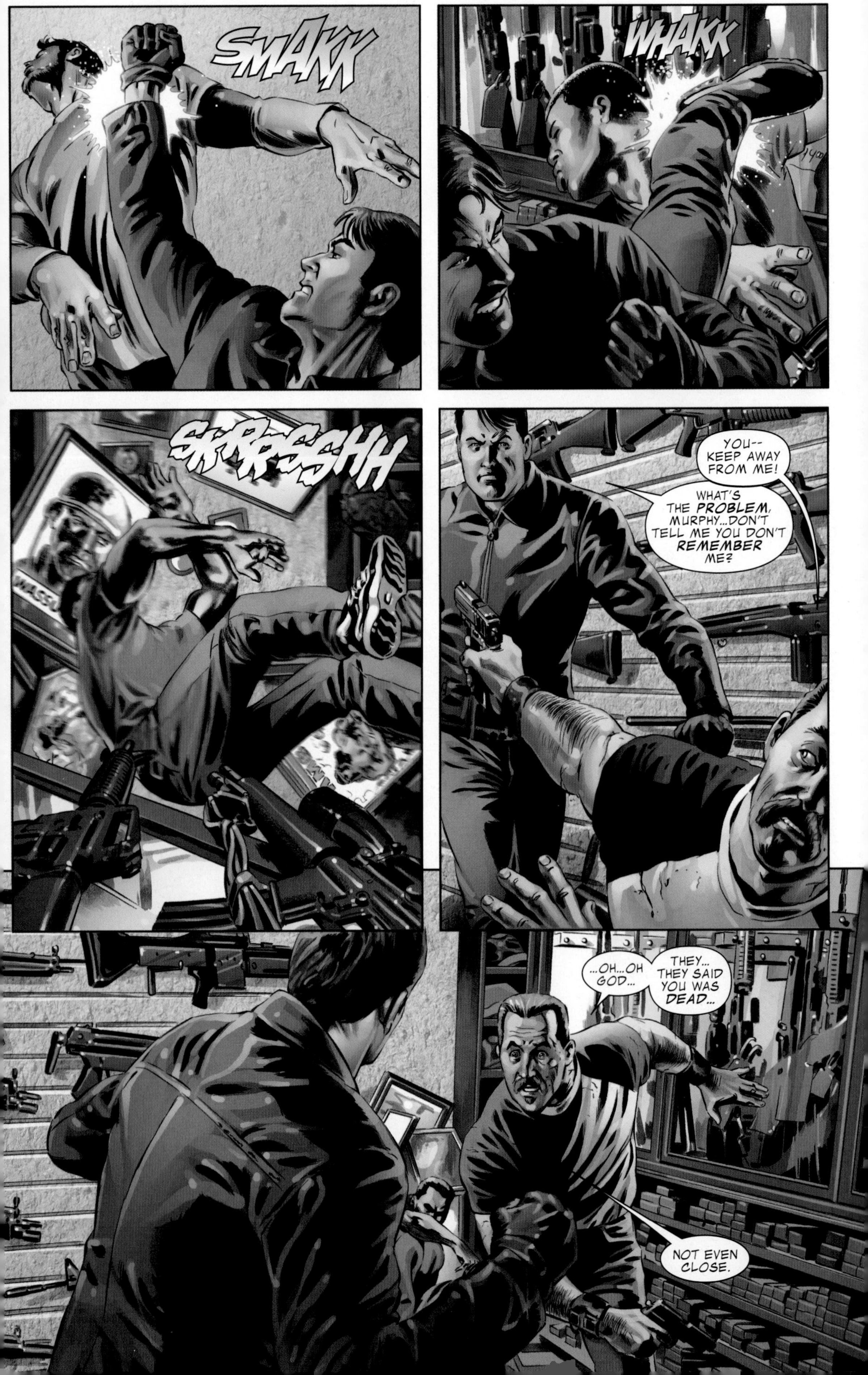
SMAKK
WHAKK
SKRRSSHH
YOU--
KEEP AWAY
FROM ME!
WHAT'S THE PROBLEM, MURPHY...DON'T TELL ME YOU DON'T REMEMBER ME?
...OH...OH GOD...
THEY... THEY SAID YOU WAS DEAD...
NOT EVEN CLOSE.

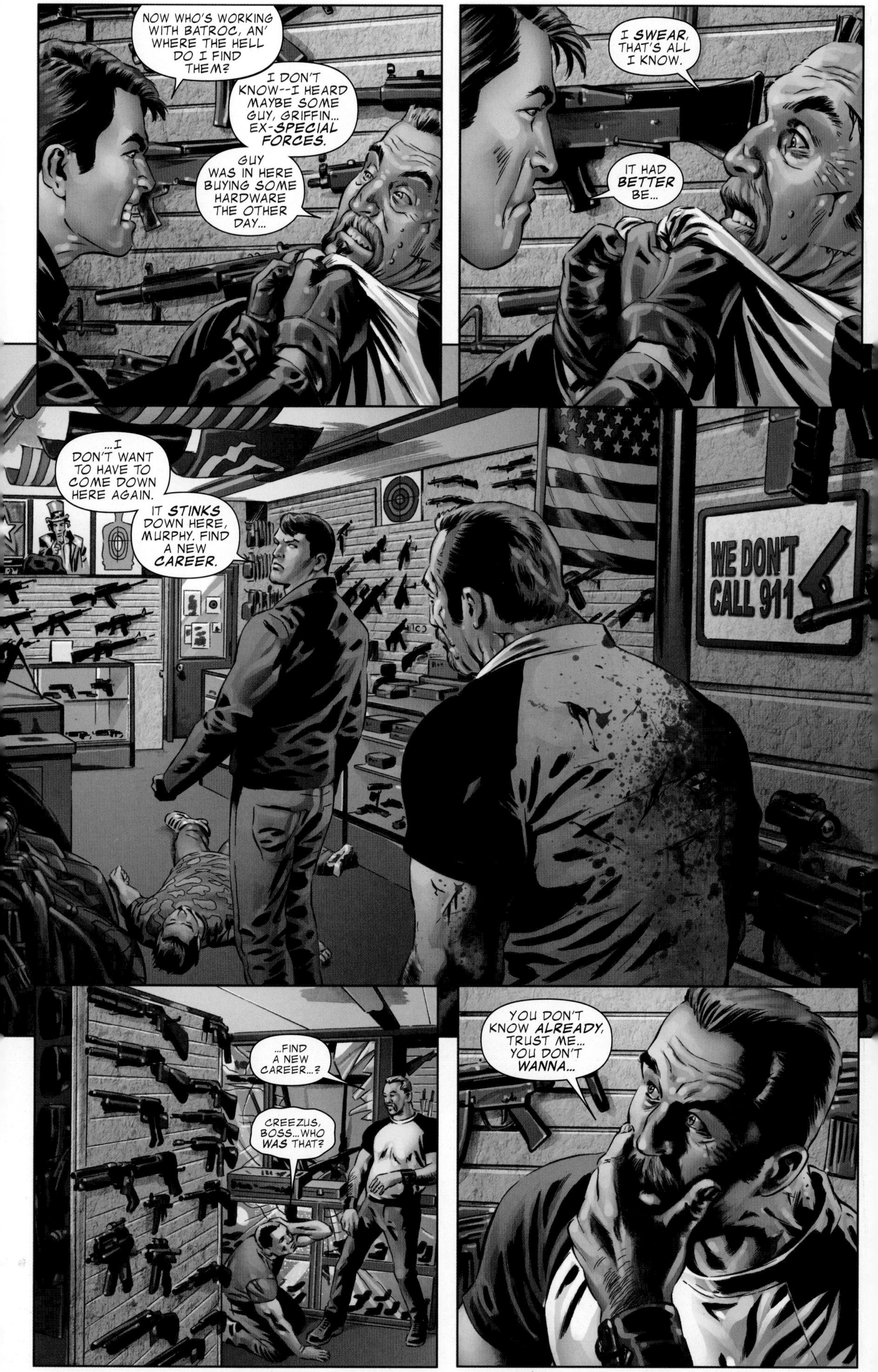
NOW WHO'S WORKING WITH BATROC, AN' WHERE THE HELL DO I FIND THEM?
I DON'T KNOW--I HEARD MAYBE SOME GUY, GRIFFIN... EX-SPECIAL FORCES.
GUY WAS IN HERE BUYING SOME HARDWARE THE OTHER DAY...
I SWEAR, THAT'S ALL I KNOW.
IT HAD BETTER BE...
...I DON'T WANT TO HAVE TO COME DOWN HERE AGAIN.
IT STINKS DOWN HERE, MURPHY. FIND A NEW CAREER.
WE DON'T CALL 911
...FIND A NEW CAREER...?
CREEZUS, BOSS...WHO WAS THAT?
YOU DON'T KNOW ALREADY, TRUST ME... YOU DON'T WANNA...

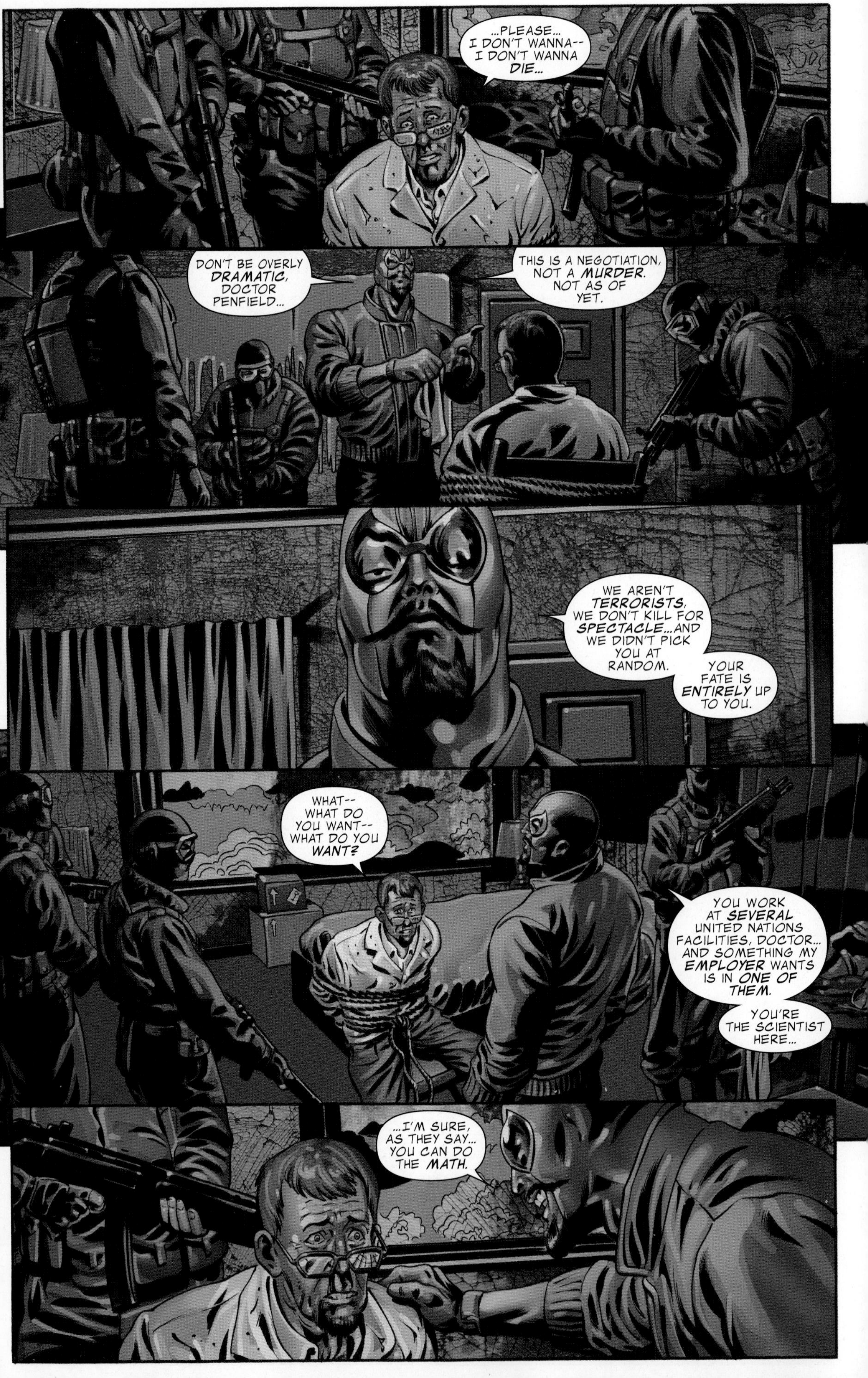
...PLEASE... I DON'T WANNA-- I DON'T WANNA DIE...
DON'T BE OVERLY DRAMATIC, DOCTOR PENFIELD...
THIS IS A NEGOTIATION, NOT A MURDER. NOT AS OF YET.
WE AREN'T TERRORISTS, WE DON'T KILL FOR SPECTACLE...AND WE DIDN'T PICK YOU AT RANDOM.
YOUR FATE IS ENTIRELY UP TO YOU.
WHAT-- WHAT DO YOU WANT-- WHAT DO YOU WANT?
YOU WORK AT SEVERAL UNITED NATIONS FACILITIES, DOCTOR... AND SOMETHING MY EMPLOYER WANTS IS IN ONE OF THEM.
YOU'RE THE SCIENTIST HERE...
...I'M SURE, AS THEY SAY... YOU CAN DO THE MATH.

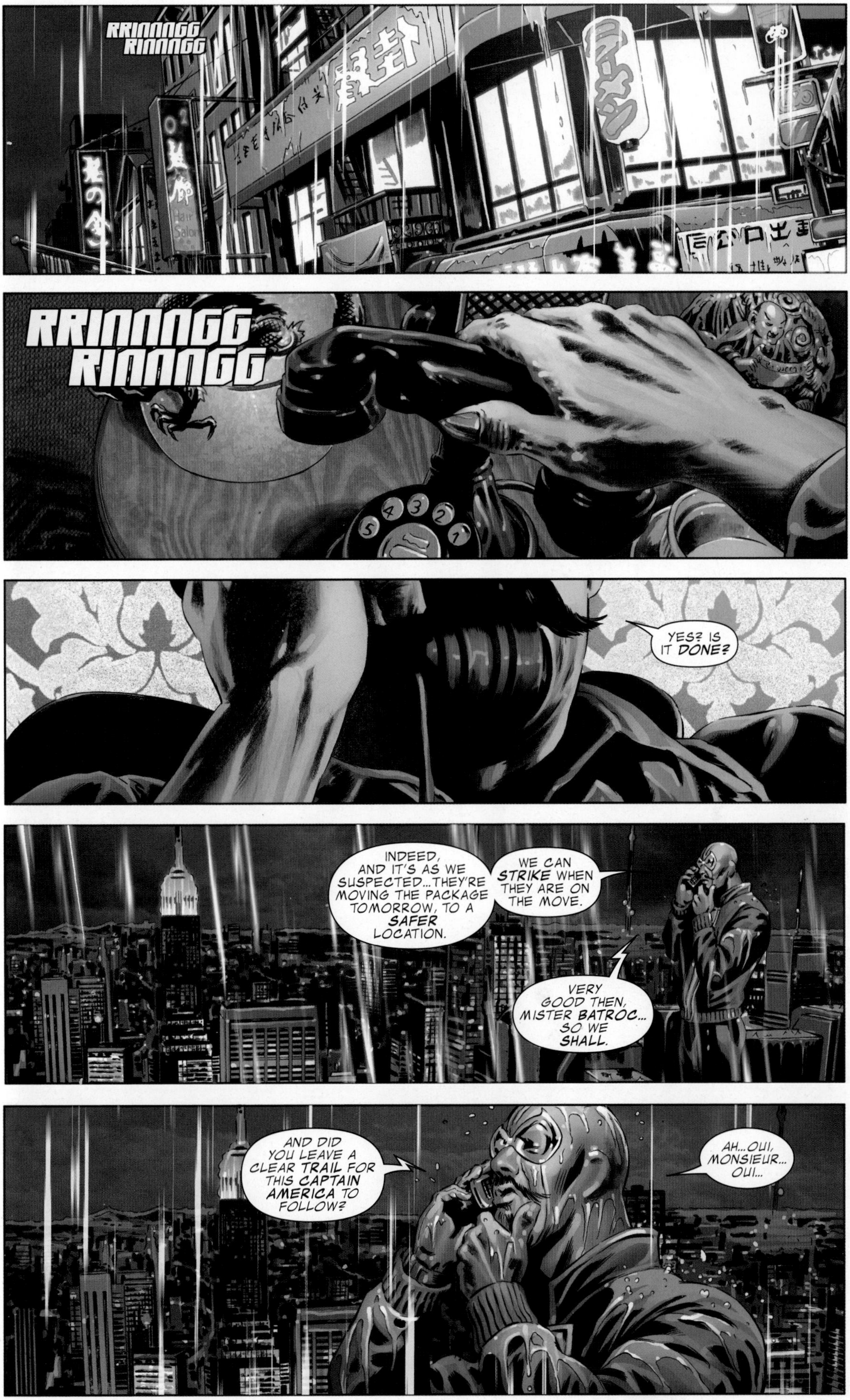
RRINNNGG
RINNNGG
RRINNNGG
RINNNGG
YES? IS IT DONE?
INDEED, AND IT'S AS WE SUSPECTED...THEY'RE MOVING THE PACKAGE TOMORROW, TO A SAFER LOCATION.
WE CAN STRIKE WHEN THEY ARE ON THE MOVE.
VERY GOOD THEN, MISTER BATROC... SO WE SHALL.
AND DID YOU LEAVE A CLEAR TRAIL FOR THIS CAPTAIN AMERICA TO FOLLOW?
AH...OUI, MONSIEUR... OUI...

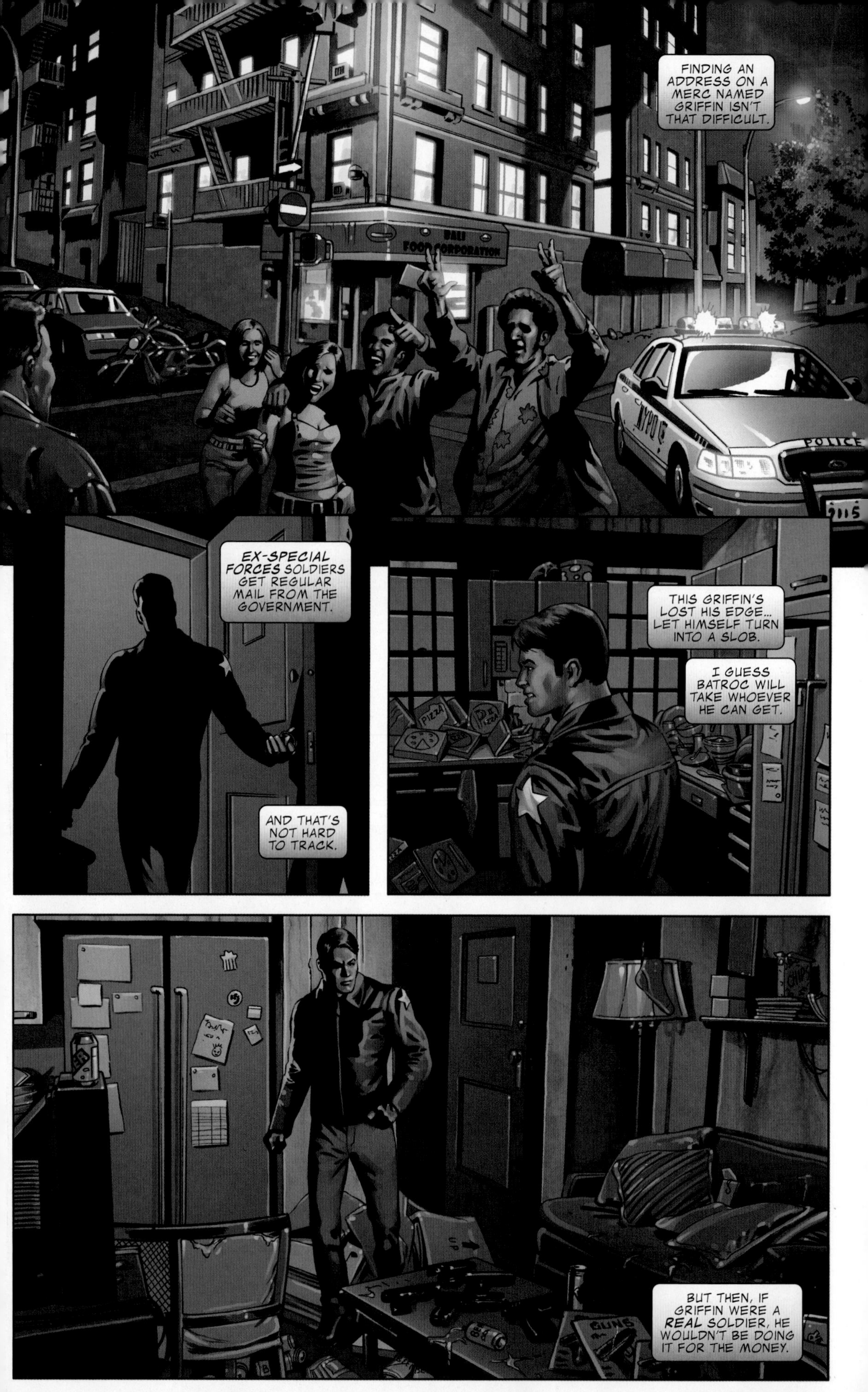
FINDING AN ADDRESS ON A MERC NAMED GRIFFIN ISN'T THAT DIFFICULT.
FOOD CORPORATION
POLICE
NYPD
EX-SPECIAL FORCES SOLDIERS GET REGULAR MAIL FROM THE GOVERNMENT.
AND THAT'S NOT HARD TO TRACK.
THIS GRIFFIN'S LOST HIS EDGE... LET HIMSELF TURN INTO A SLOB.
I GUESS BATROC WILL TAKE WHOEVER HE CAN GET.
PIZZA
BUT THEN, IF GRIFFIN WERE A REAL SOLDIER, HE WOULDN'T BE DOING IT FOR THE MONEY.
GUNS

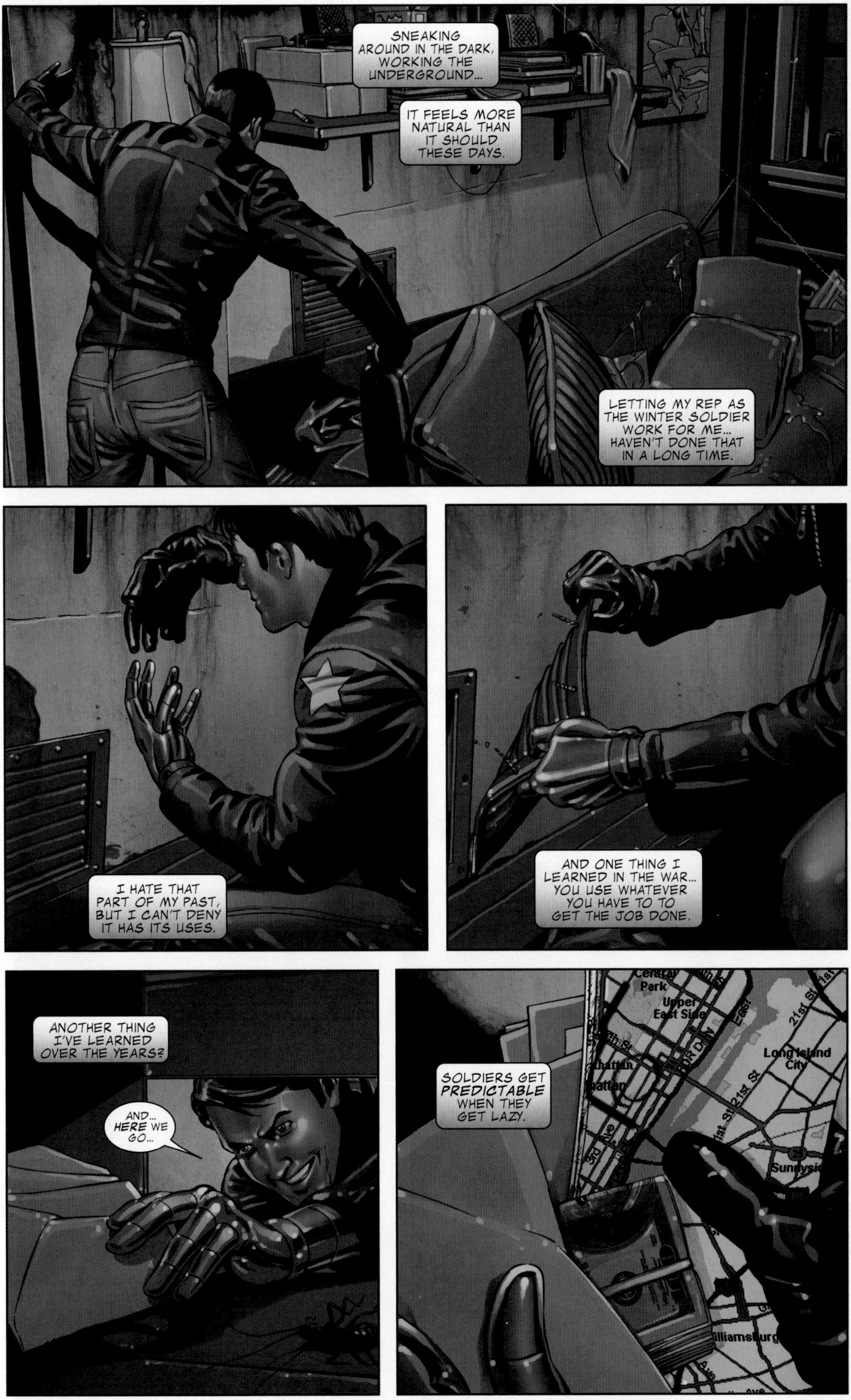
SNEAKING AROUND IN THE DARK, WORKING THE UNDERGROUND...
IT FEELS MORE NATURAL THAN IT SHOULD THESE DAYS.
LETTING MY REP AS THE WINTER SOLDIER WORK FOR ME... HAVEN'T DONE THAT IN A LONG TIME.
I HATE THAT PART OF MY PAST, BUT I CAN'T DENY IT HAS ITS USES.
AND ONE THING I LEARNED IN THE WAR... YOU USE WHATEVER YOU HAVE TO TO GET THE JOB DONE.
ANOTHER THING I'VE LEARNED OVER THE YEARS?
AND... *HERE* WE GO...
SOLDIERS GET ***PREDICTABLE*** WHEN THEY GET LAZY.
Central Park
Upper East Side
Long Island City

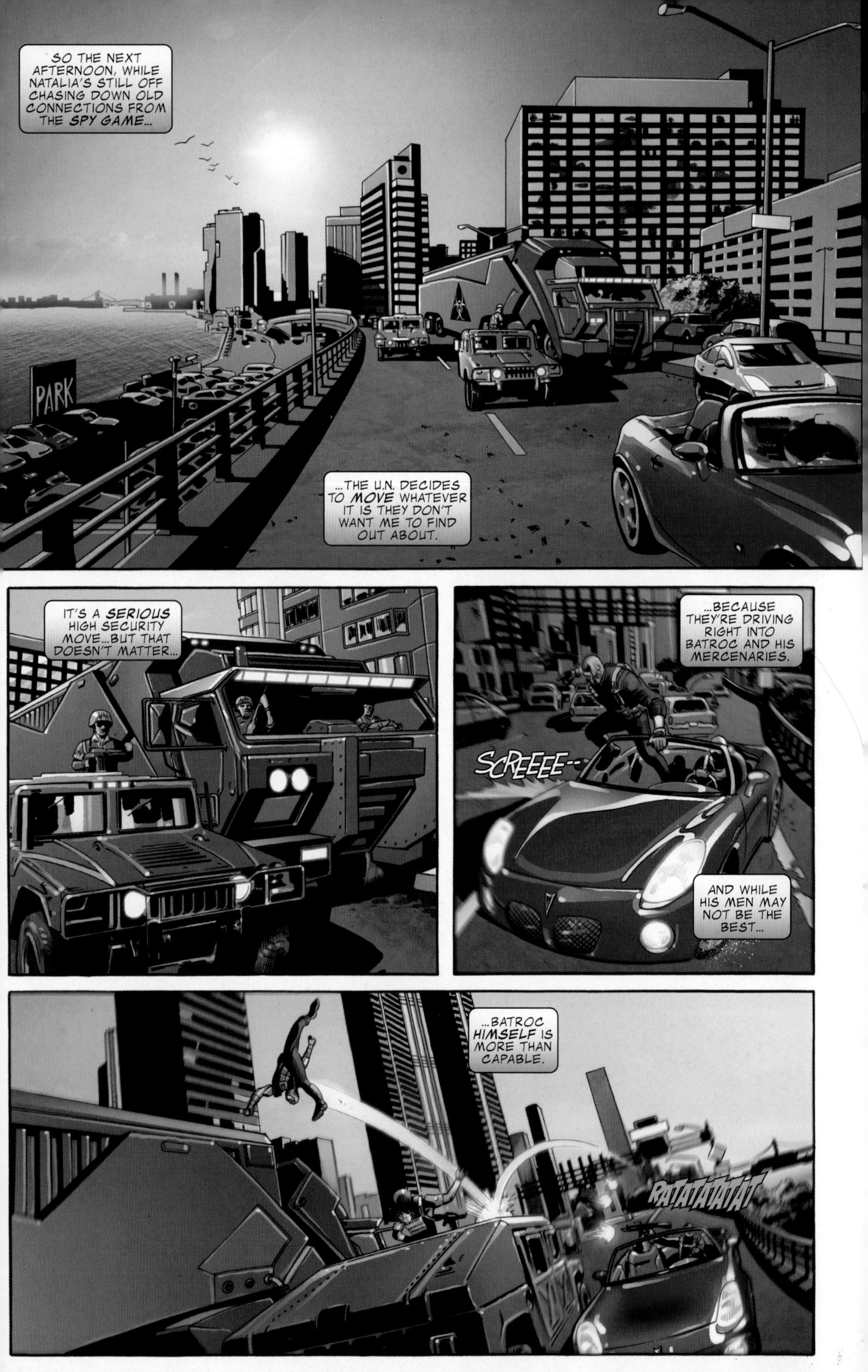
SO THE NEXT AFTERNOON, WHILE NATALIA'S STILL OFF CHASING DOWN OLD CONNECTIONS FROM THE SPY GAME...
PARK
...THE U.N. DECIDES TO MOVE WHATEVER IT IS THEY DON'T WANT ME TO FIND OUT ABOUT.
IT'S A SERIOUS HIGH SECURITY MOVE...BUT THAT DOESN'T MATTER...
...BECAUSE THEY'RE DRIVING RIGHT INTO BATROC AND HIS MERCENARIES.
SCREEEE--
AND WHILE HIS MEN MAY NOT BE THE BEST...
...BATROC HIMSELF IS MORE THAN CAPABLE.
RATATATATAT

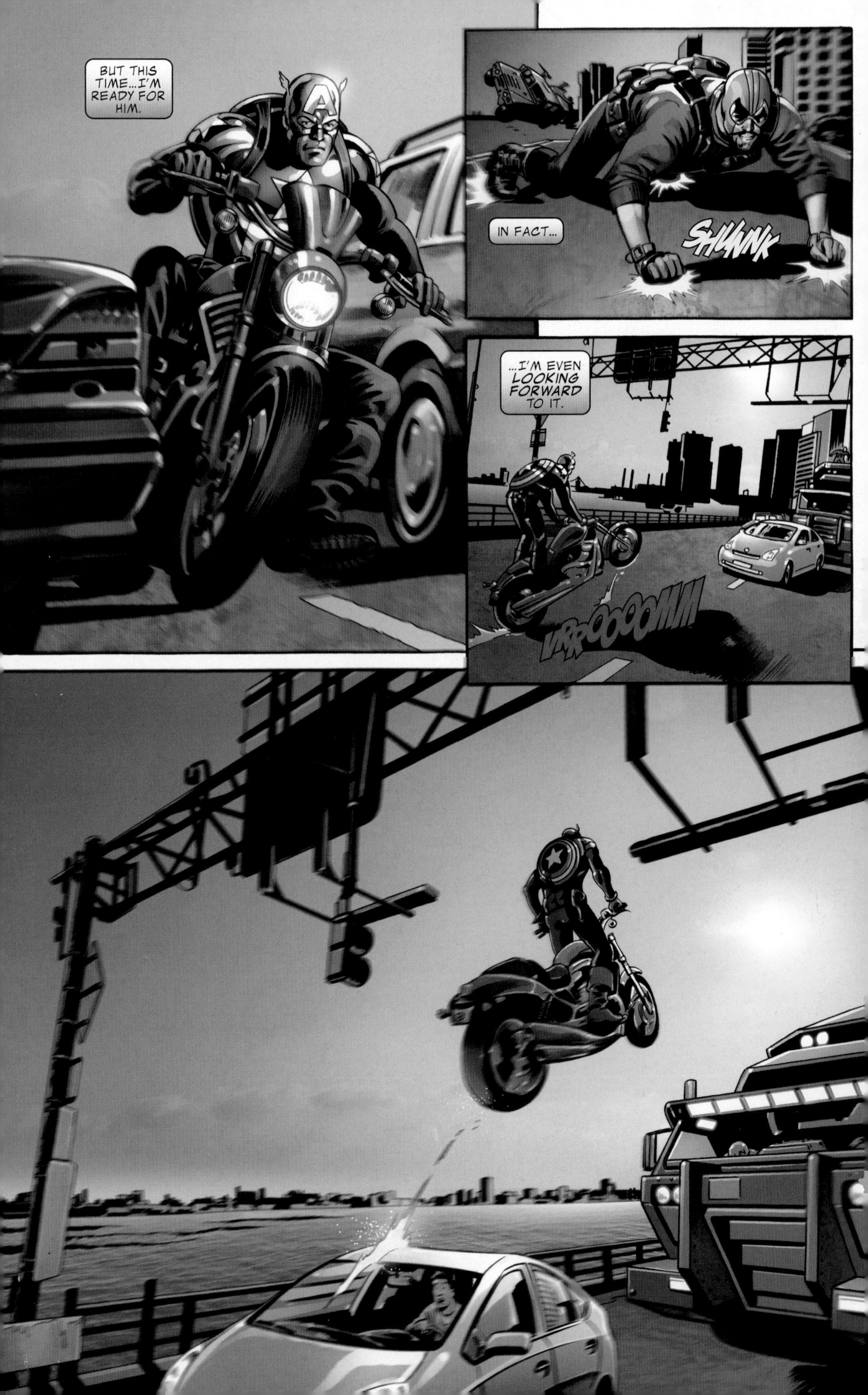
BUT THIS TIME...I'M READY FOR HIM.
IN FACT...
SHUNK
...I'M EVEN LOOKING FORWARD TO IT.
VRROOOOMM

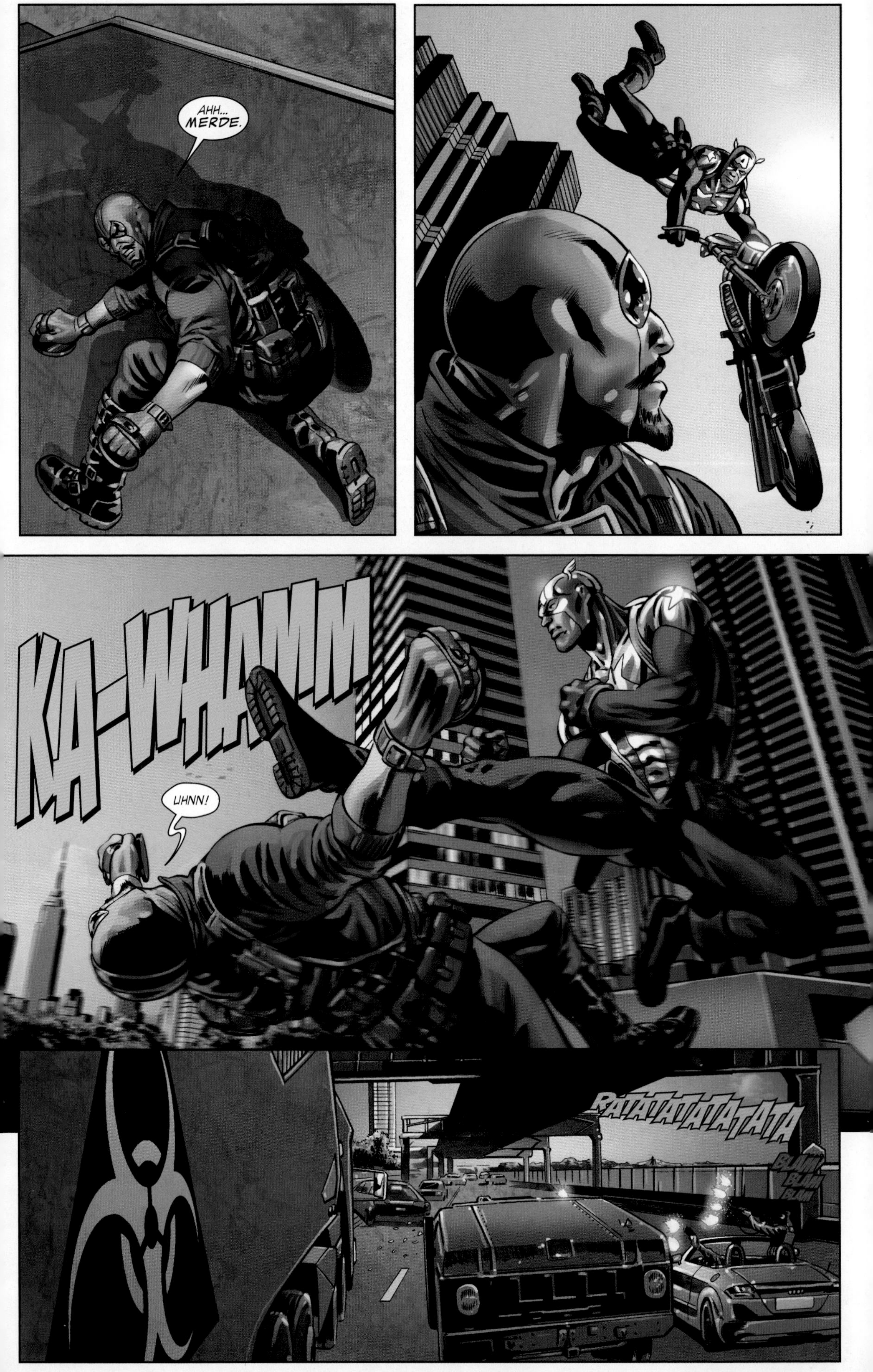
AHH... MERDE.
KA-WHAMM
UHNN!
RATATATATATATA
BLAM BLAM BLAM

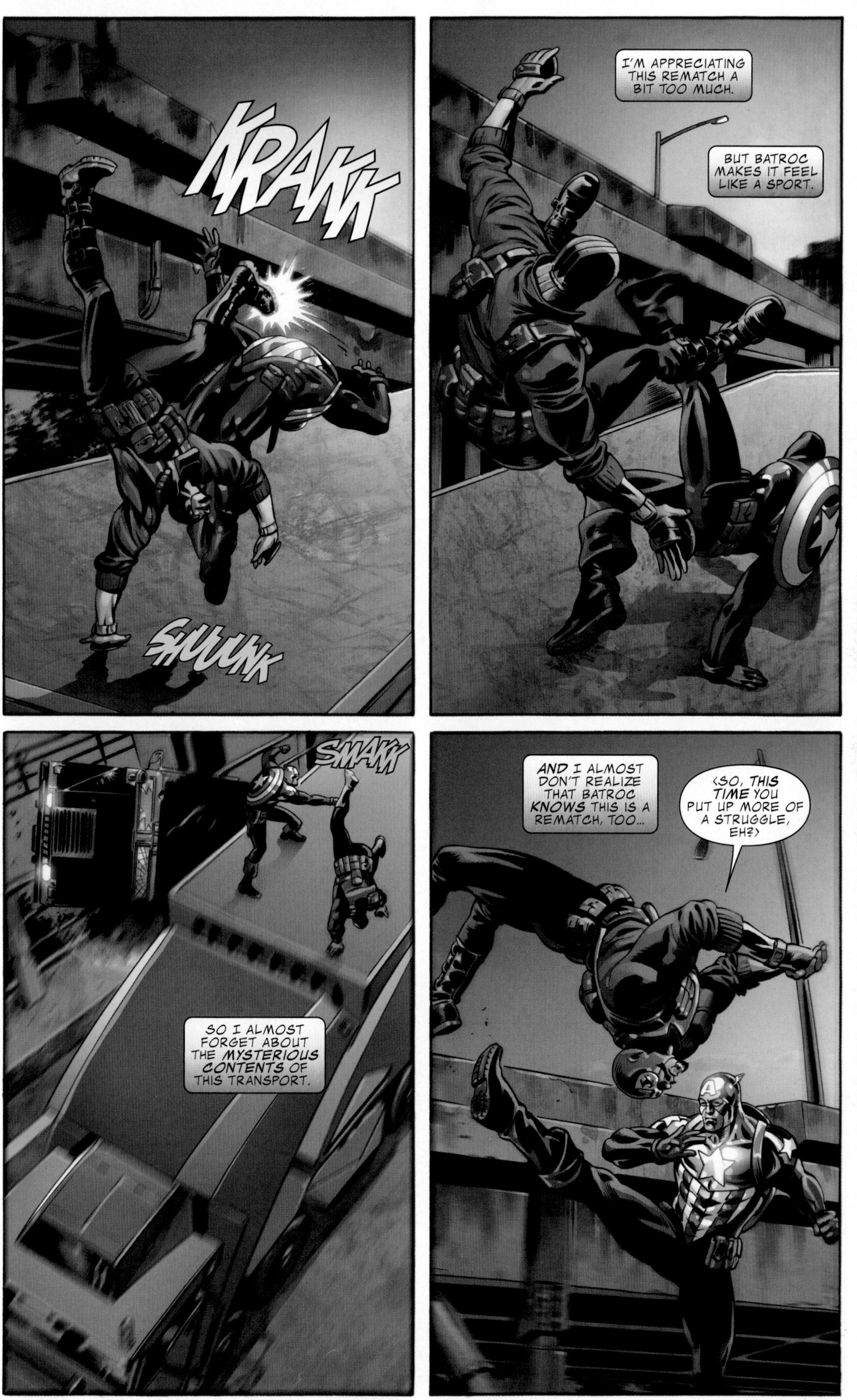
KRAKK
SHUUUNK
I'M APPRECIATING THIS REMATCH A BIT TOO MUCH.
BUT BATROC MAKES IT FEEL LIKE A SPORT.
SMAKK
SO I ALMOST FORGET ABOUT THE MYSTERIOUS CONTENTS OF THIS TRANSPORT.
AND I ALMOST DON'T REALIZE THAT BATROC KNOWS THIS IS A REMATCH, TOO...
‹SO, THIS TIME YOU PUT UP MORE OF A STRUGGLE, EH?›

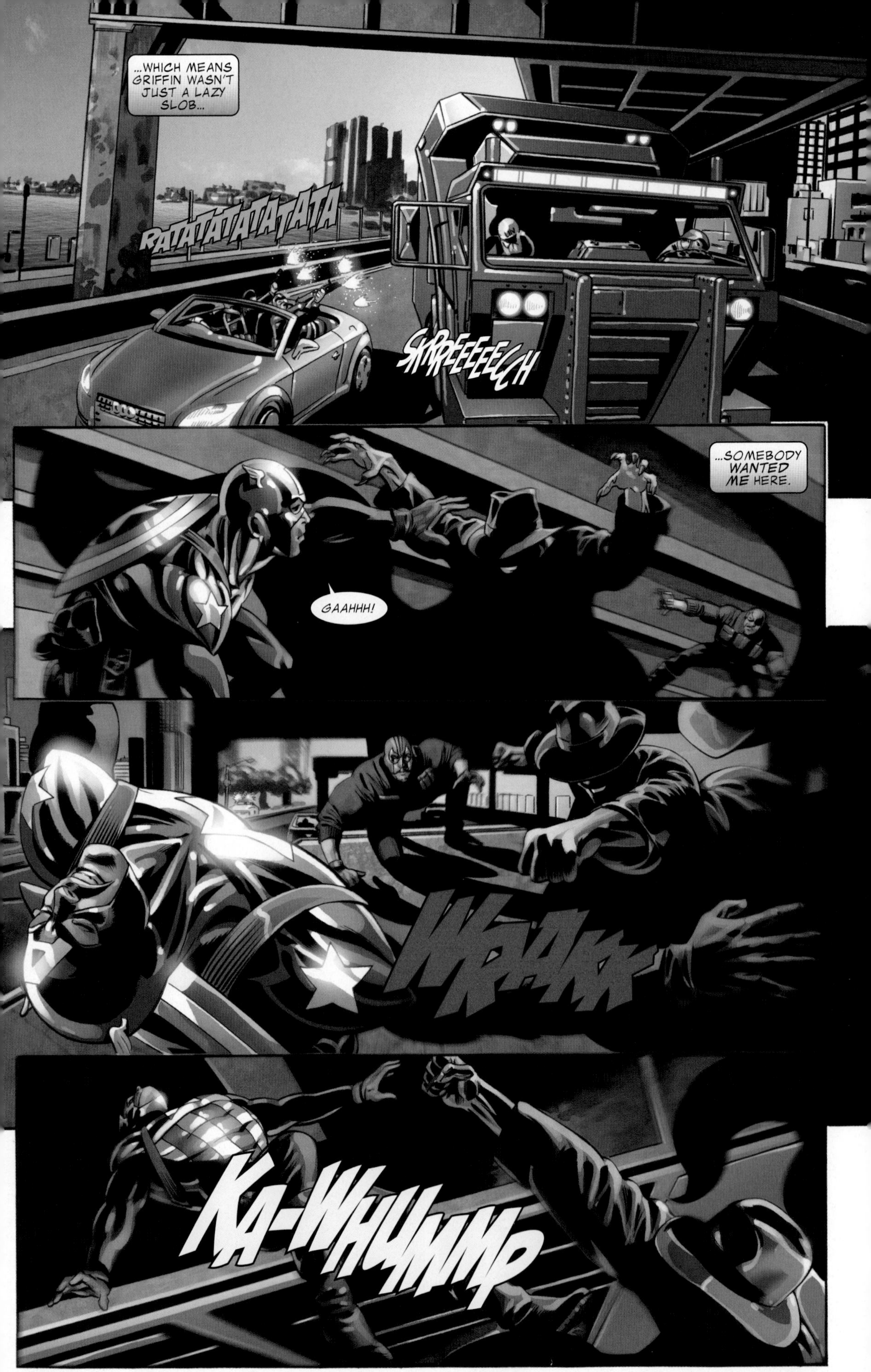
...WHICH MEANS GRIFFIN WASN'T JUST A LAZY SLOB...
RATATATATATATA
SKRREEEEECH
...SOMEBODY WANTED ME HERE.
GAAHHH!
WHAKK
KA-WHUMMP

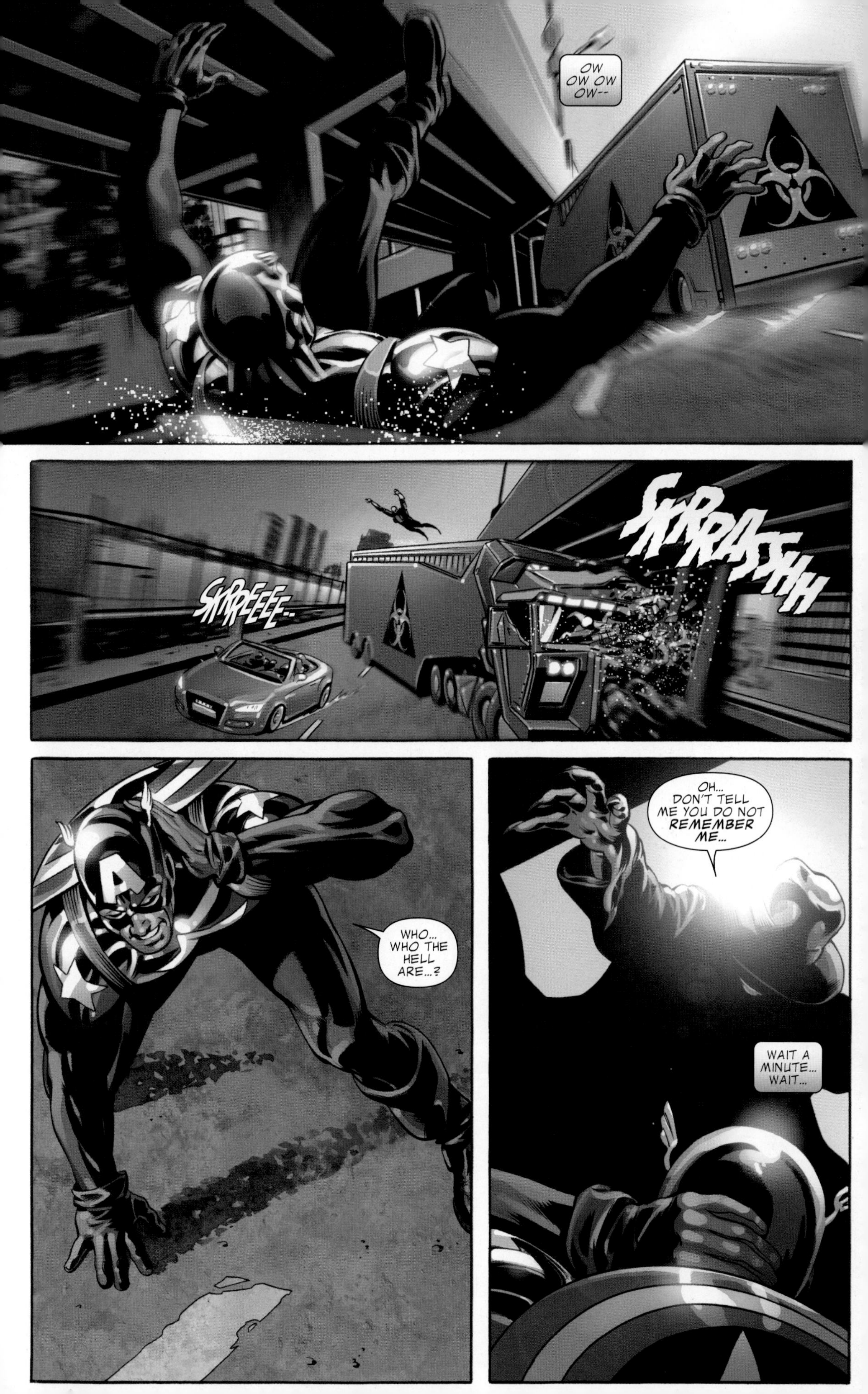
OW OW OW OW--
SKRASHH
SKREEEE--
WHO... WHO THE HELL ARE...?
OH... DON'T TELL ME YOU DO NOT REMEMBER ME...
WAIT A MINUTE... WAIT...

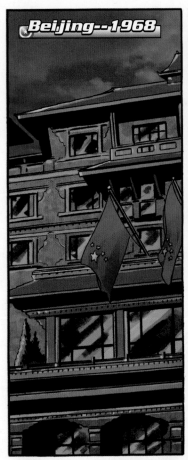

<...AND THE CHAIRMAN THOUGHT MY VIEWS, WHILE *VALID*, WERE *TOO REVOLUTIONARY*, EVEN FOR HIM.>

<EVEN *HE* CANNOT FACE WHAT IS COMING. WHAT WE *KNOW* IS COMING.>

<EVEN HE CANNOT FACE FACTS.>

<HUMANKIND WILL DESTROY THIS PLANET...WE WILL BLEED IT DRY LIKE A CANCER...>

<WE WILL--->

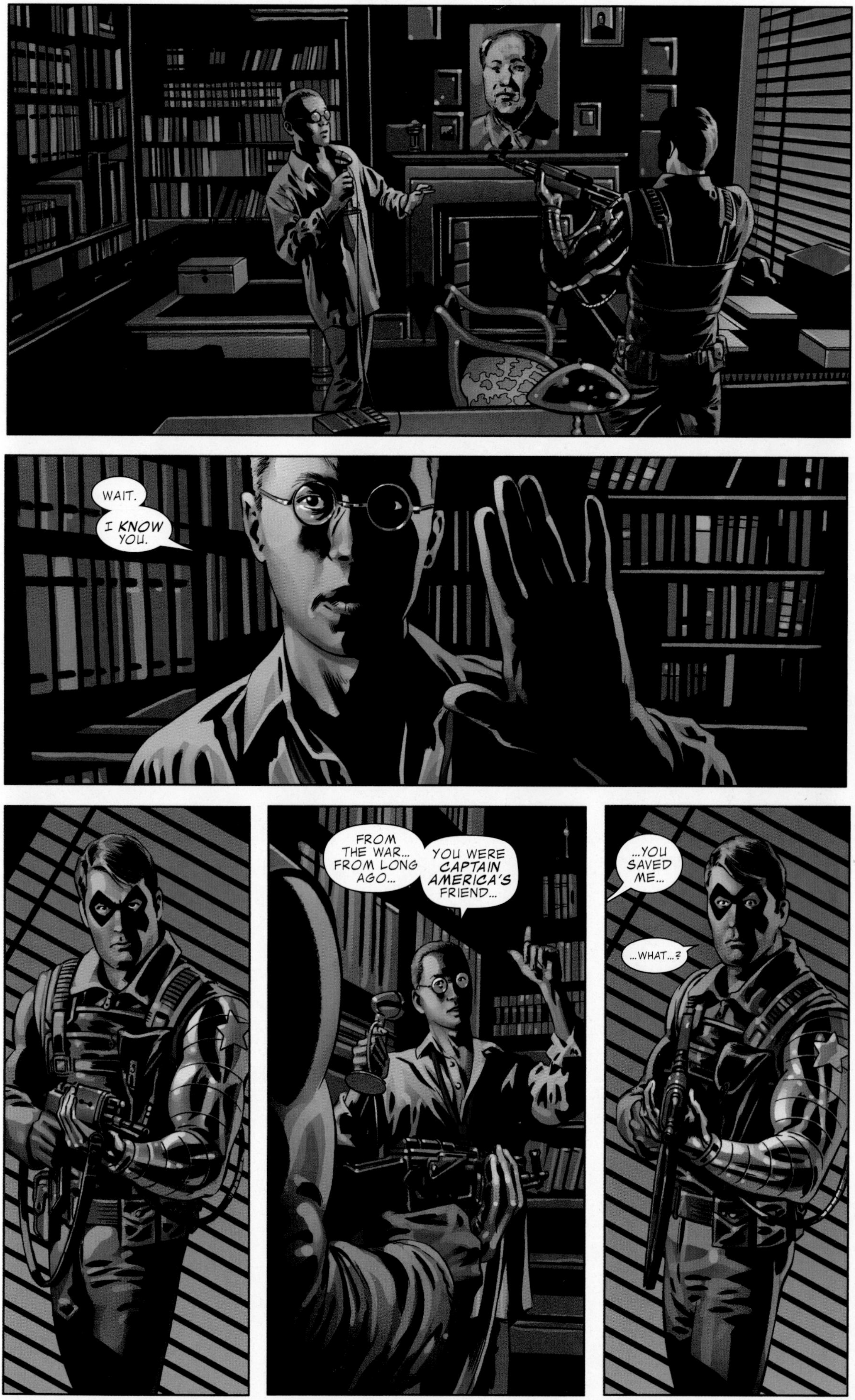
WAIT.
I KNOW YOU.
FROM THE WAR... FROM LONG AGO...
YOU WERE CAPTAIN AMERICA'S FRIEND...
...YOU SAVED ME...
...WHAT...?

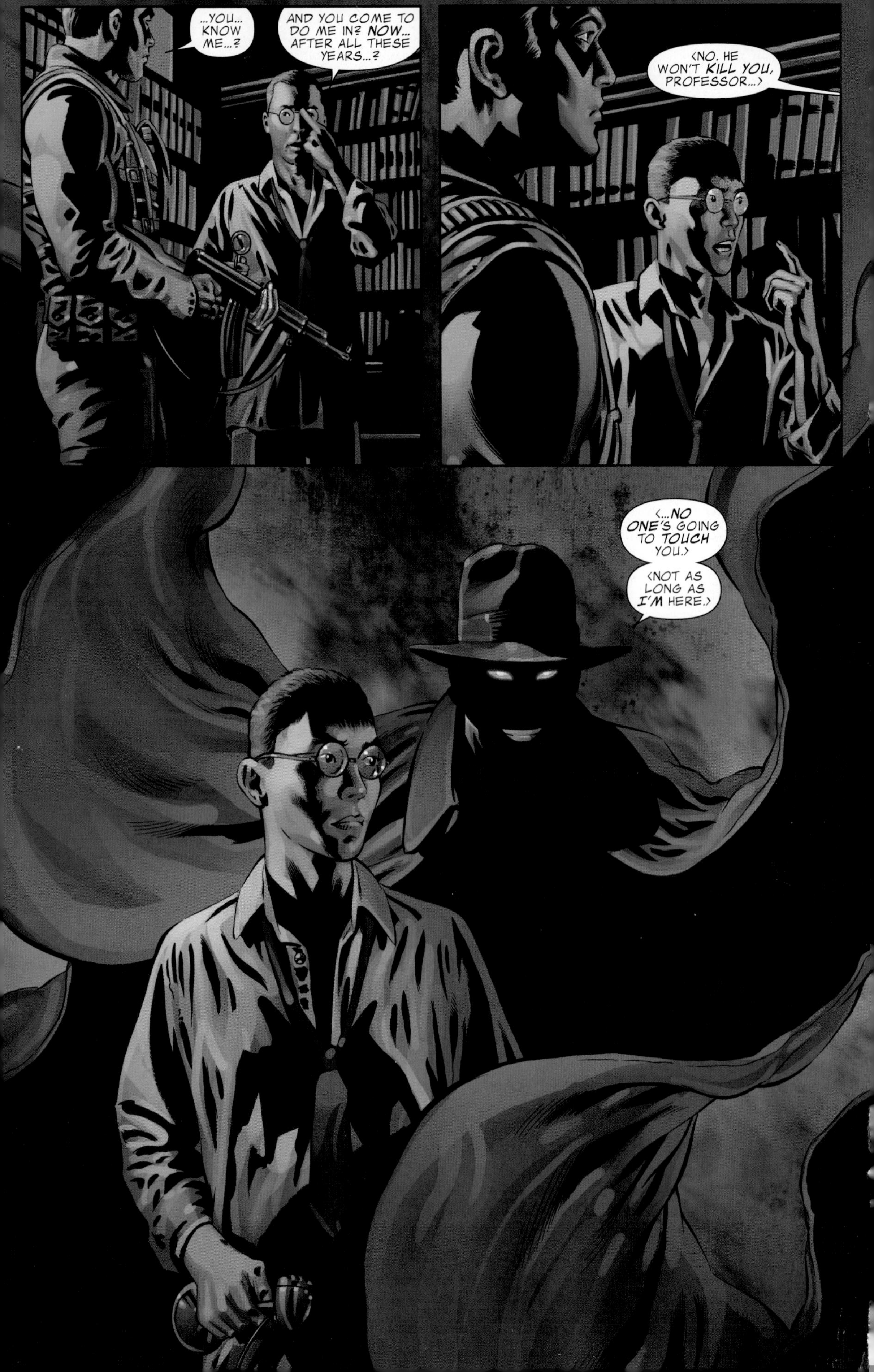
...YOU... KNOW ME...?
AND YOU COME TO DO ME IN? NOW... AFTER ALL THESE YEARS...?
<NO. HE WON'T KILL YOU, PROFESSOR...>
<...NO ONE'S GOING TO TOUCH YOU.>
<NOT AS LONG AS I'M HERE.>

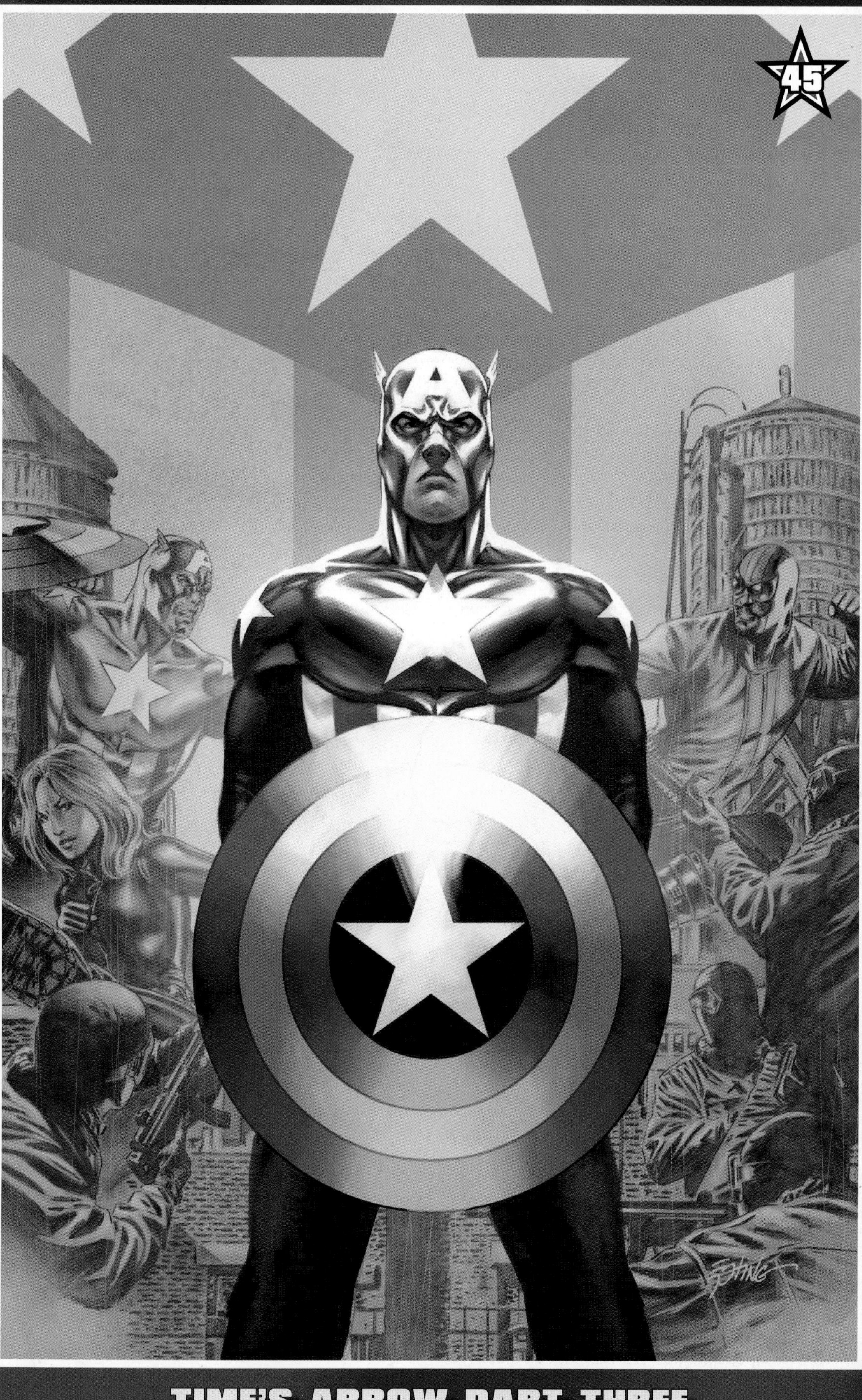
45

TIME'S ARROW PART THREE

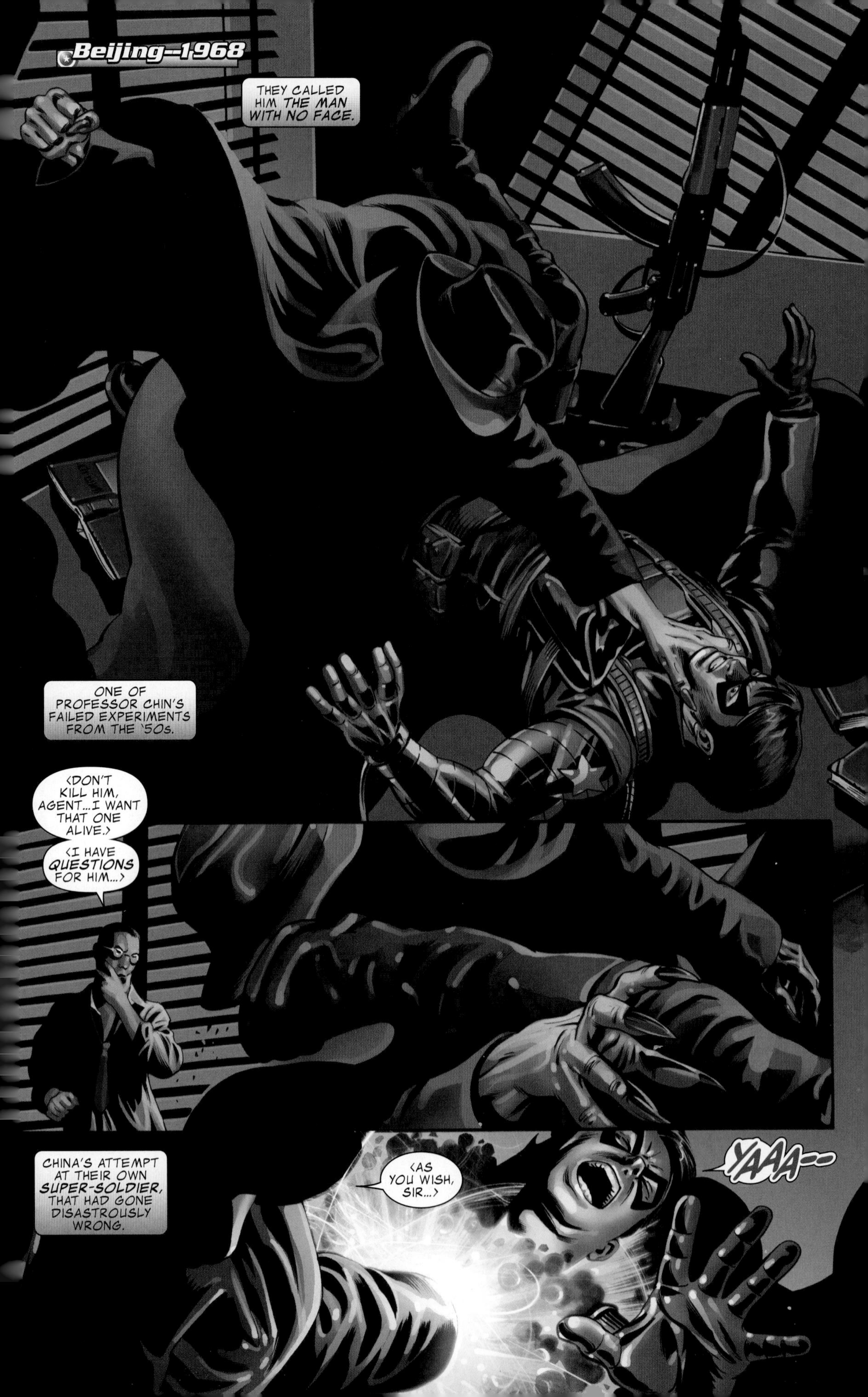
Beijing--1968
THEY CALLED HIM THE MAN WITH NO FACE.
ONE OF PROFESSOR CHIN'S FAILED EXPERIMENTS FROM THE '50s.
<DON'T KILL HIM, AGENT...I WANT THAT ONE ALIVE.>
<I HAVE QUESTIONS FOR HIM...>
CHINA'S ATTEMPT AT THEIR OWN SUPER-SOLDIER, THAT HAD GONE DISASTROUSLY WRONG.
<AS YOU WISH, SIR...>
YAAA--

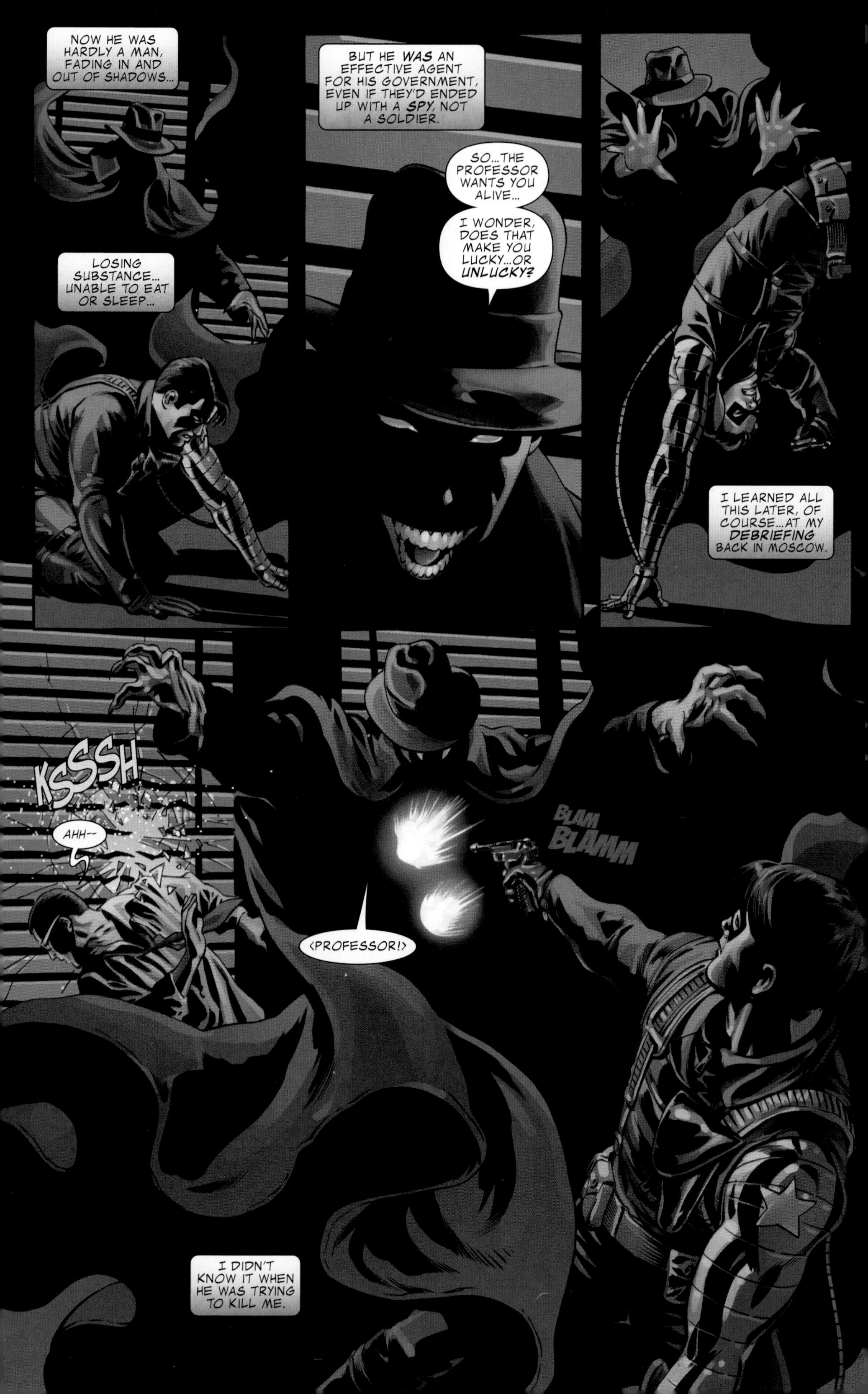
NOW HE WAS HARDLY A MAN, FADING IN AND OUT OF SHADOWS...
LOSING SUBSTANCE... UNABLE TO EAT OR SLEEP...
BUT HE WAS AN EFFECTIVE AGENT FOR HIS GOVERNMENT, EVEN IF THEY'D ENDED UP WITH A SPY, NOT A SOLDIER.
SO...THE PROFESSOR WANTS YOU ALIVE...
I WONDER, DOES THAT MAKE YOU LUCKY...OR UNLUCKY?
I LEARNED ALL THIS LATER, OF COURSE...AT MY DEBRIEFING BACK IN MOSCOW.
KSSSH
AHH--
BLAM BLAMM
<PROFESSOR!>
I DIDN'T KNOW IT WHEN HE WAS TRYING TO KILL ME.

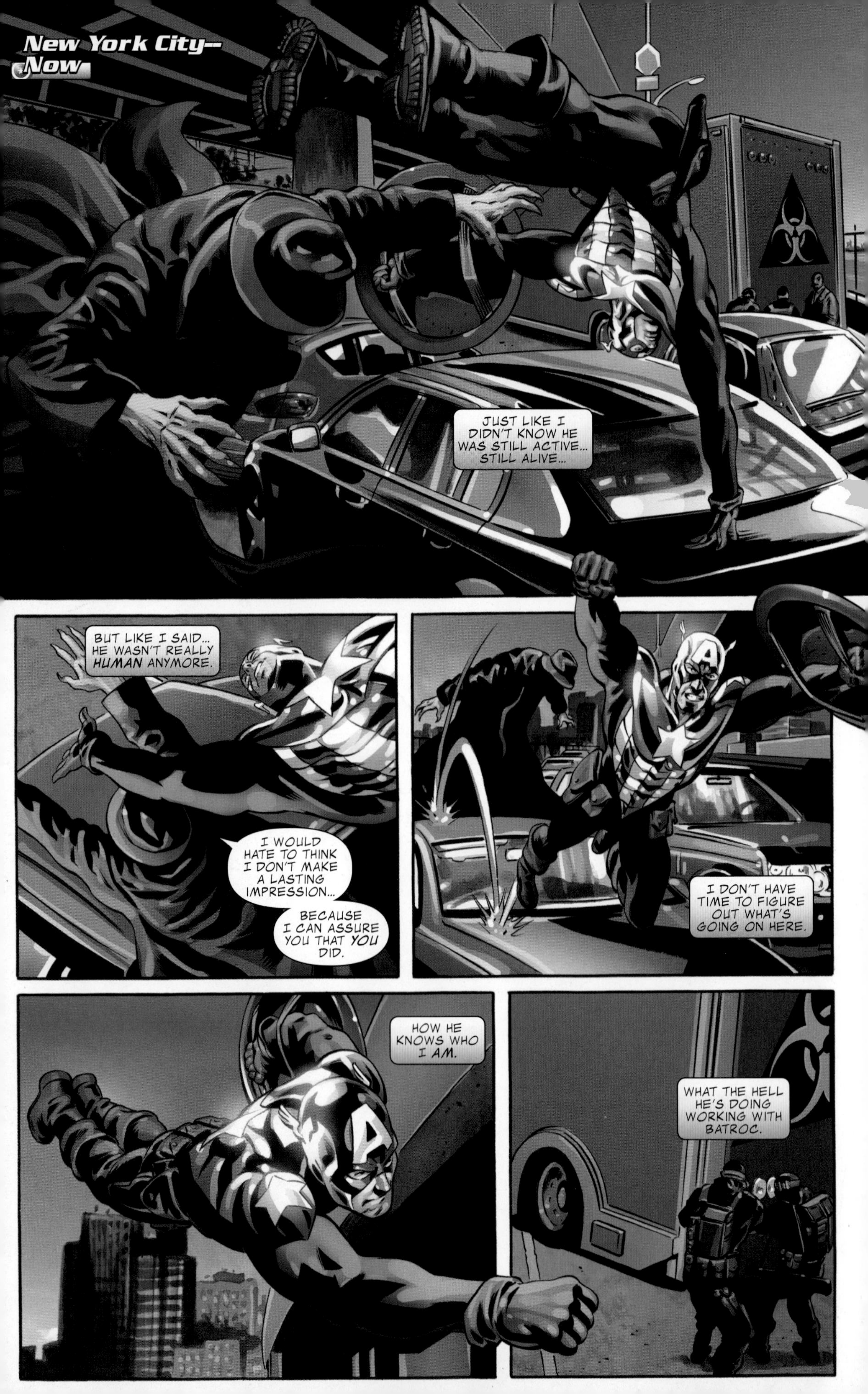

New York City--
Now
JUST LIKE I DIDN'T KNOW HE WAS STILL ACTIVE... STILL ALIVE...
BUT LIKE I SAID... HE WASN'T REALLY HUMAN ANYMORE.
I WOULD HATE TO THINK I DON'T MAKE A LASTING IMPRESSION...
BECAUSE I CAN ASSURE YOU THAT YOU DID.
I DON'T HAVE TIME TO FIGURE OUT WHAT'S GOING ON HERE.
HOW HE KNOWS WHO I AM.
WHAT THE HELL HE'S DOING WORKING WITH BATROC.

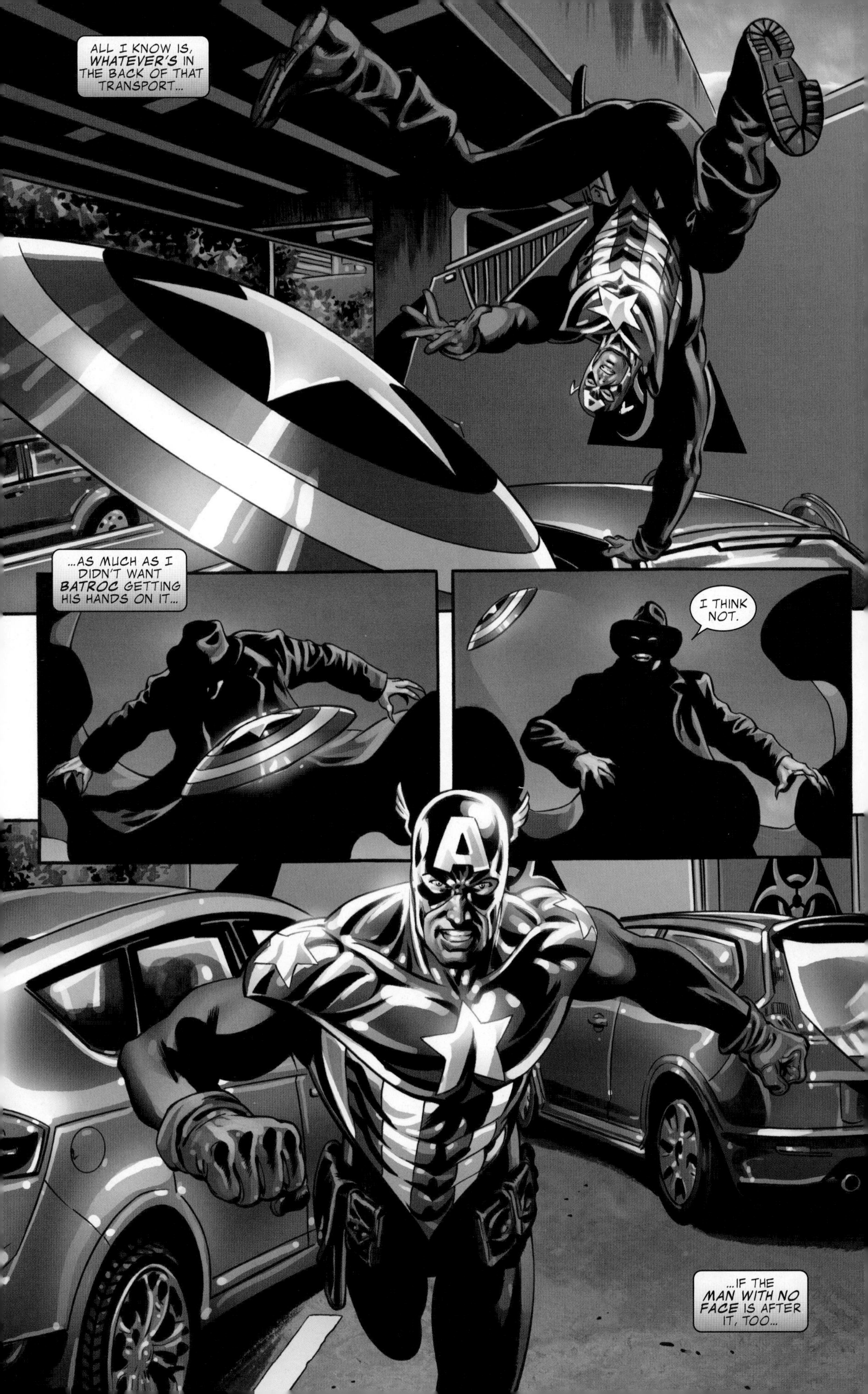
ALL I KNOW IS, *WHATEVER'S* IN THE BACK OF THAT TRANSPORT...
...AS MUCH AS I DIDN'T WANT *BATROC* GETTING HIS HANDS ON IT...
I THINK NOT.
...IF THE *MAN WITH NO FACE* IS AFTER IT, TOO...

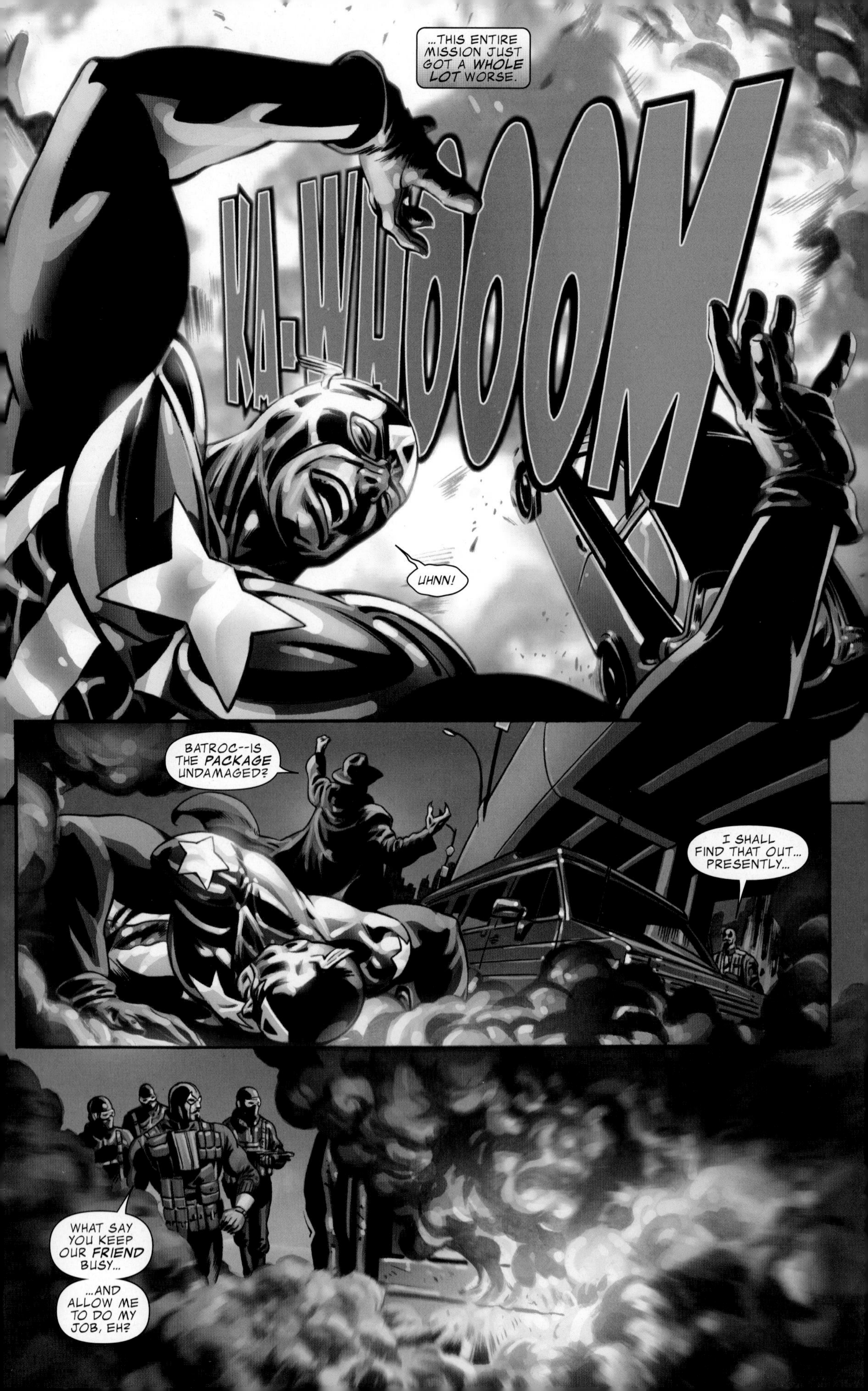
...THIS ENTIRE MISSION JUST GOT A WHOLE LOT WORSE.
KA-WHOOOOM
UHNN!
BATROC--IS THE PACKAGE UNDAMAGED?
I SHALL FIND THAT OUT... PRESENTLY...
WHAT SAY YOU KEEP OUR FRIEND BUSY...
...AND ALLOW ME TO DO MY JOB, EH?

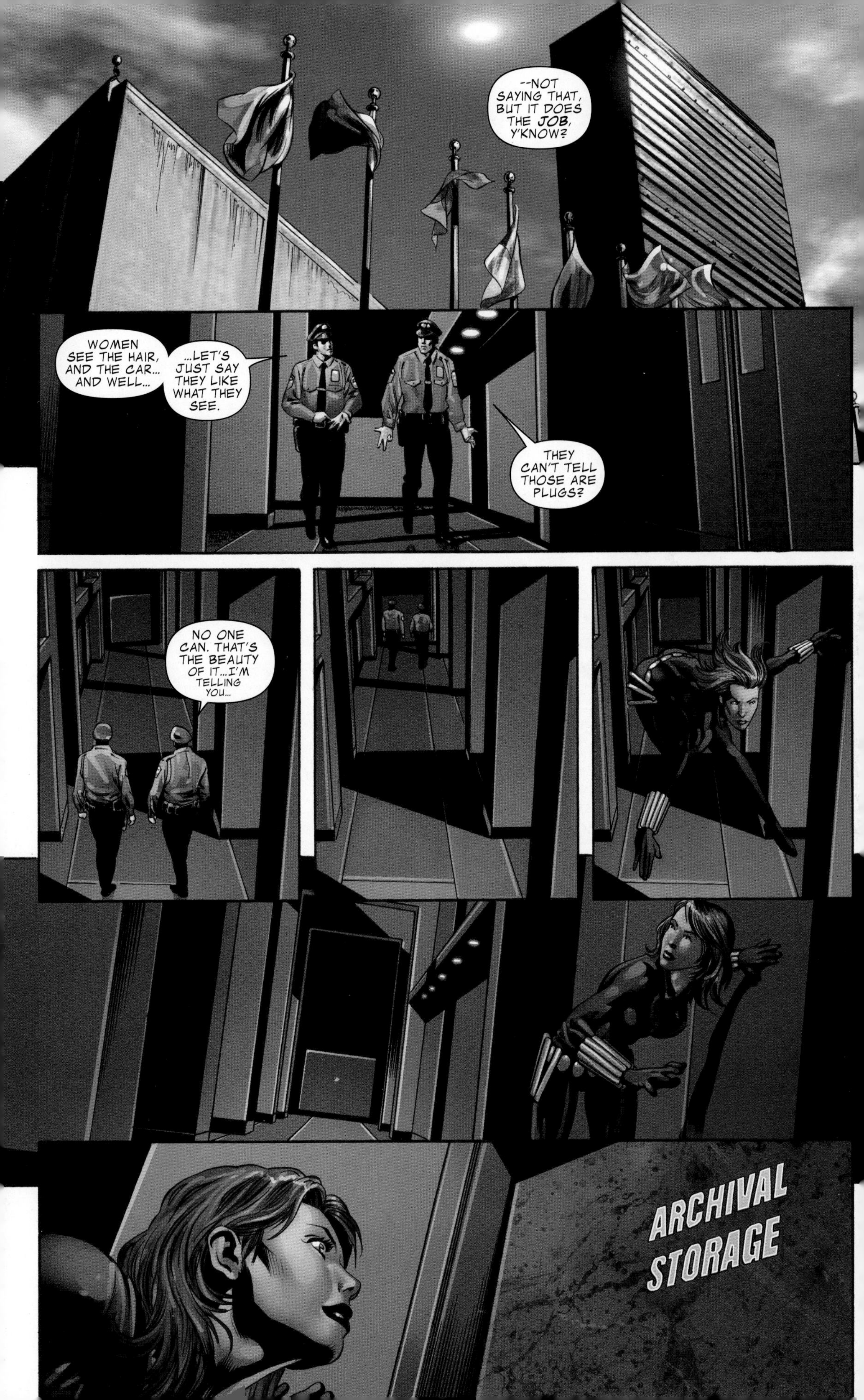
--NOT SAYING THAT, BUT IT DOES THE JOB, Y'KNOW?
WOMEN SEE THE HAIR, AND THE CAR... AND WELL...
...LET'S JUST SAY THEY LIKE WHAT THEY SEE.
THEY CAN'T TELL THOSE ARE PLUGS?
NO ONE CAN. THAT'S THE BEAUTY OF IT...I'M TELLING YOU...
ARCHIVAL STORAGE

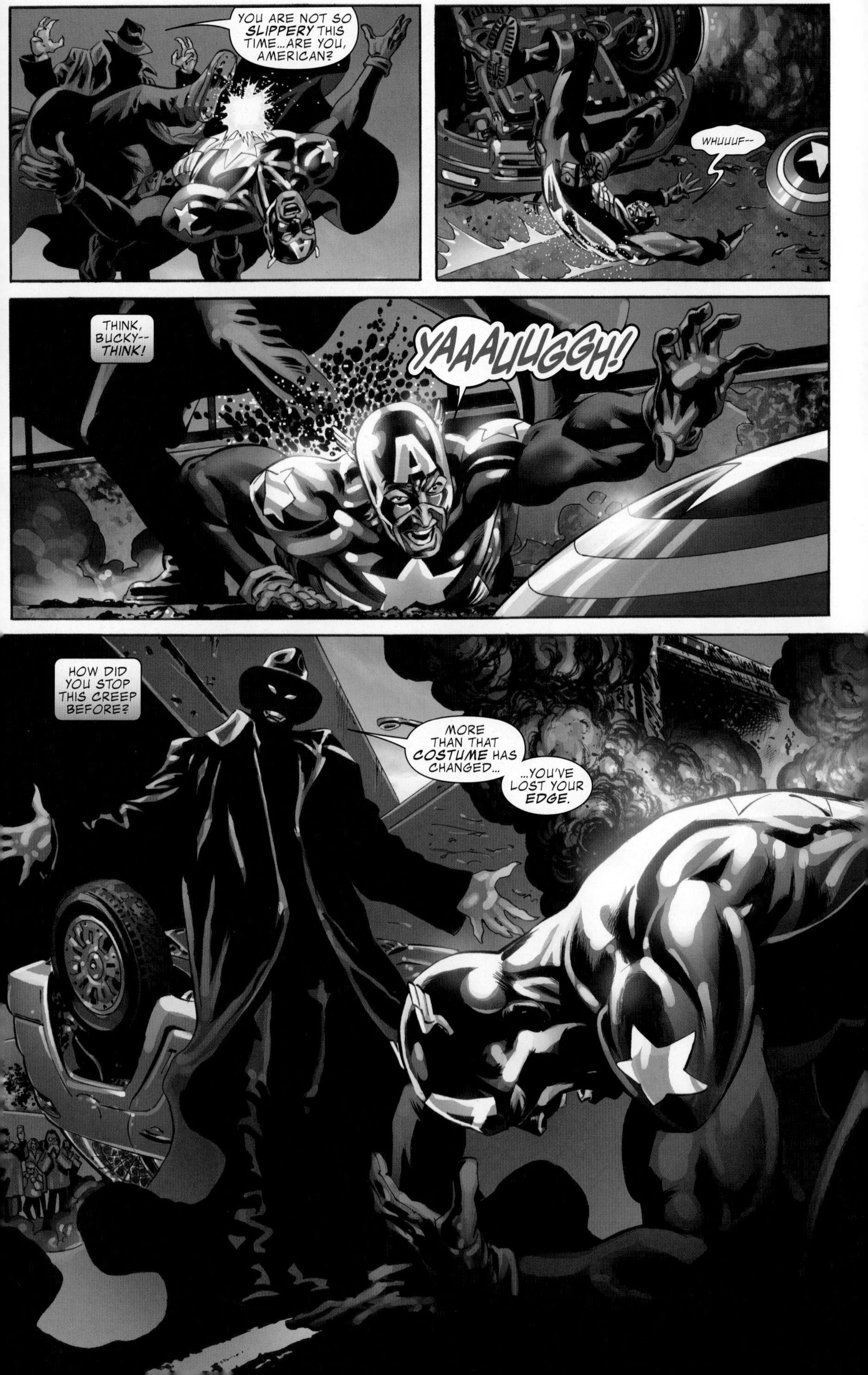
YOU ARE NOT SO SLIPPERY THIS TIME...ARE YOU, AMERICAN?
WHUUUF--
THINK, BUCKY--THINK!
YAAAUUGGH!
HOW DID YOU STOP THIS CREEP BEFORE?
MORE THAN THAT COSTUME HAS CHANGED...
...YOU'VE LOST YOUR EDGE.

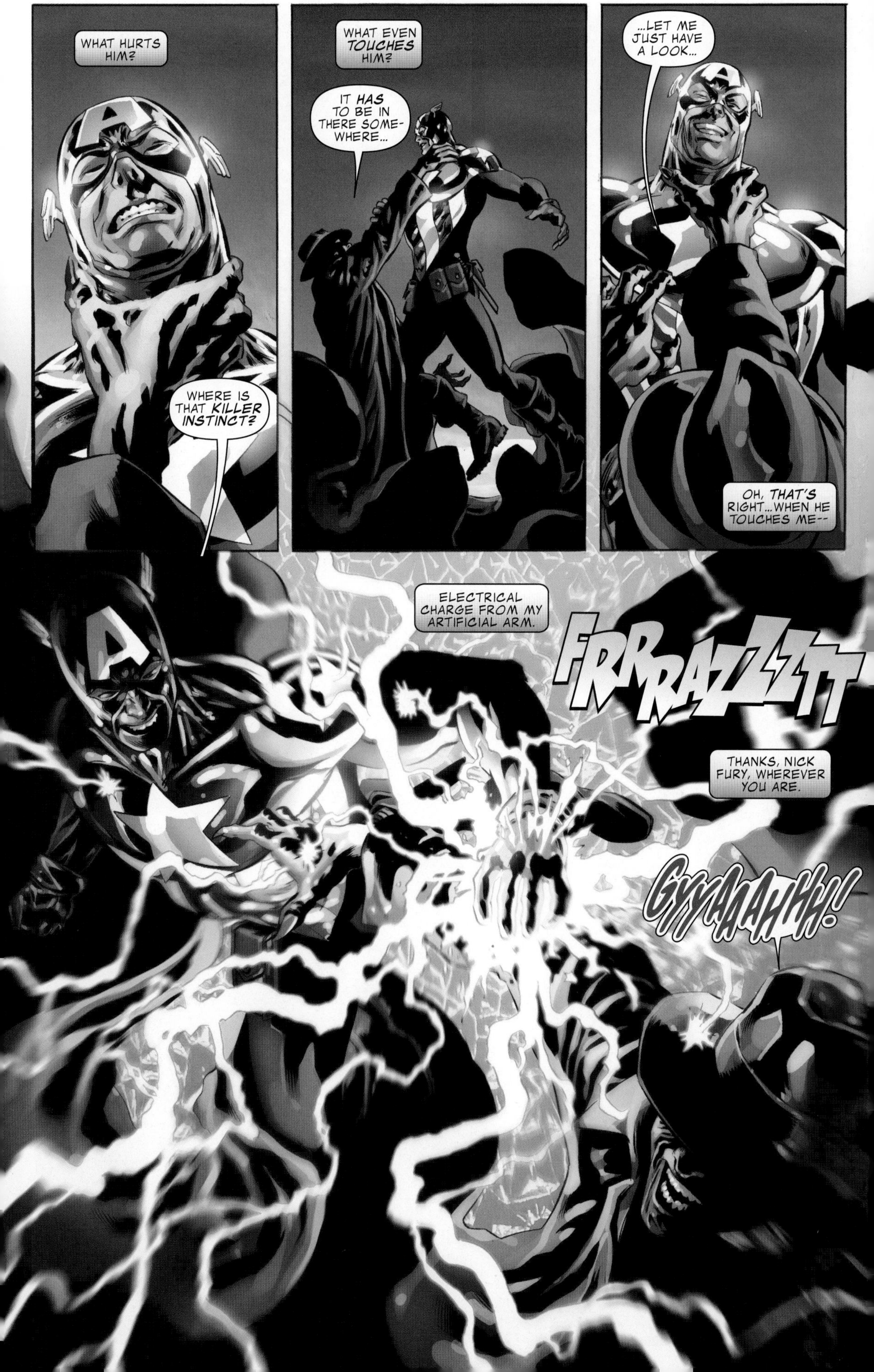
WHAT HURTS HIM?
WHERE IS THAT KILLER INSTINCT?
WHAT EVEN TOUCHES HIM?
IT HAS TO BE IN THERE SOME-WHERE...
...LET ME JUST HAVE A LOOK...
OH, THAT'S RIGHT...WHEN HE TOUCHES ME--
ELECTRICAL CHARGE FROM MY ARTIFICIAL ARM.
FRRRAZZZTT
THANKS, NICK FURY, WHEREVER YOU ARE.
GYYAAAAHHH!

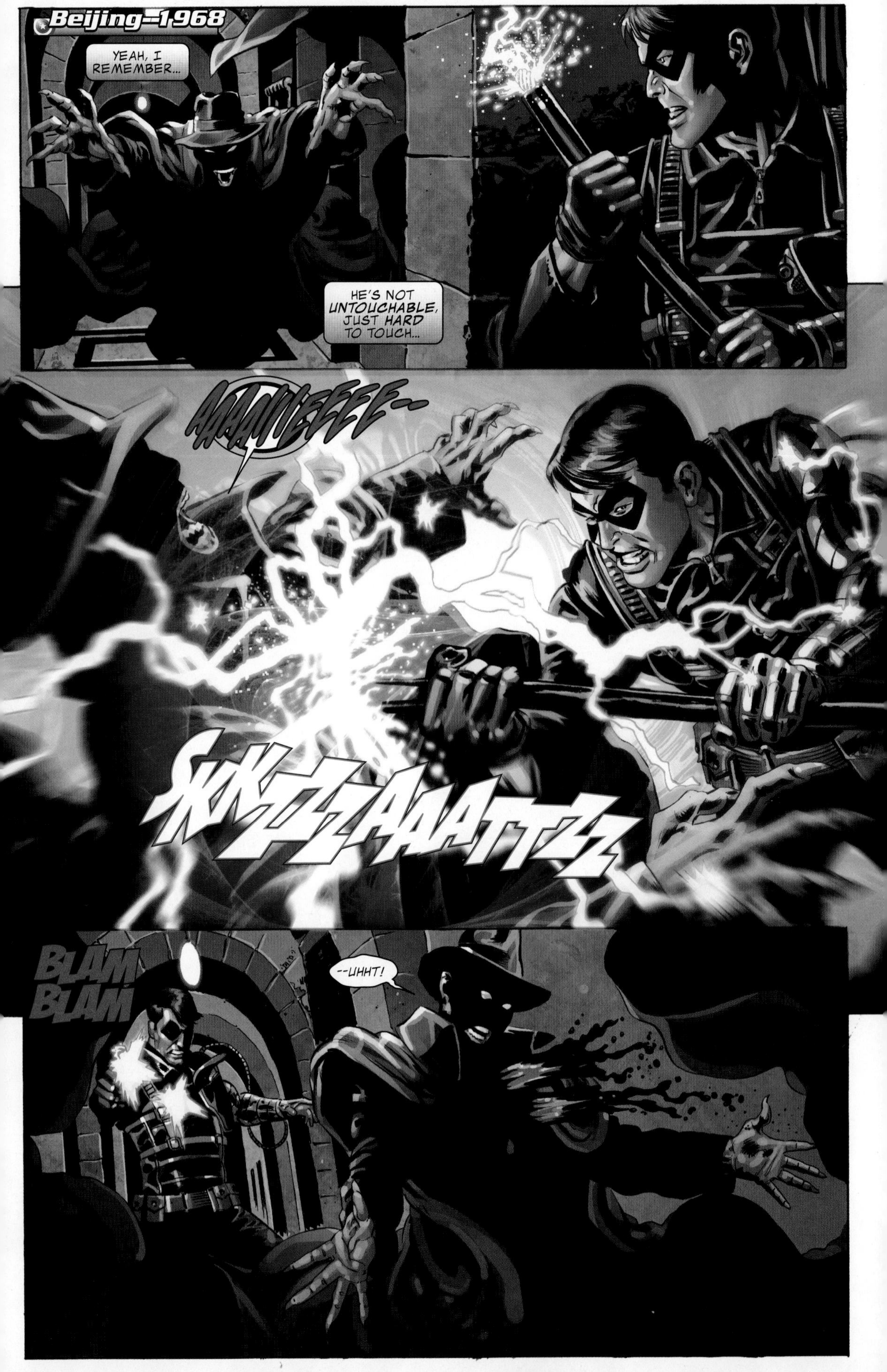
Beijing--1968
YEAH, I REMEMBER...
HE'S NOT UNTOUCHABLE, JUST HARD TO TOUCH...
AAAAIIEEEE--
SKKZZZAAATTZZ
BLAM BLAM
--UHHT!

...AND NOT EASY TO *KEEP* DOWN.

<AGENT?>

<STAY *BACK*, LEADER! IT'S NOT SAFE!>

THIS WAS ONE OF THE FEW MISSIONS THAT WENT BELLY-UP ON ME.

WHERE ESCAPE SUDDENLY TOOK PRIORITY OVER ALL OTHER OBJECTIVES.

A SOVIET AGENT COULDN'T BE FOUND HUNTING SCIENTISTS IN CHINA.

<NO, AGENT-- *STOP HIM!*>

<DON'T LET HIM GO *THAT WAY!*>

IT WAS ESCAPE AT ALL COSTS...

BLAM BLAM BLAM

...BY ANY MEANS NECESSARY.

<NOT THAT WAY!>

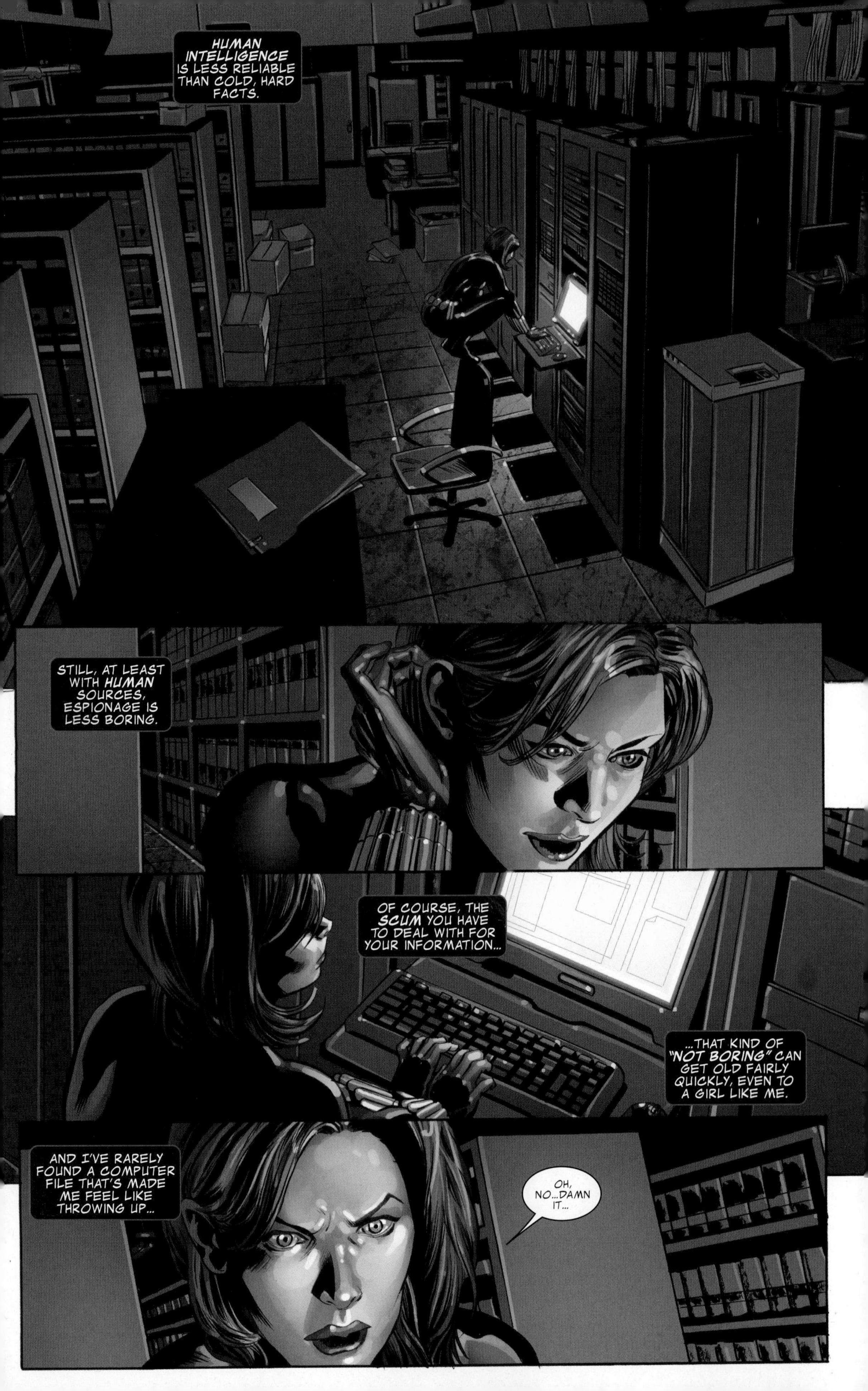
HUMAN INTELLIGENCE IS LESS RELIABLE THAN COLD, HARD FACTS.
STILL, AT LEAST WITH HUMAN SOURCES, ESPIONAGE IS LESS BORING.
OF COURSE, THE SCUM YOU HAVE TO DEAL WITH FOR YOUR INFORMATION...
...THAT KIND OF "NOT BORING" CAN GET OLD FAIRLY QUICKLY, EVEN TO A GIRL LIKE ME.
AND I'VE RARELY FOUND A COMPUTER FILE THAT'S MADE ME FEEL LIKE THROWING UP...
OH, NO...DAMN IT...

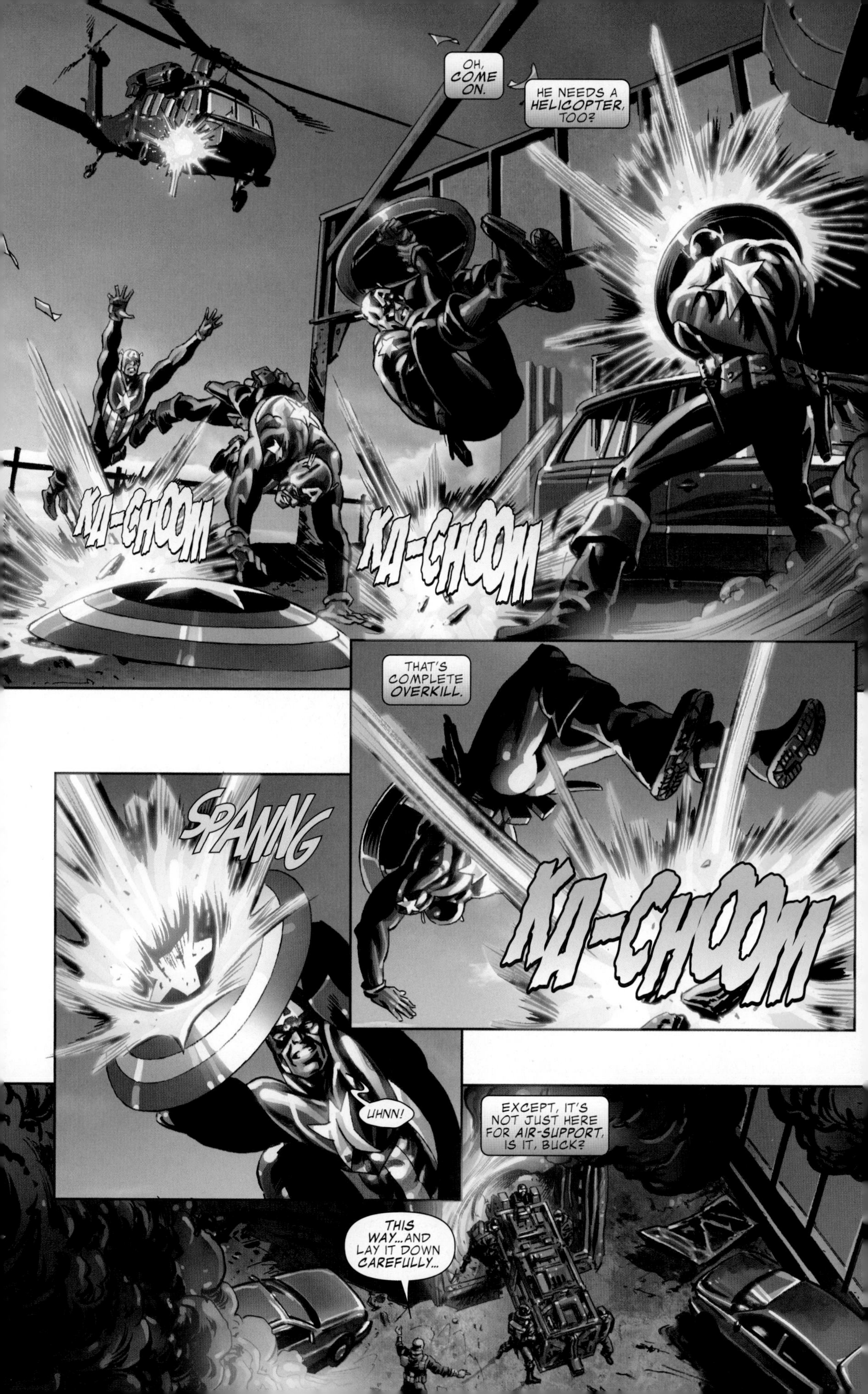
OH, COME ON.
HE NEEDS A HELICOPTER, TOO?
KA-CHOOM
KA-CHOOM
THAT'S COMPLETE OVERKILL.
KA-CHOOM
SPANNG
UHNN!
EXCEPT, IT'S NOT JUST HERE FOR AIR-SUPPORT. IS IT, BUCK?
THIS WAY...AND LAY IT DOWN CAREFULLY...

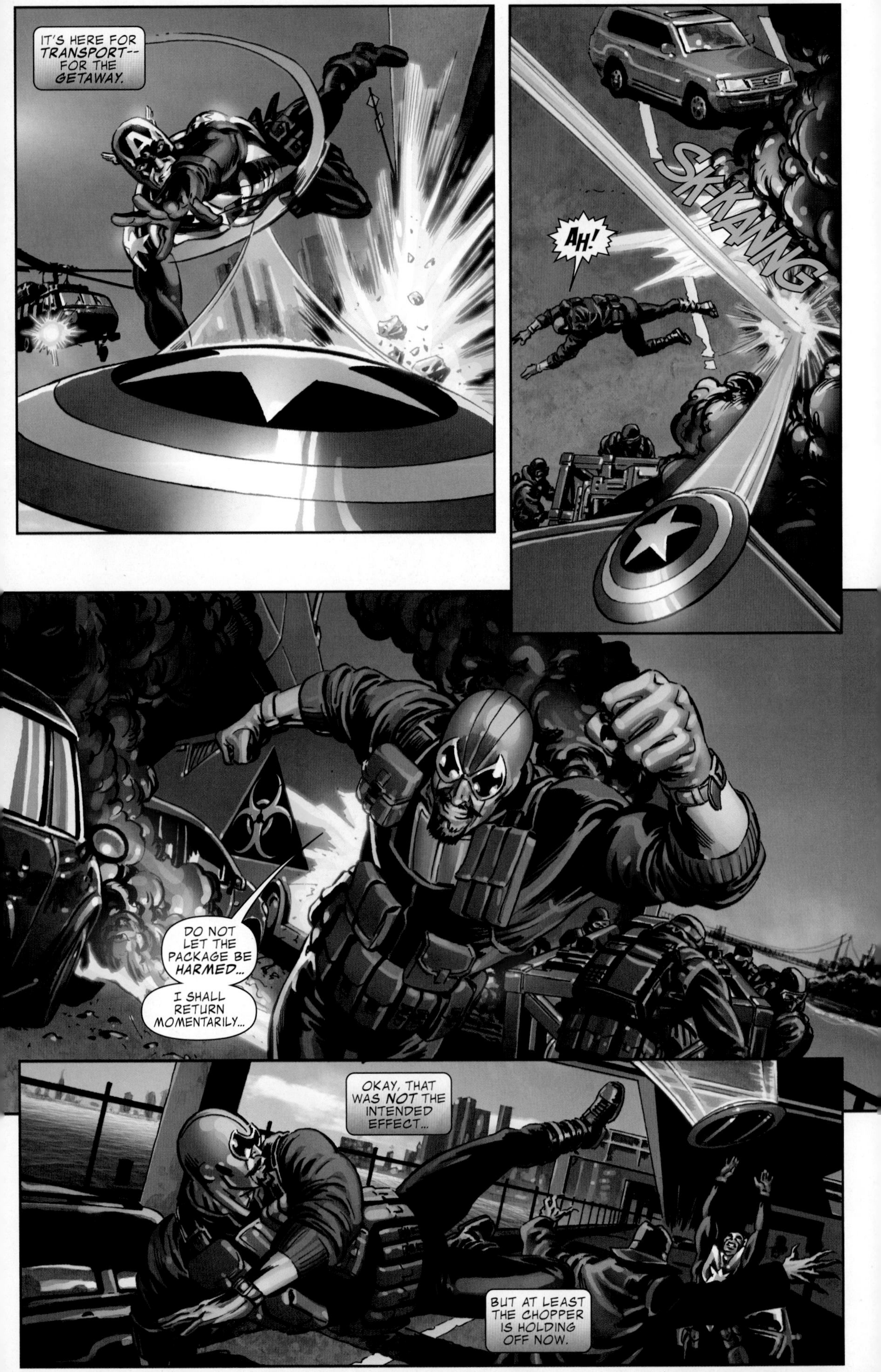
IT'S HERE FOR TRANSPORT-- FOR THE GETAWAY.
SK-KANNG
AH!
DO NOT LET THE PACKAGE BE HARMED...
I SHALL RETURN MOMENTARILY...
OKAY, THAT WAS NOT THE INTENDED EFFECT...
BUT AT LEAST THE CHOPPER IS HOLDING OFF NOW.

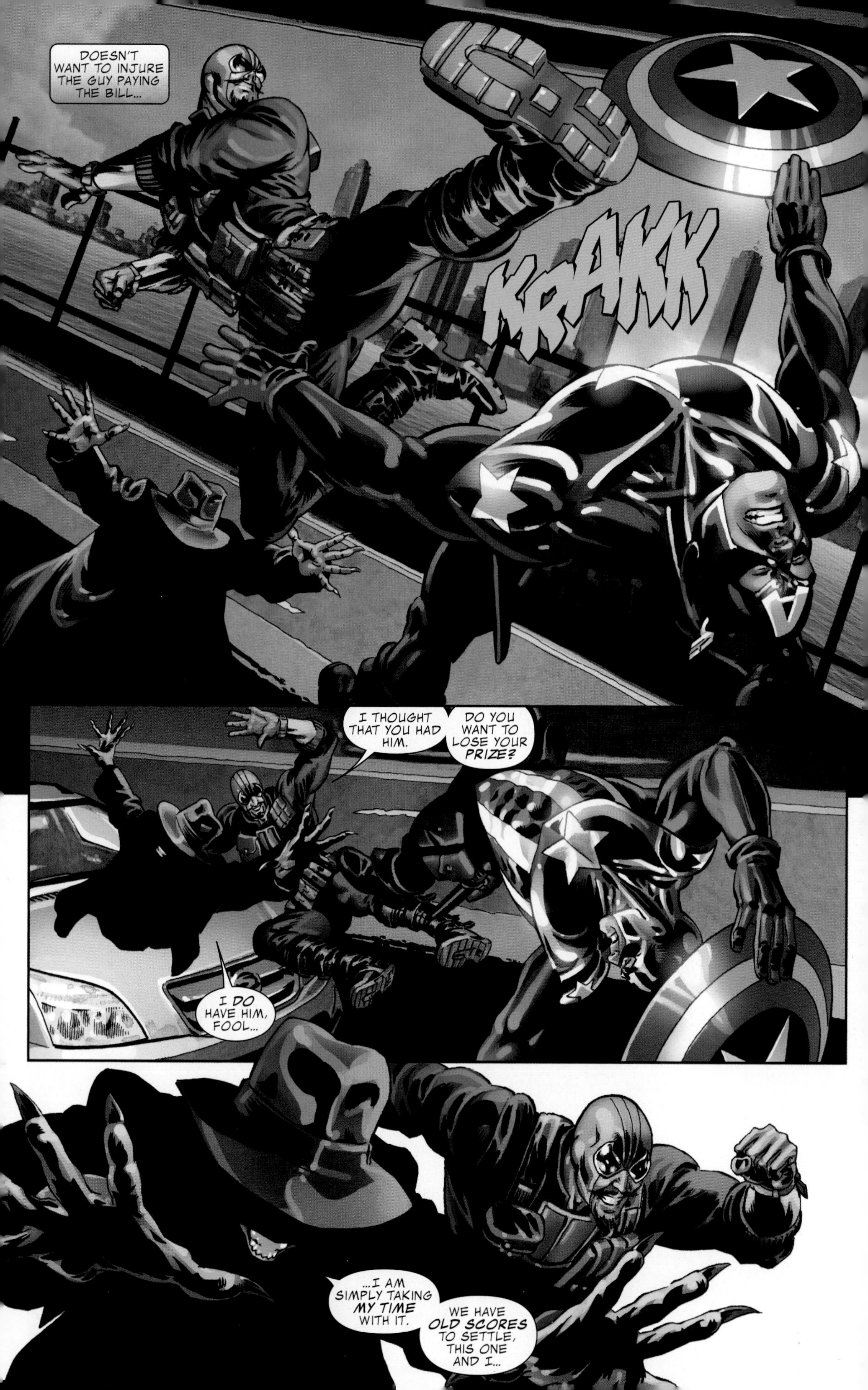
DOESN'T WANT TO INJURE THE GUY PAYING THE BILL...
KRAKK
I THOUGHT THAT YOU HAD HIM.
DO YOU WANT TO LOSE YOUR PRIZE?
I DO HAVE HIM, FOOL...
...I AM SIMPLY TAKING MY TIME WITH IT.
WE HAVE OLD SCORES TO SETTLE, THIS ONE AND I...

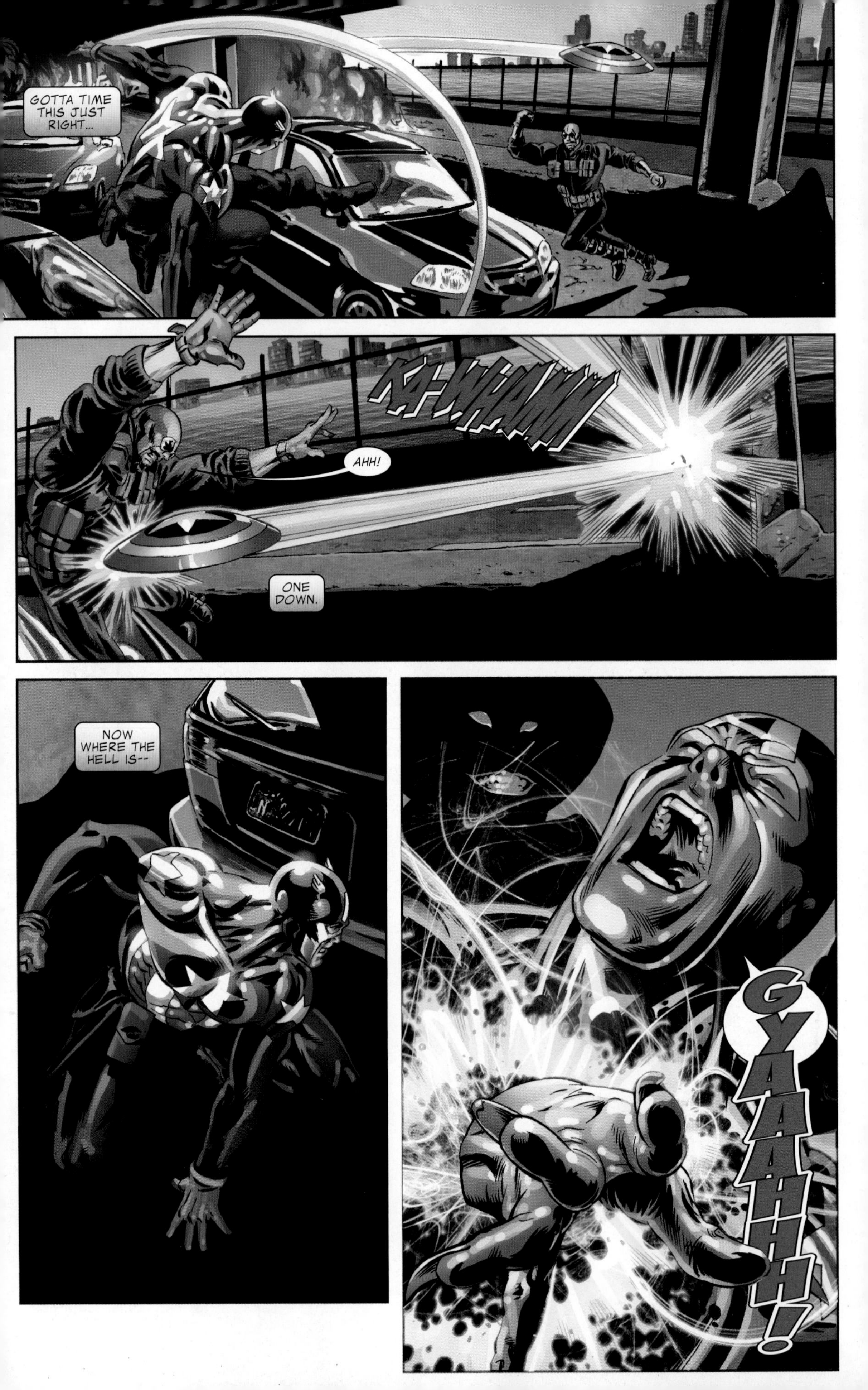
GOTTA TIME THIS JUST RIGHT...
KA-WHAMM
AHH!
ONE DOWN.
NOW WHERE THE HELL IS--
GYAAHHH!

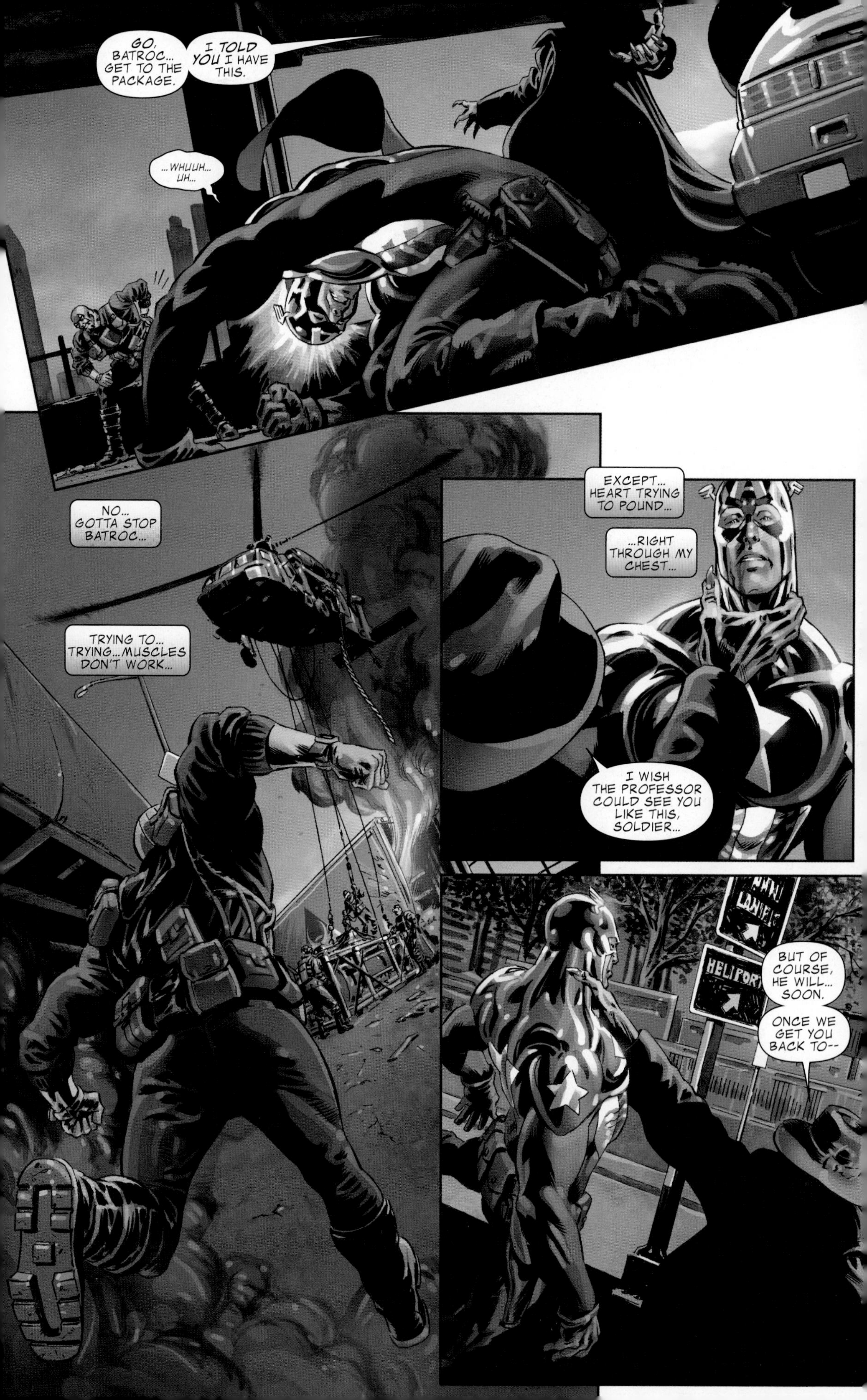
GO, BATROC... GET TO THE PACKAGE.
I TOLD YOU I HAVE THIS.
...WHUUH... UH...
NO... GOTTA STOP BATROC...
TRYING TO... TRYING...MUSCLES DON'T WORK...
EXCEPT... HEART TRYING TO POUND...
...RIGHT THROUGH MY CHEST...
I WISH THE PROFESSOR COULD SEE YOU LIKE THIS, SOLDIER...
HELIPORT
BUT OF COURSE, HE WILL... SOON.
ONCE WE GET YOU BACK TO--

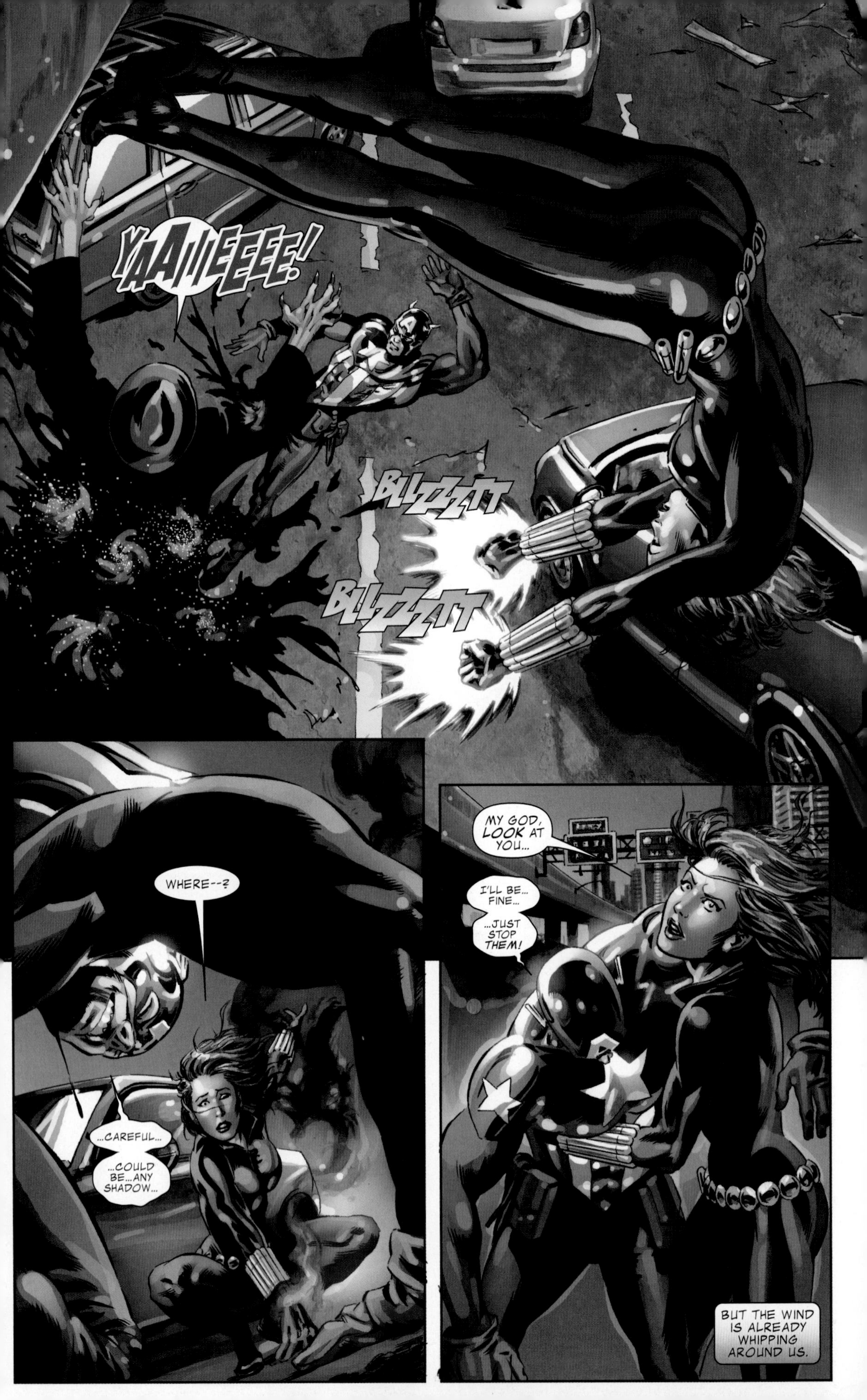
YAAIIEEEE!
BLLZZZZTT
BLLZZZZTT
WHERE--?
...CAREFUL...
...COULD BE...ANY SHADOW...
MY GOD, LOOK AT YOU...
I'LL BE... FINE...
...JUST STOP THEM!
BUT THE WIND IS ALREADY WHIPPING AROUND US.

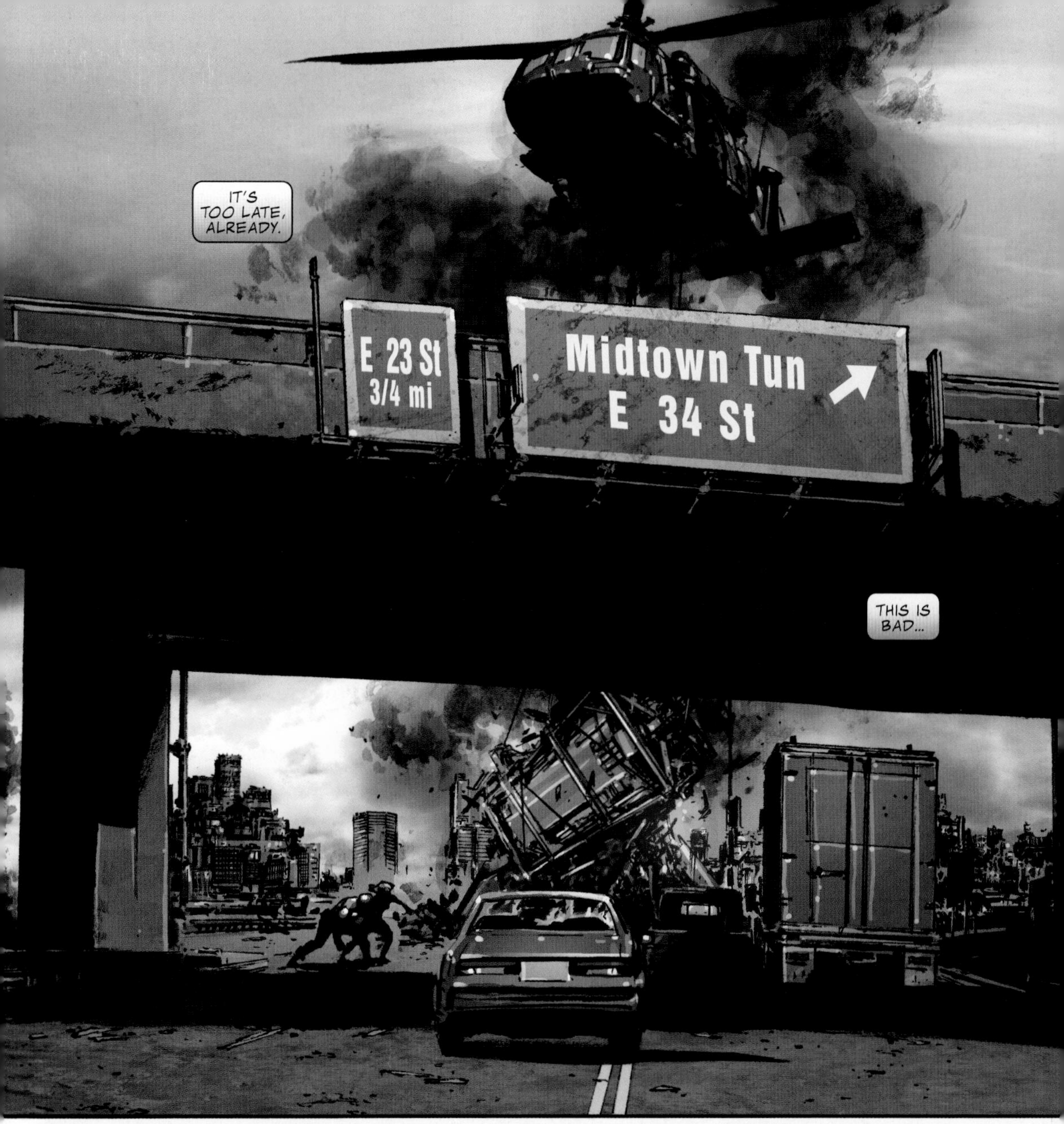
IT'S TOO LATE, ALREADY.
E 23 St
3/4 mi
Midtown Tun
E 34 St
THIS IS BAD...

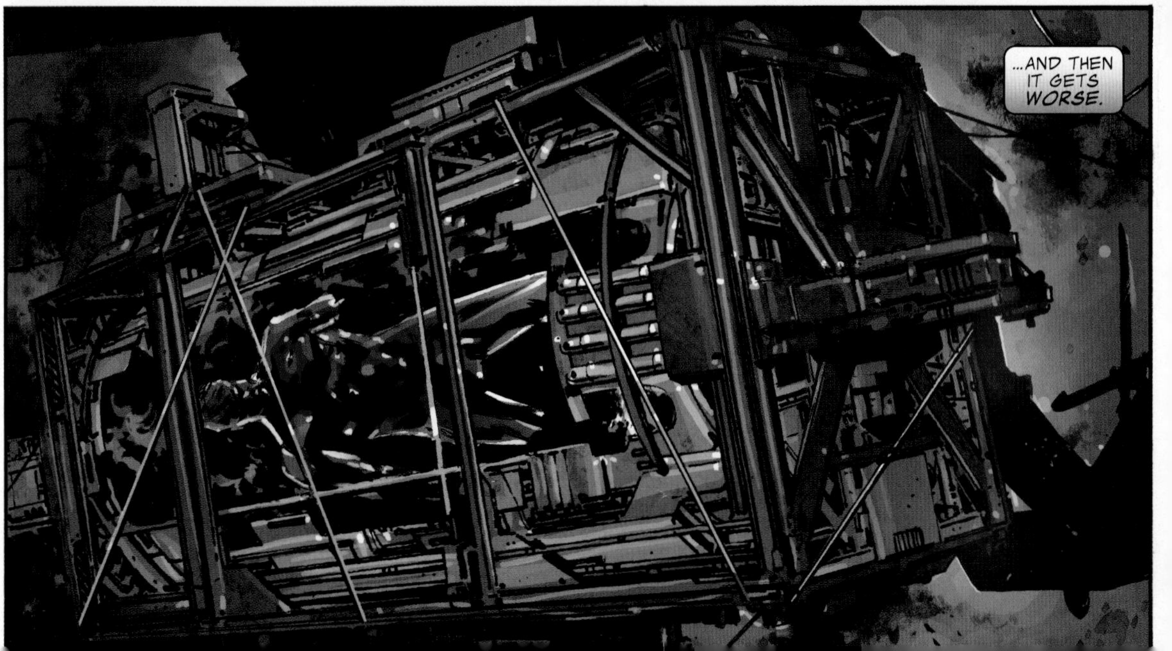
...AND THEN IT GETS WORSE.

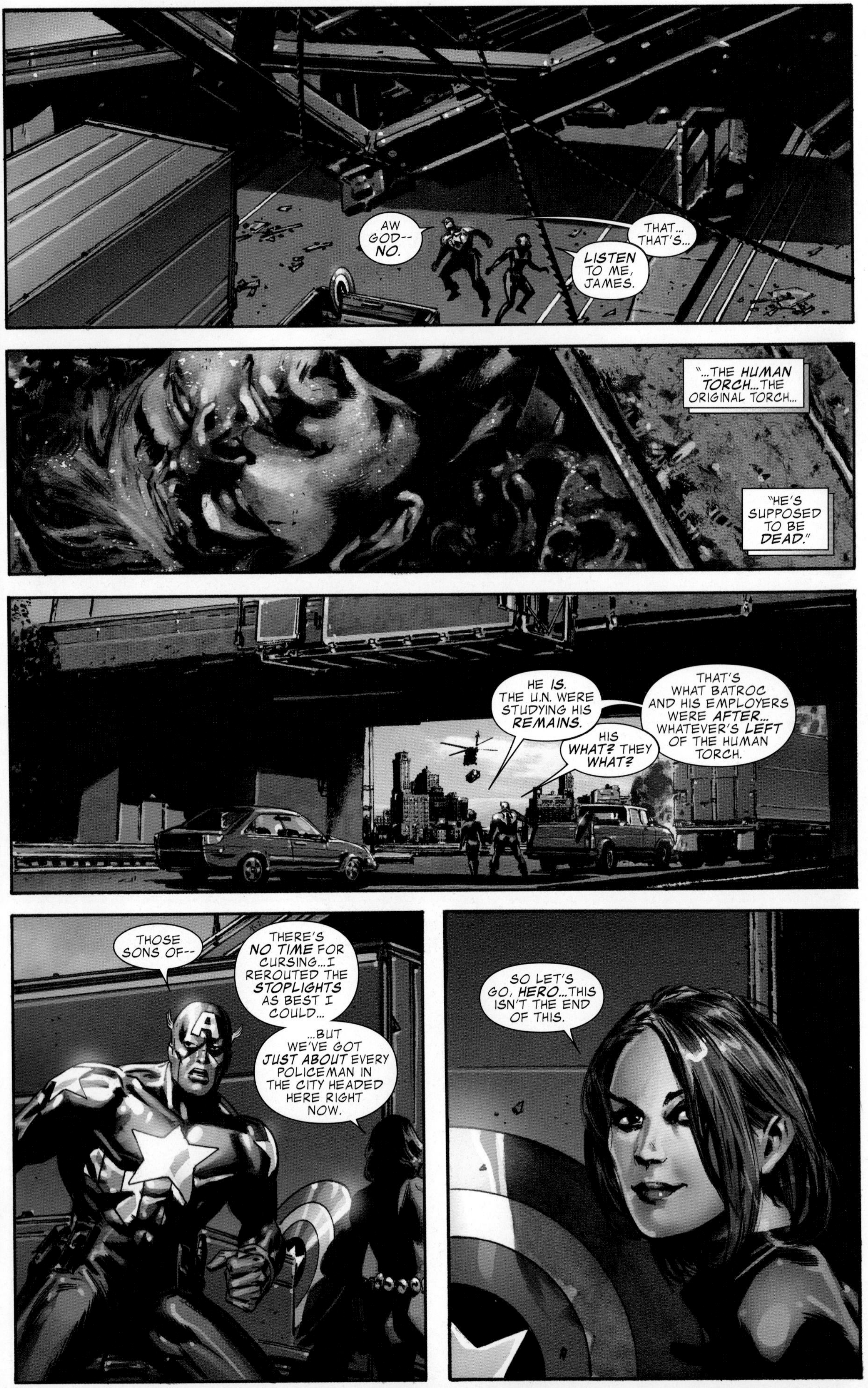
AW GOD-- NO.
THAT... THAT'S...
LISTEN TO ME, JAMES.
"...THE HUMAN TORCH...THE ORIGINAL TORCH...
"HE'S SUPPOSED TO BE DEAD."
HE IS. THE U.N. WERE STUDYING HIS REMAINS.
HIS WHAT? THEY WHAT?
THAT'S WHAT BATROC AND HIS EMPLOYERS WERE AFTER... WHATEVER'S LEFT OF THE HUMAN TORCH.
THOSE SONS OF--
THERE'S NO TIME FOR CURSING...I REROUTED THE STOPLIGHTS AS BEST I COULD...
...BUT WE'VE GOT JUST ABOUT EVERY POLICEMAN IN THE CITY HEADED HERE RIGHT NOW.
SO LET'S GO, HERO...THIS ISN'T THE END OF THIS.

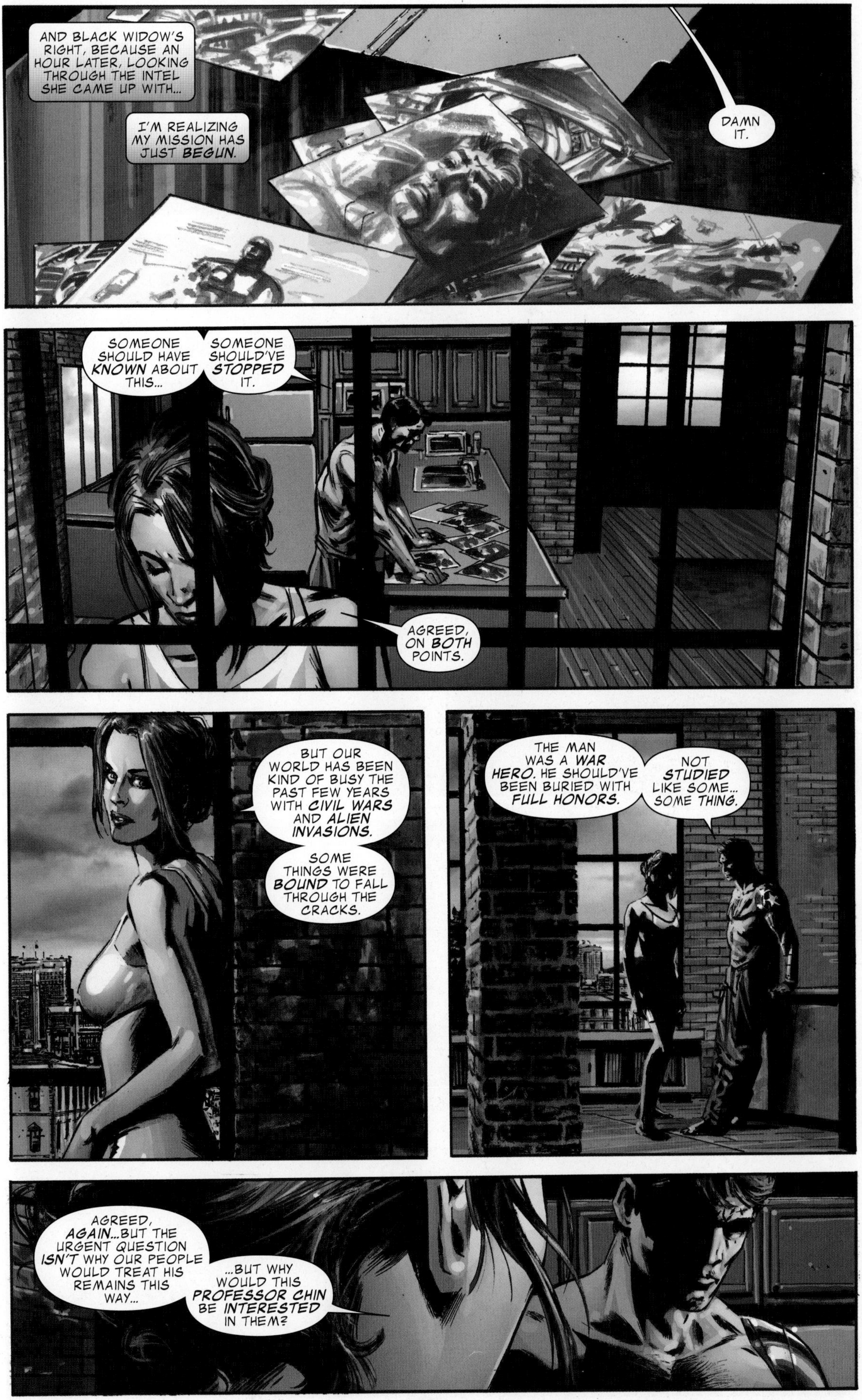
AND BLACK WIDOW'S RIGHT, BECAUSE AN HOUR LATER, LOOKING THROUGH THE INTEL SHE CAME UP WITH...
I'M REALIZING MY MISSION HAS JUST BEGUN.
DAMN IT.
SOMEONE SHOULD HAVE KNOWN ABOUT THIS...
SOMEONE SHOULD'VE STOPPED IT.
AGREED, ON BOTH POINTS.
BUT OUR WORLD HAS BEEN KIND OF BUSY THE PAST FEW YEARS WITH CIVIL WARS AND ALIEN INVASIONS.
SOME THINGS WERE BOUND TO FALL THROUGH THE CRACKS.
THE MAN WAS A WAR HERO. HE SHOULD'VE BEEN BURIED WITH FULL HONORS.
NOT STUDIED LIKE SOME... SOME THING.
AGREED, AGAIN...BUT THE URGENT QUESTION ISN'T WHY OUR PEOPLE WOULD TREAT HIS REMAINS THIS WAY...
...BUT WHY WOULD THIS PROFESSOR CHIN BE INTERESTED IN THEM?

SO I TELL HER WHAT I SAW THAT DAY...

BUT NOT WHAT I DID.

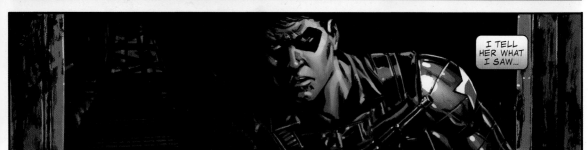

I TELL HER WHAT I SAW...

...THE THINGS IN THAT LAB, THE EXPERIMENTS, THE VICTIMS...

...BECAUSE THAT'S HOW I KNOW THE ANSWER TO HER QUESTION.

BECAUSE I'VE SEEN WHAT KIND OF SCIENCE CHIN PRACTICES.

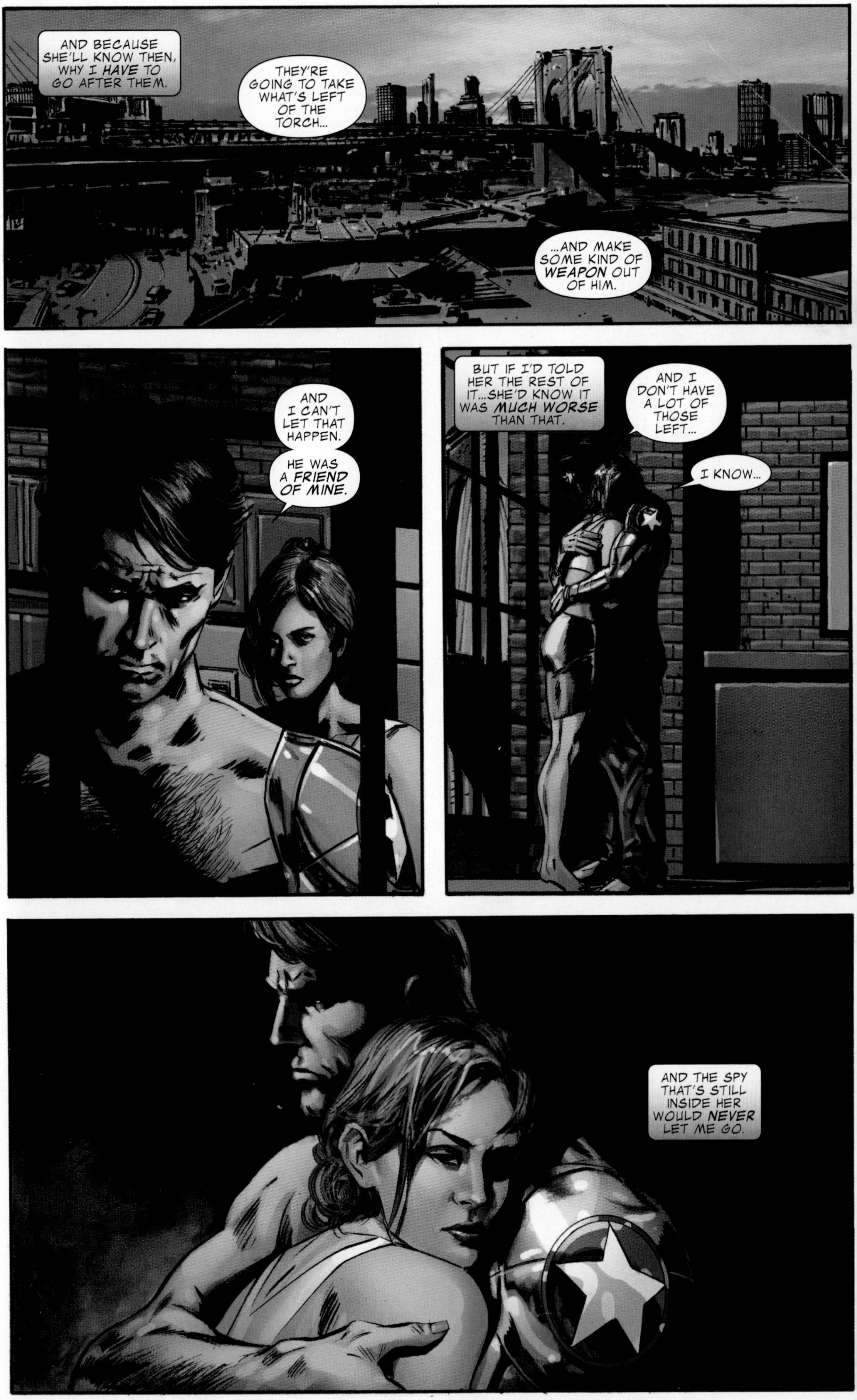
AND BECAUSE SHE'LL KNOW THEN, WHY I HAVE TO GO AFTER THEM.
THEY'RE GOING TO TAKE WHAT'S LEFT OF THE TORCH...
...AND MAKE SOME KIND OF WEAPON OUT OF HIM.
AND I CAN'T LET THAT HAPPEN.
HE WAS A FRIEND OF MINE.
BUT IF I'D TOLD HER THE REST OF IT...SHE'D KNOW IT WAS MUCH WORSE THAN THAT.
AND I DON'T HAVE A LOT OF THOSE LEFT...
I KNOW...
AND THE SPY THAT'S STILL INSIDE HER WOULD NEVER LET ME GO.

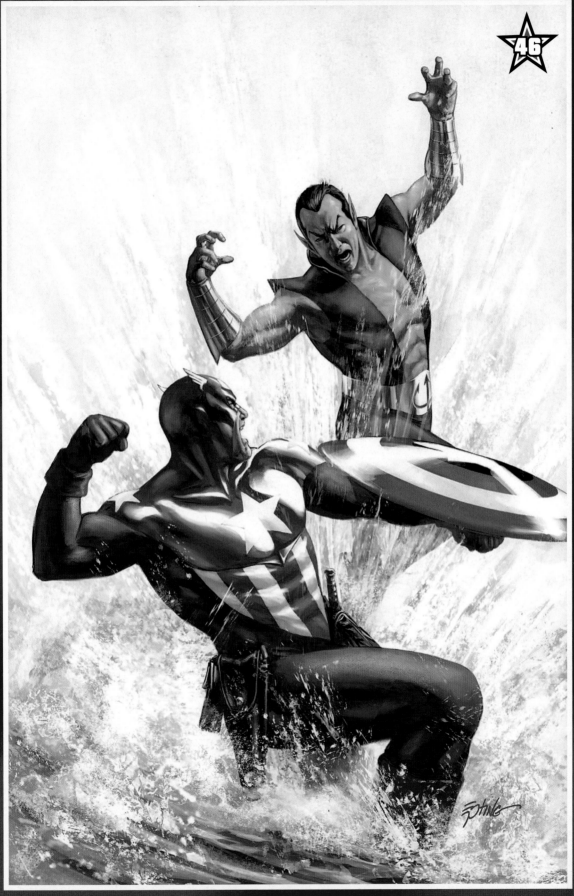

OLD FRIENDS AND ENEMIES PART ONE

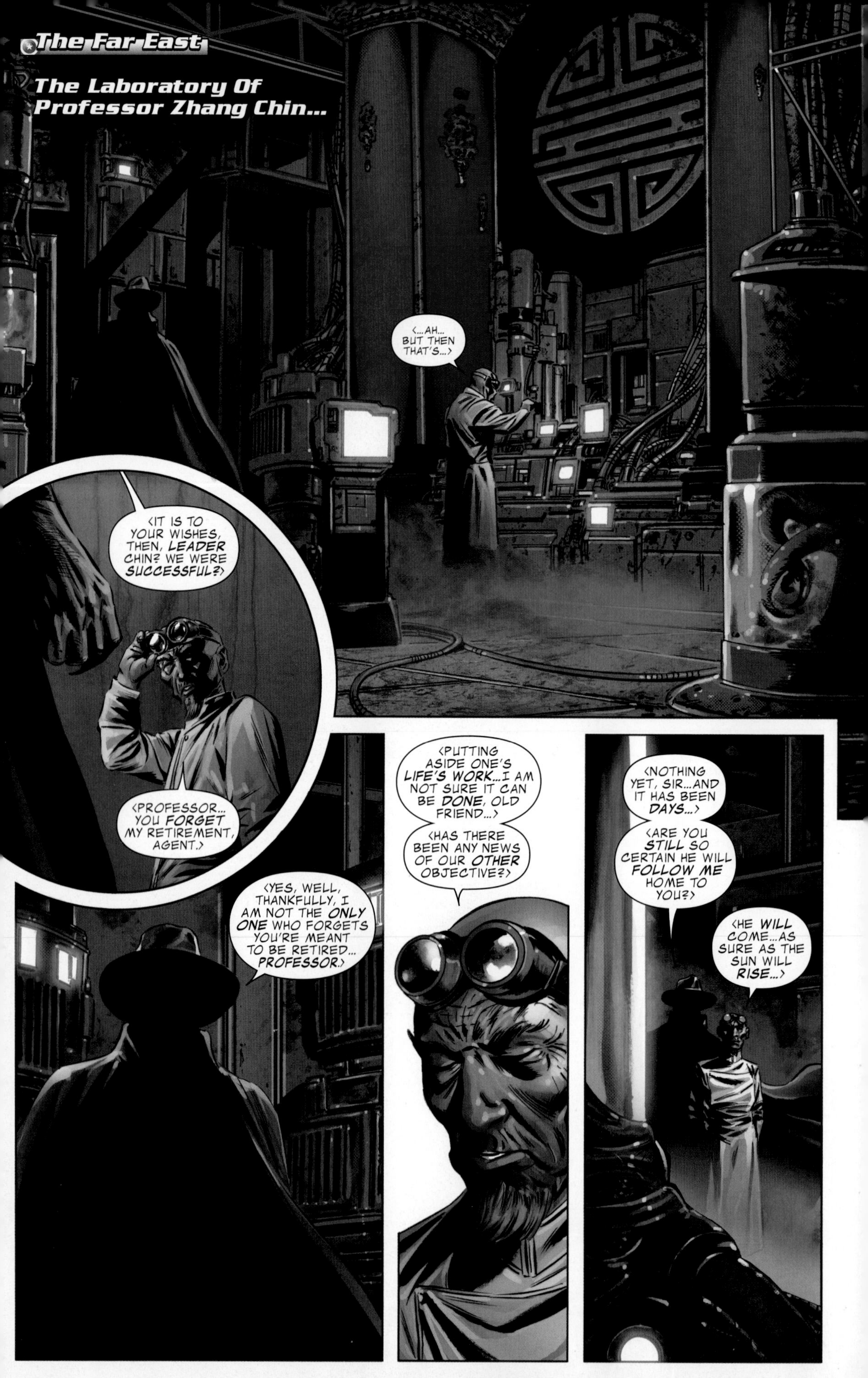
The Far East
The Laboratory Of Professor Zhang Chin...
‹...AH... BUT THEN THAT'S...›
‹IT IS TO YOUR WISHES, THEN, LEADER CHIN? WE WERE SUCCESSFUL?›
‹PROFESSOR... YOU FORGET MY RETIREMENT, AGENT.›
‹YES, WELL, THANKFULLY, I AM NOT THE ONLY ONE WHO FORGETS YOU'RE MEANT TO BE RETIRED... PROFESSOR.›
‹PUTTING ASIDE ONE'S LIFE'S WORK...I AM NOT SURE IT CAN BE DONE, OLD FRIEND...›
‹HAS THERE BEEN ANY NEWS OF OUR OTHER OBJECTIVE?›
‹NOTHING YET, SIR...AND IT HAS BEEN DAYS...›
‹ARE YOU STILL SO CERTAIN HE WILL FOLLOW ME HOME TO YOU?›
‹HE WILL COME...AS SURE AS THE SUN WILL RISE...›

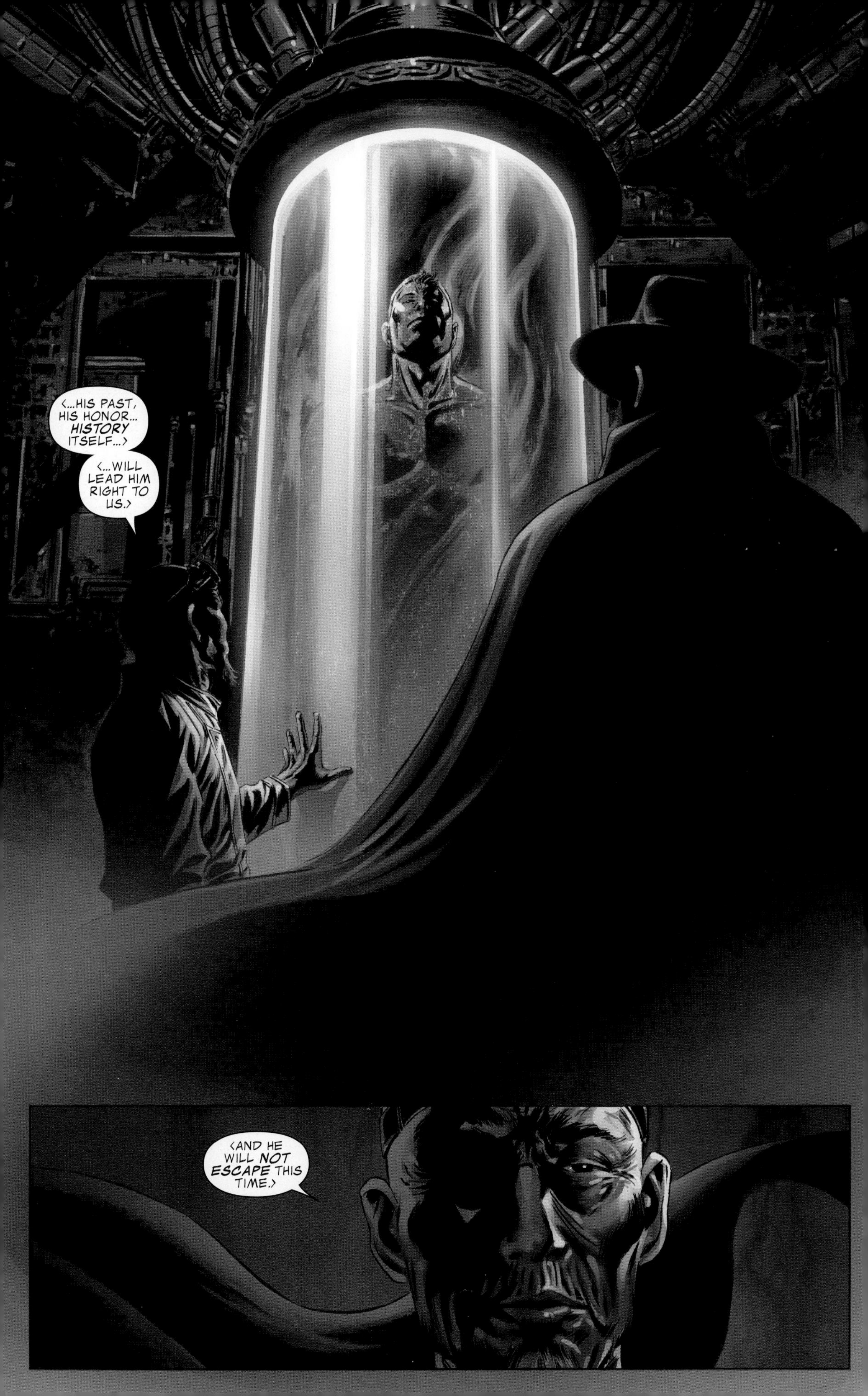
‹...HIS PAST, HIS HONOR... *HISTORY* ITSELF...›
‹...WILL LEAD HIM RIGHT TO US.›
‹AND HE WILL *NOT ESCAPE* THIS TIME.›

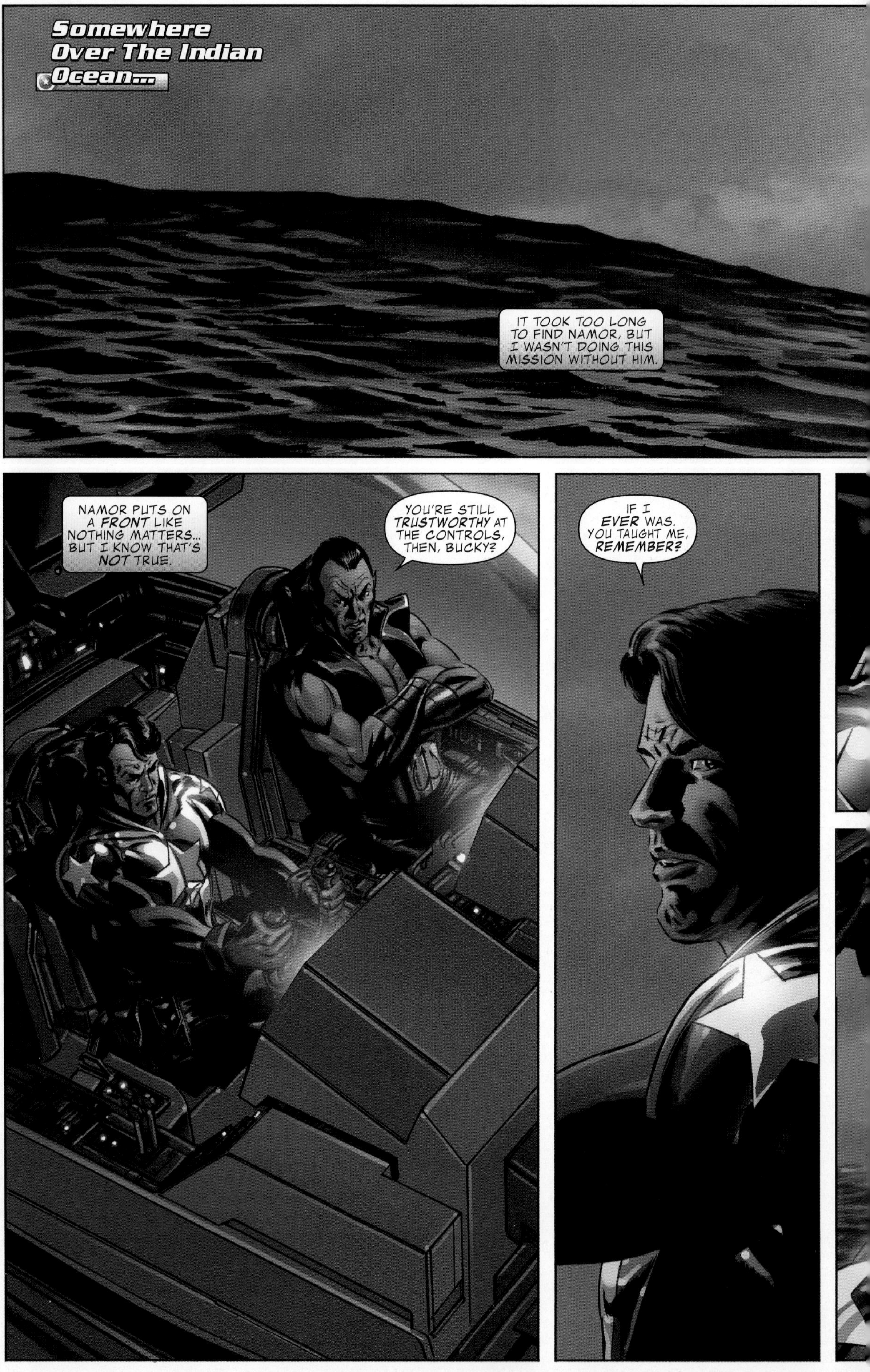
Somewhere Over The Indian Ocean...
IT TOOK TOO LONG TO FIND NAMOR, BUT I WASN'T DOING THIS MISSION WITHOUT HIM.
NAMOR PUTS ON A FRONT LIKE NOTHING MATTERS... BUT I KNOW THAT'S NOT TRUE.
YOU'RE STILL TRUSTWORTHY AT THE CONTROLS, THEN, BUCKY?
IF I EVER WAS. YOU TAUGHT ME, REMEMBER?

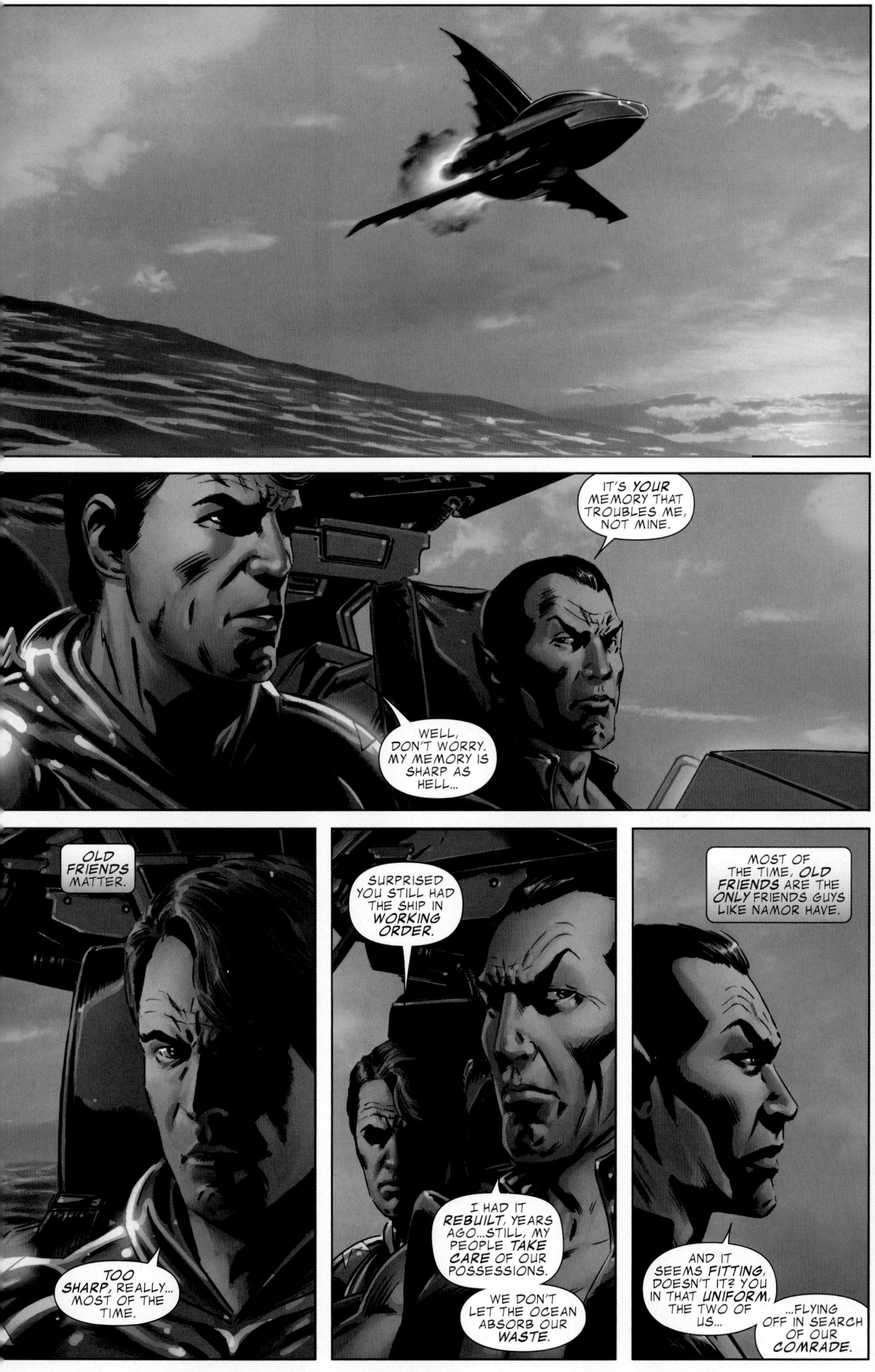
IT'S YOUR MEMORY THAT TROUBLES ME, NOT MINE.
WELL, DON'T WORRY. MY MEMORY IS SHARP AS HELL...
OLD FRIENDS MATTER.
TOO SHARP, REALLY... MOST OF THE TIME.
SURPRISED YOU STILL HAD THE SHIP IN WORKING ORDER.
I HAD IT REBUILT, YEARS AGO...STILL, MY PEOPLE TAKE CARE OF OUR POSSESSIONS.
WE DON'T LET THE OCEAN ABSORB OUR WASTE.
MOST OF THE TIME, OLD FRIENDS ARE THE ONLY FRIENDS GUYS LIKE NAMOR HAVE.
AND IT SEEMS FITTING, DOESN'T IT? YOU IN THAT UNIFORM, THE TWO OF US...
...FLYING OFF IN SEARCH OF OUR COMRADE.

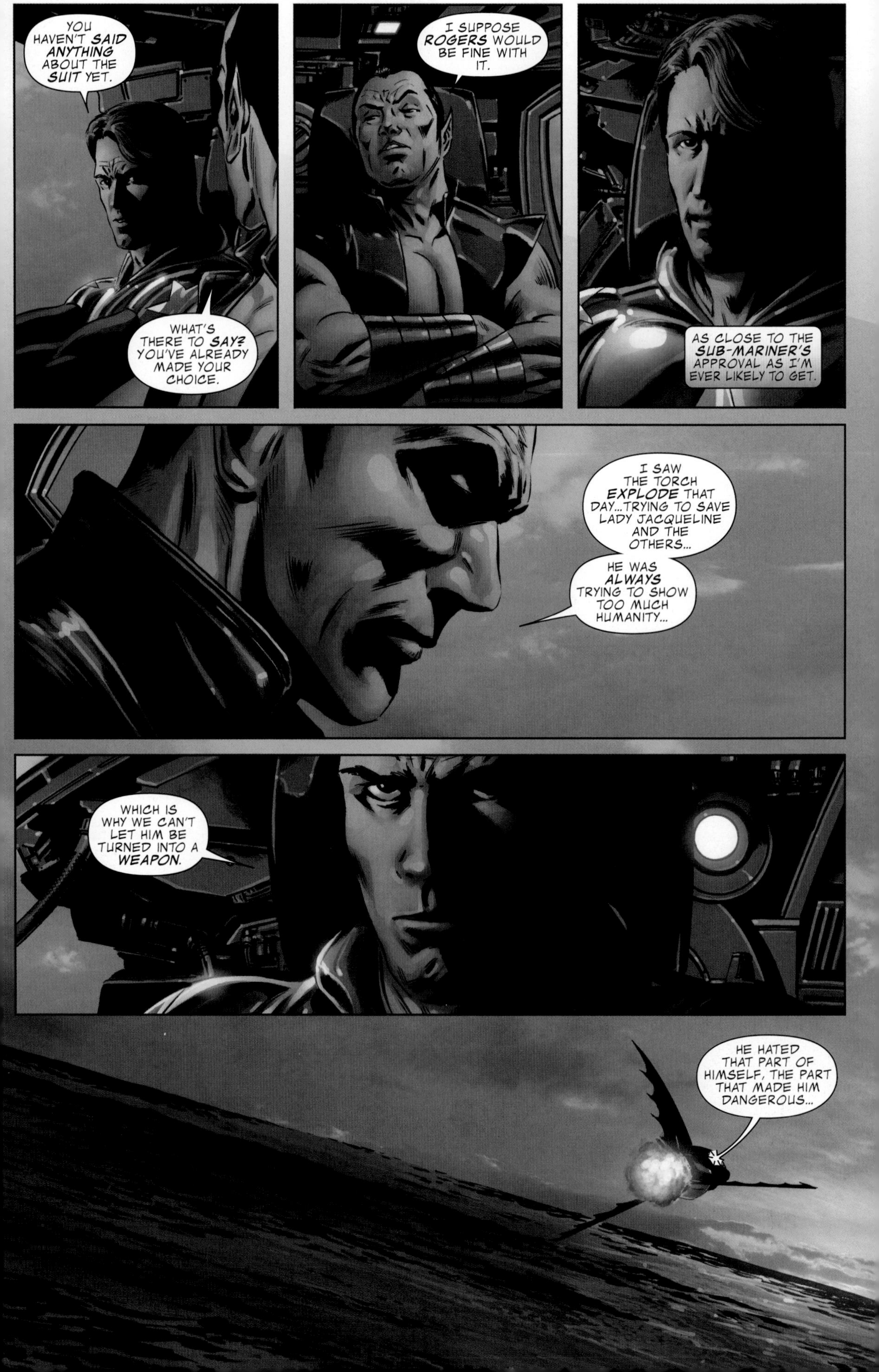
YOU HAVEN'T SAID ANYTHING ABOUT THE SUIT YET.
WHAT'S THERE TO SAY? YOU'VE ALREADY MADE YOUR CHOICE.
I SUPPOSE ROGERS WOULD BE FINE WITH IT.
AS CLOSE TO THE SUB-MARINER'S APPROVAL AS I'M EVER LIKELY TO GET.
I SAW THE TORCH EXPLODE THAT DAY...TRYING TO SAVE LADY JACQUELINE AND THE OTHERS...
HE WAS ALWAYS TRYING TO SHOW TOO MUCH HUMANITY...
WHICH IS WHY WE CAN'T LET HIM BE TURNED INTO A WEAPON.
HE HATED THAT PART OF HIMSELF, THE PART THAT MADE HIM DANGEROUS...

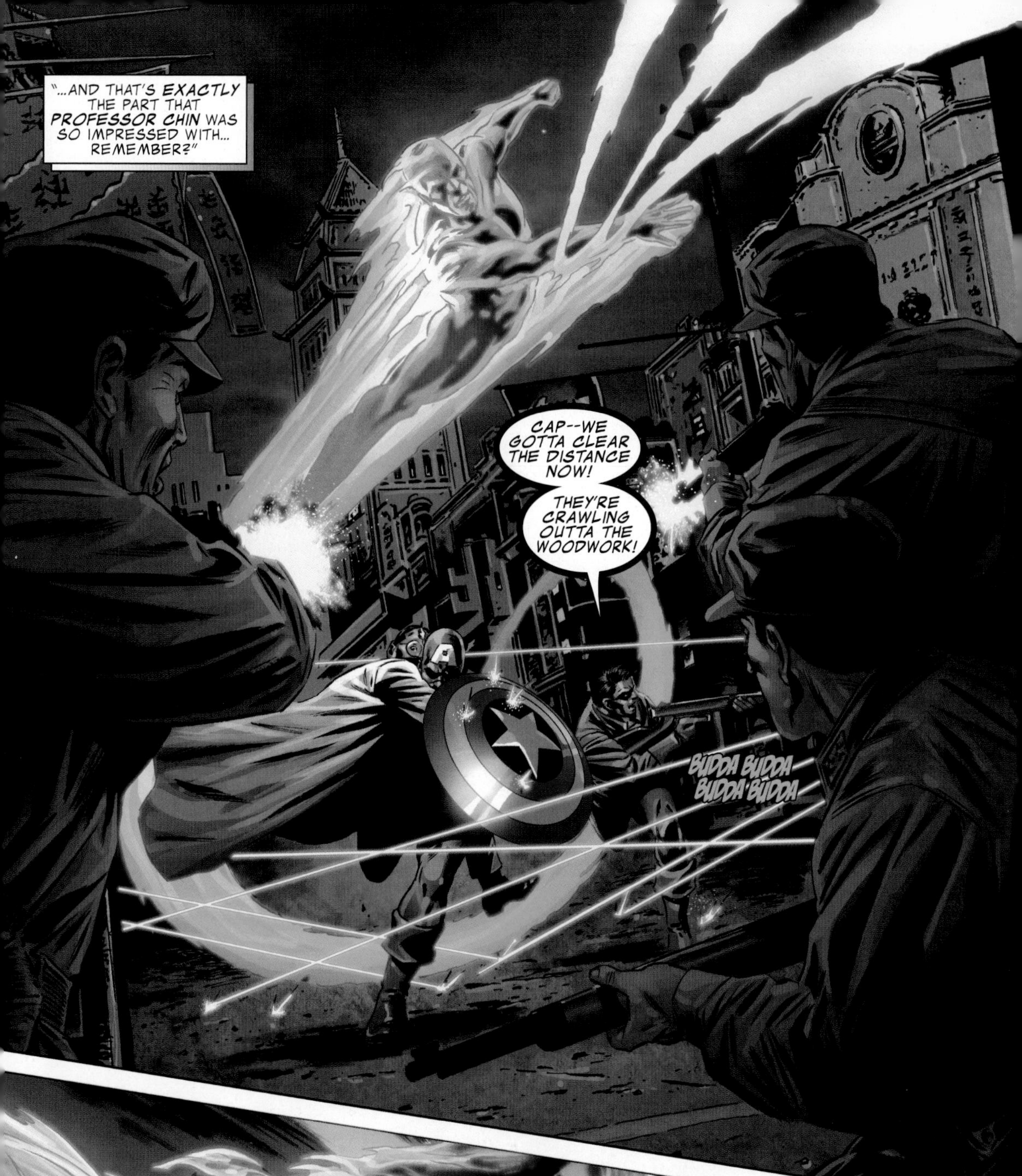
"...AND THAT'S EXACTLY THE PART THAT PROFESSOR CHIN WAS SO IMPRESSED WITH... REMEMBER?"
CAP--WE GOTTA CLEAR THE DISTANCE NOW!
THEY'RE CRAWLING OUTTA THE WOODWORK!
BUDDA BUDDA BUDDA BUDDA
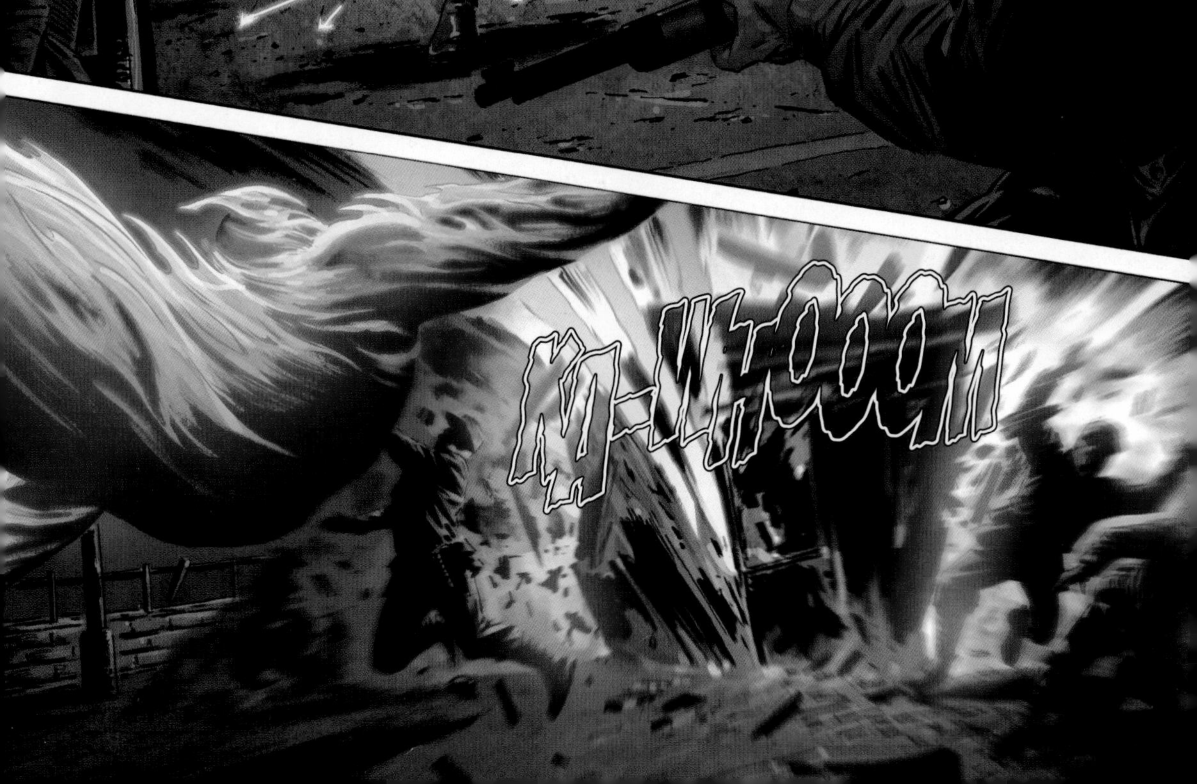
KA-WHOOOM

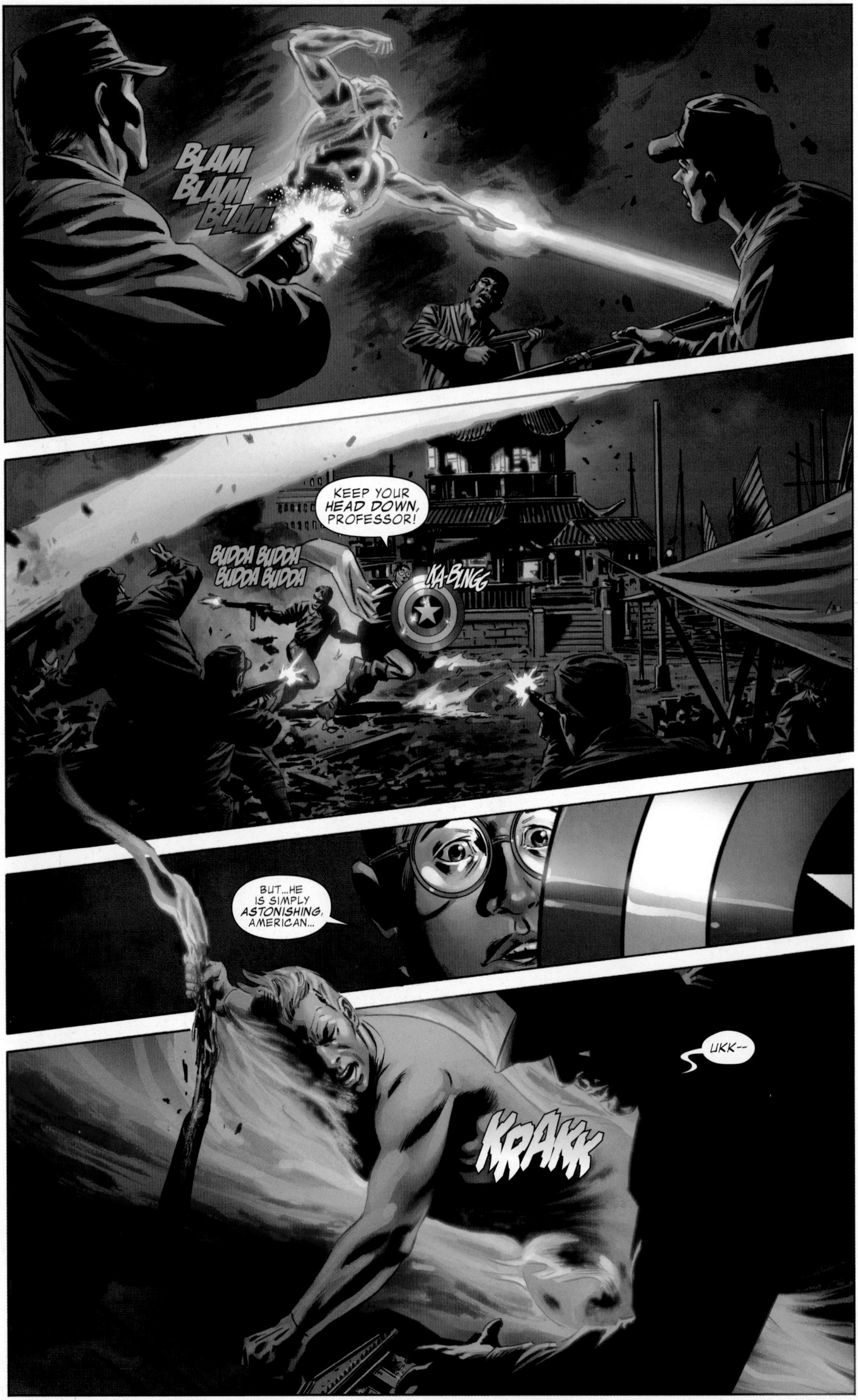
BLAM
BLAM
BLAM
KEEP YOUR HEAD DOWN, PROFESSOR!
BUDDA BUDDA BUDDA BUDDA
KA-BLNGG
BUT...HE IS SIMPLY ASTONISHING, AMERICAN...
UKK--
KRAKK

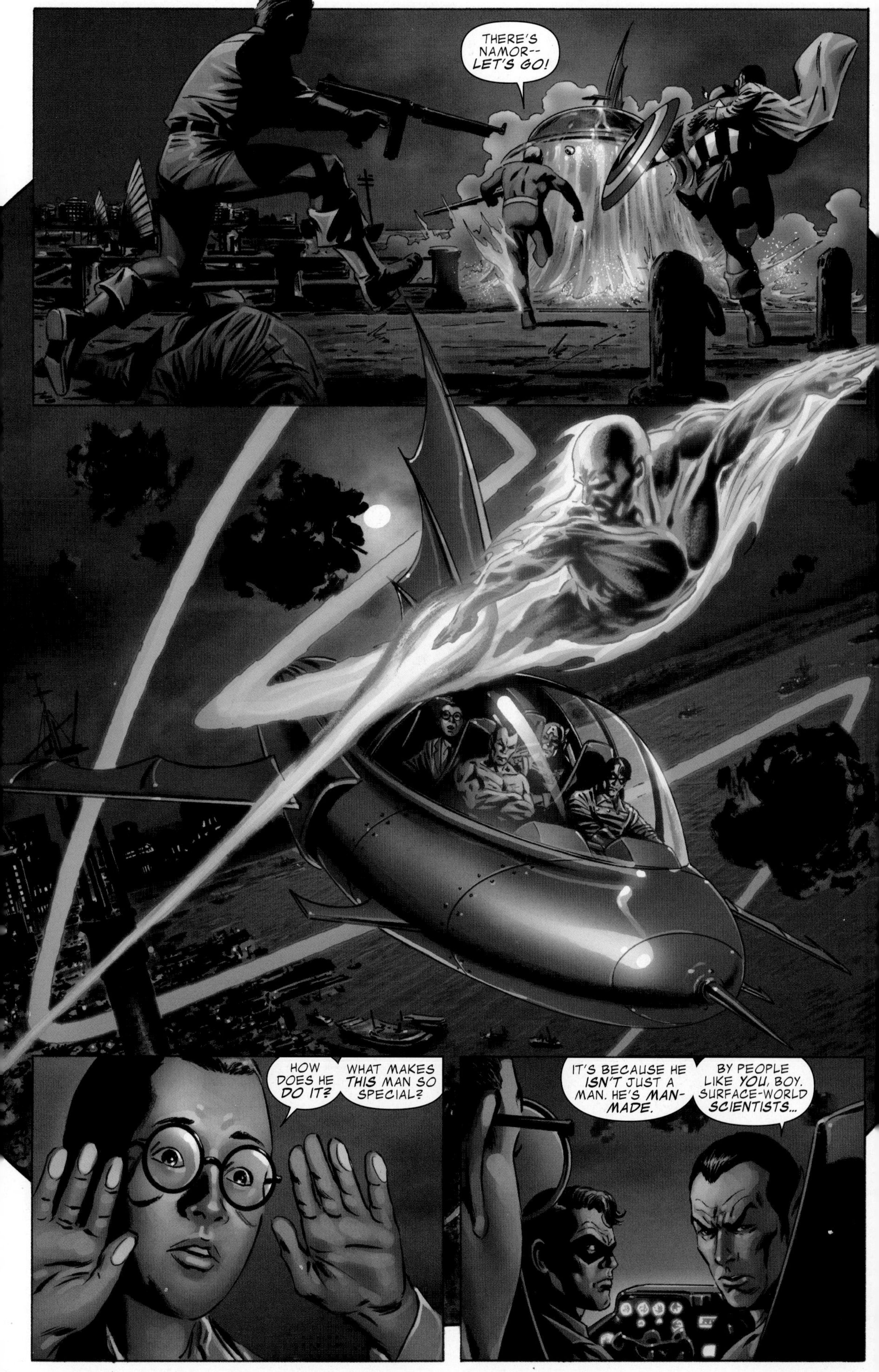
THERE'S NAMOR-- LET'S GO!
HOW DOES HE DO IT?
WHAT MAKES THIS MAN SO SPECIAL?
IT'S BECAUSE HE ISN'T JUST A MAN. HE'S MAN-MADE.
BY PEOPLE LIKE YOU, BOY. SURFACE-WORLD SCIENTISTS...

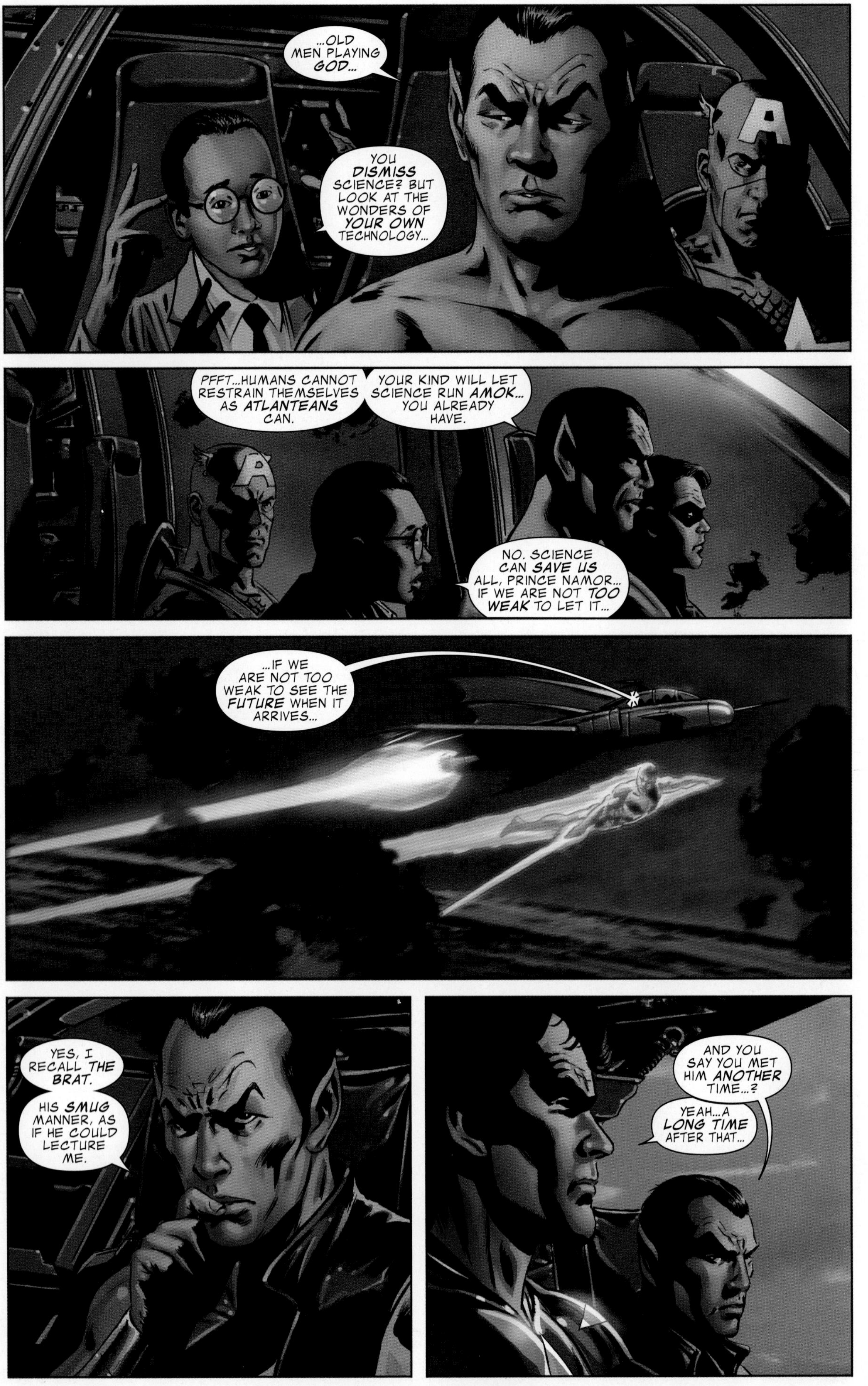
...OLD MEN PLAYING GOD...
YOU DISMISS SCIENCE? BUT LOOK AT THE WONDERS OF YOUR OWN TECHNOLOGY...
PFFT...HUMANS CANNOT RESTRAIN THEMSELVES AS ATLANTEANS CAN.
YOUR KIND WILL LET SCIENCE RUN AMOK... YOU ALREADY HAVE.
NO. SCIENCE CAN SAVE US ALL, PRINCE NAMOR... IF WE ARE NOT TOO WEAK TO LET IT...
...IF WE ARE NOT TOO WEAK TO SEE THE FUTURE WHEN IT ARRIVES...
YES, I RECALL THE BRAT.
HIS SMUG MANNER, AS IF HE COULD LECTURE ME.
AND YOU SAY YOU MET HIM ANOTHER TIME...?
YEAH...A LONG TIME AFTER THAT...

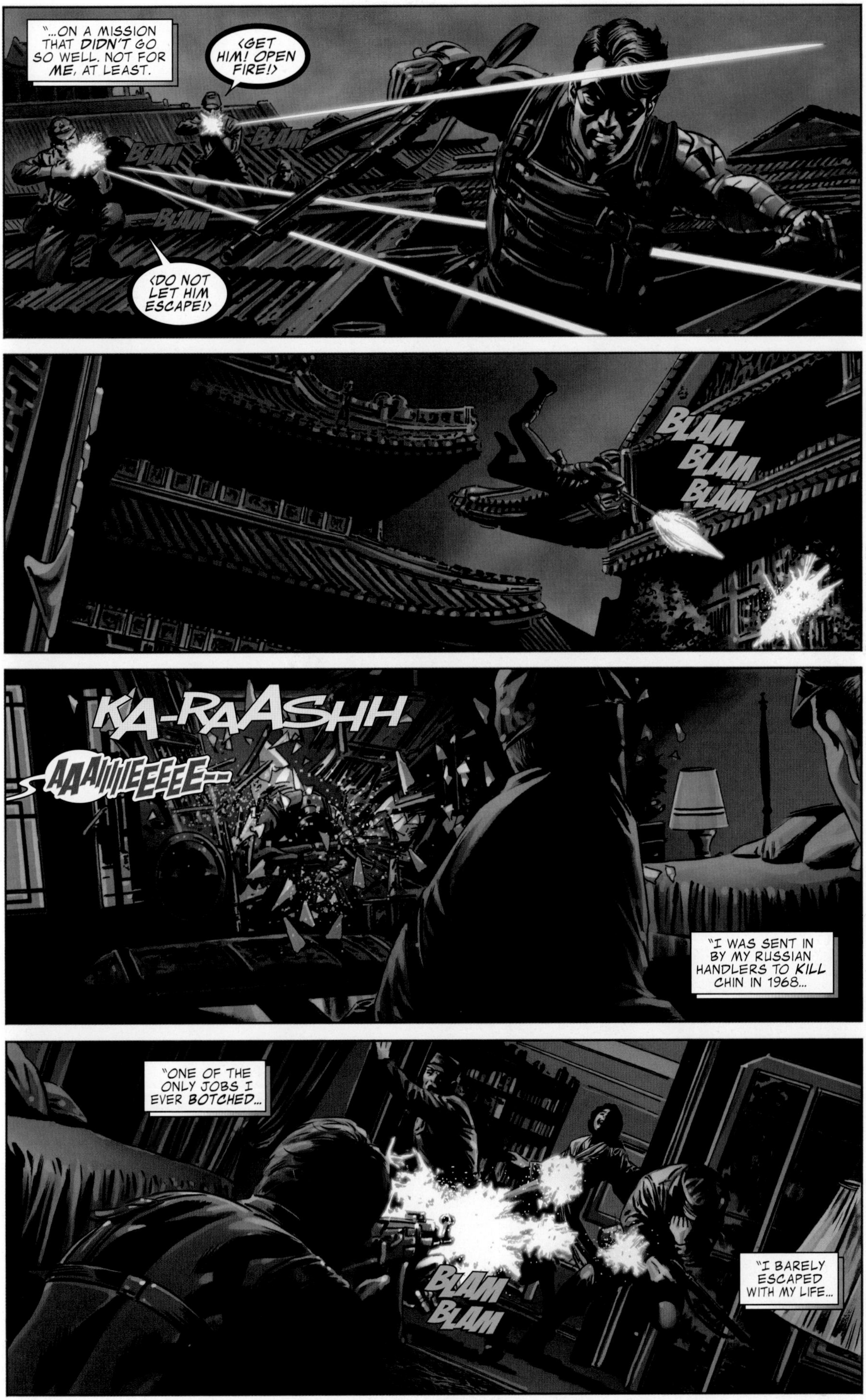
"...ON A MISSION THAT DIDN'T GO SO WELL. NOT FOR ME, AT LEAST.
<GET HIM! OPEN FIRE!>
BLAM
BLAM
BLAM
<DO NOT LET HIM ESCAPE!>
BLAM
BLAM
BLAM
KA-RAASHH
AAAIIIIEEEE--
"I WAS SENT IN BY MY RUSSIAN HANDLERS TO KILL CHIN IN 1968...
"ONE OF THE ONLY JOBS I EVER BOTCHED...
BLAM
BLAM
"I BARELY ESCAPED WITH MY LIFE...

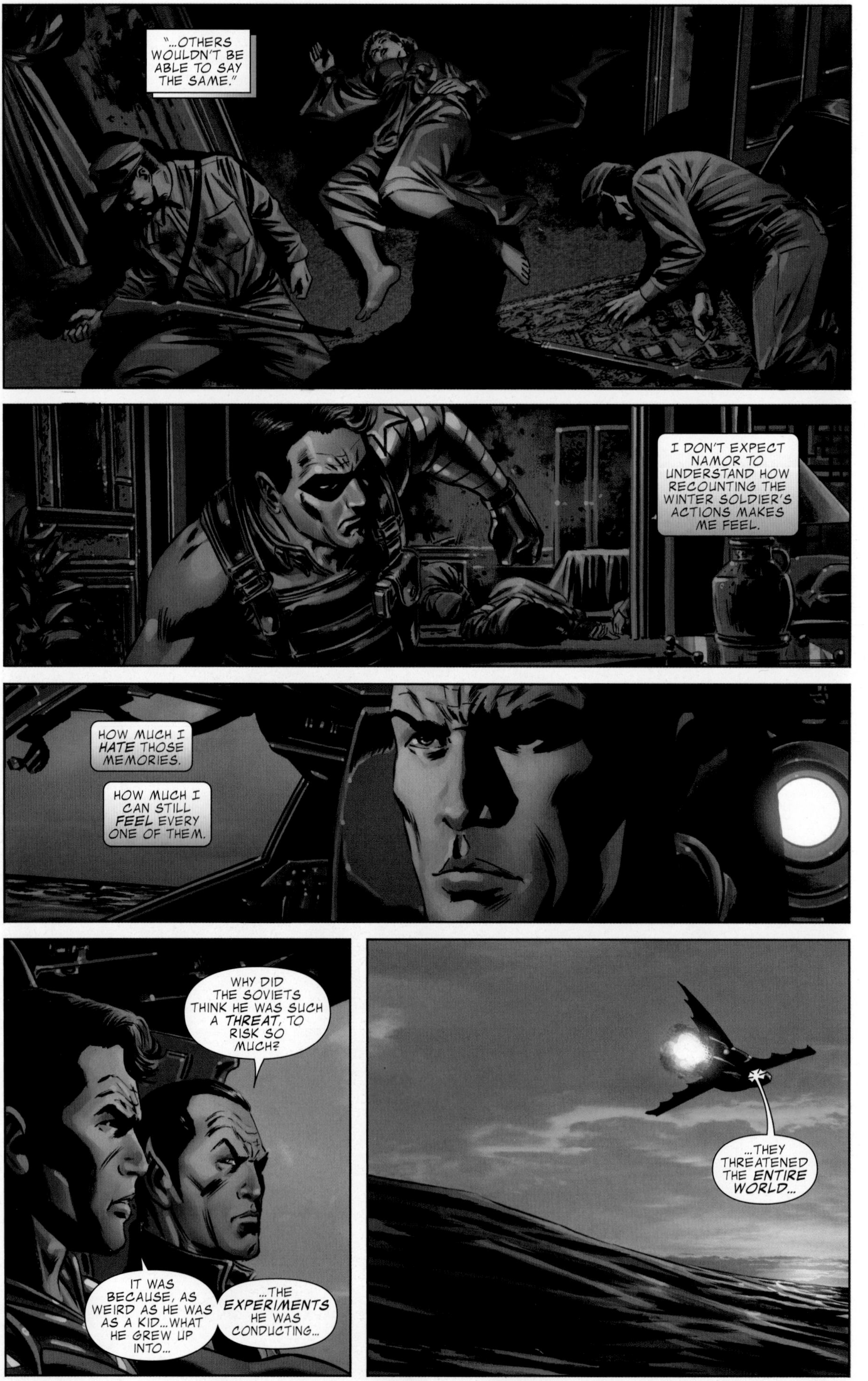
"...OTHERS WOULDN'T BE ABLE TO SAY THE SAME."
I DON'T EXPECT NAMOR TO UNDERSTAND HOW RECOUNTING THE WINTER SOLDIER'S ACTIONS MAKES ME FEEL.
HOW MUCH I HATE THOSE MEMORIES.
HOW MUCH I CAN STILL FEEL EVERY ONE OF THEM.
WHY DID THE SOVIETS THINK HE WAS SUCH A THREAT, TO RISK SO MUCH?
IT WAS BECAUSE, AS WEIRD AS HE WAS AS A KID...WHAT HE GREW UP INTO...
...THE EXPERIMENTS HE WAS CONDUCTING...
...THEY THREATENED THE ENTIRE WORLD...

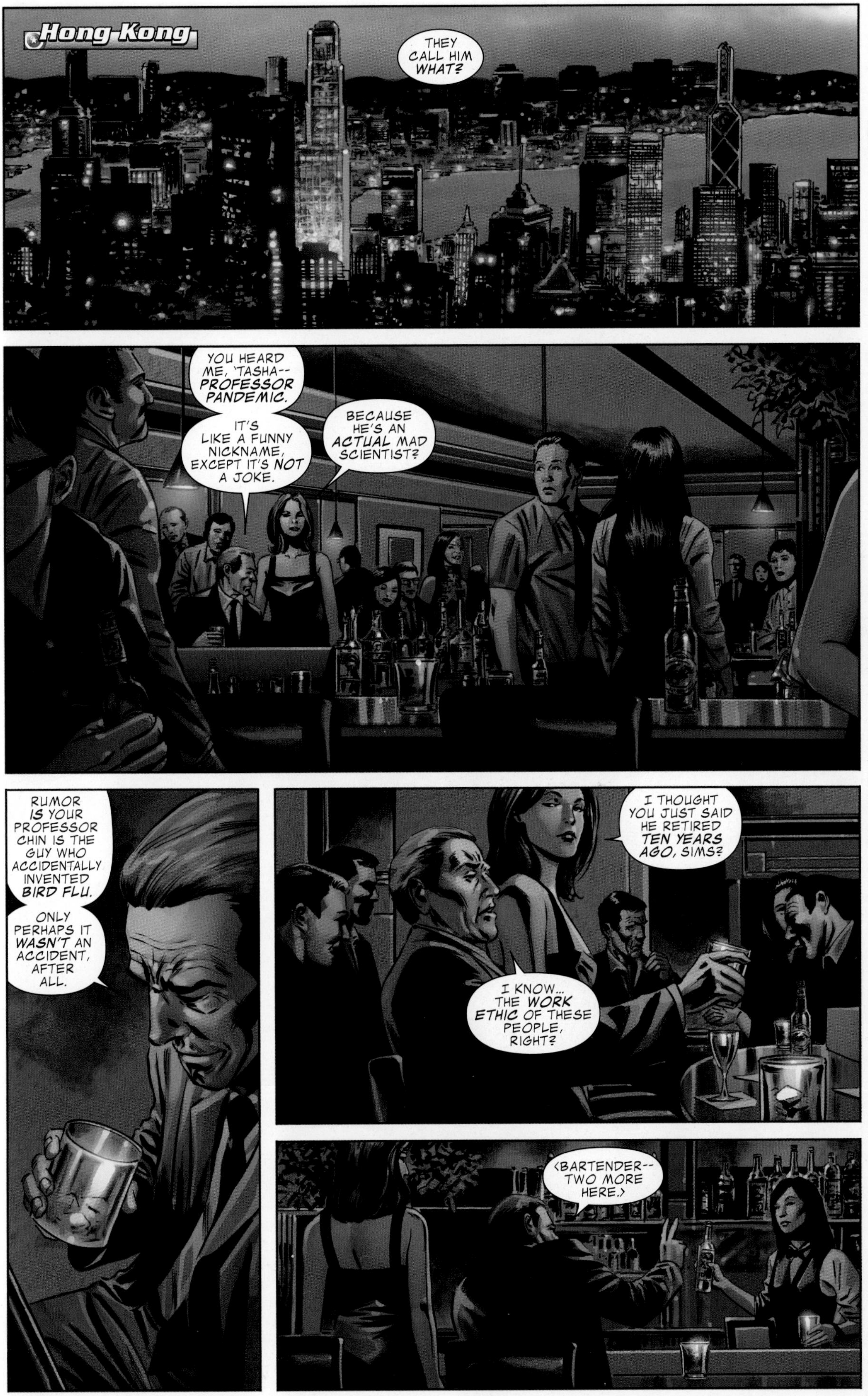
Hong Kong
THEY CALL HIM WHAT?
YOU HEARD ME, 'TASHA-- PROFESSOR PANDEMIC.
IT'S LIKE A FUNNY NICKNAME, EXCEPT IT'S NOT A JOKE.
BECAUSE HE'S AN ACTUAL MAD SCIENTIST?
RUMOR IS YOUR PROFESSOR CHIN IS THE GUY WHO ACCIDENTALLY INVENTED BIRD FLU.
ONLY PERHAPS IT WASN'T AN ACCIDENT, AFTER ALL.
I THOUGHT YOU JUST SAID HE RETIRED TEN YEARS AGO, SIMS?
I KNOW... THE WORK ETHIC OF THESE PEOPLE, RIGHT?
<BARTENDER-- TWO MORE HERE.>

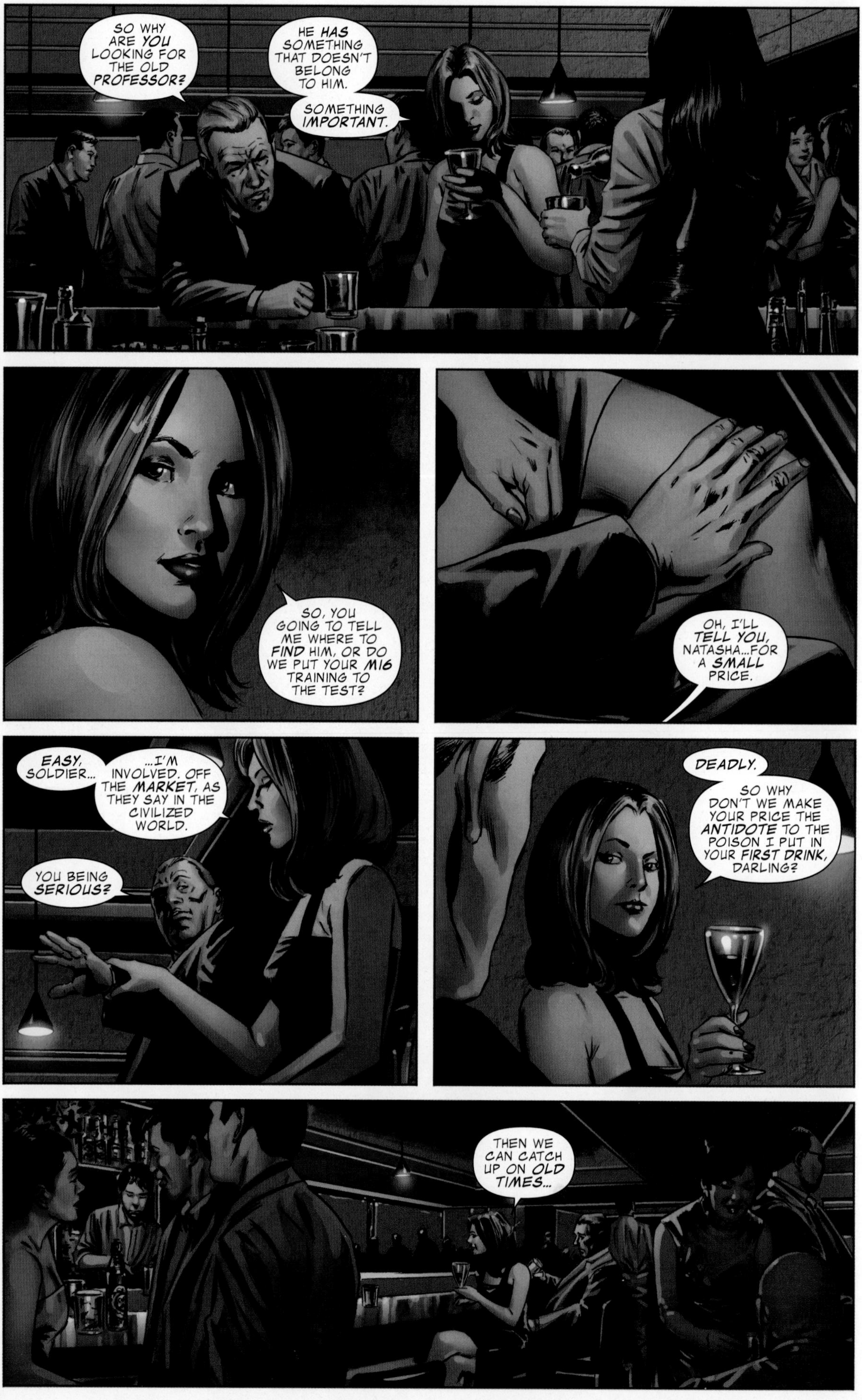
SO WHY ARE YOU LOOKING FOR THE OLD PROFESSOR?
HE HAS SOMETHING THAT DOESN'T BELONG TO HIM.
SOMETHING IMPORTANT.
SO, YOU GOING TO TELL ME WHERE TO FIND HIM, OR DO WE PUT YOUR MI6 TRAINING TO THE TEST?
OH, I'LL TELL YOU, NATASHA...FOR A SMALL PRICE.
EASY, SOLDIER...
...I'M INVOLVED. OFF THE MARKET, AS THEY SAY IN THE CIVILIZED WORLD.
YOU BEING SERIOUS?
DEADLY.
SO WHY DON'T WE MAKE YOUR PRICE THE ANTIDOTE TO THE POISON I PUT IN YOUR FIRST DRINK, DARLING?
THEN WE CAN CATCH UP ON OLD TIMES...

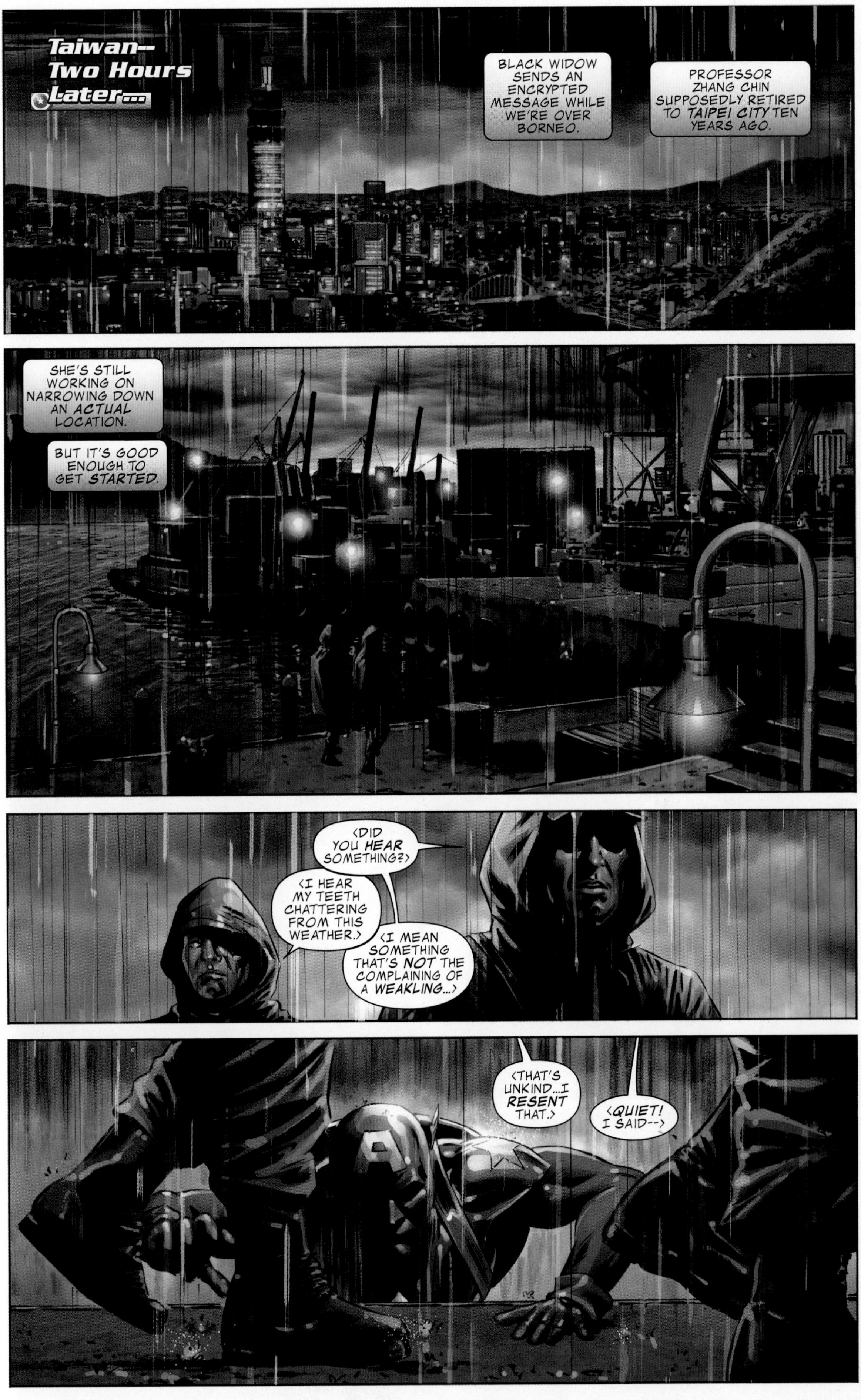
Taiwan-- Two Hours Later...
BLACK WIDOW SENDS AN ENCRYPTED MESSAGE WHILE WE'RE OVER BORNEO.
PROFESSOR ZHANG CHIN SUPPOSEDLY RETIRED TO TAIPEI CITY TEN YEARS AGO.
SHE'S STILL WORKING ON NARROWING DOWN AN ACTUAL LOCATION.
BUT IT'S GOOD ENOUGH TO GET STARTED.
<DID YOU HEAR SOMETHING?>
<I HEAR MY TEETH CHATTERING FROM THIS WEATHER.>
<I MEAN SOMETHING THAT'S NOT THE COMPLAINING OF A WEAKLING...>
<THAT'S UNKIND...I RESENT THAT.>
<QUIET! I SAID-->

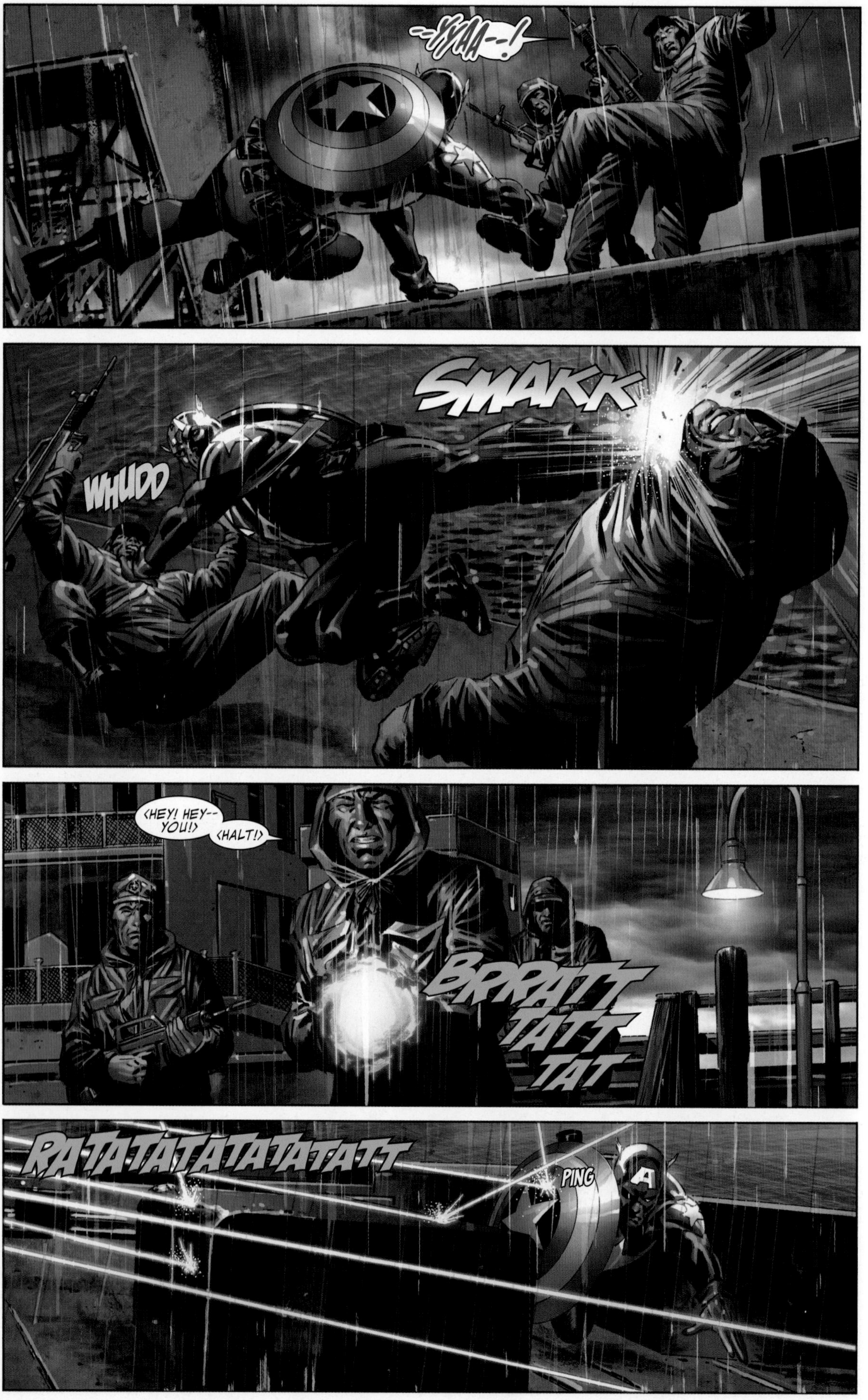

--YYAA--!
SMAKK
WHUDD
‹HEY! HEY--YOU!›
‹HALT!›
BRRATT TATT TAT
RATATATATATATATT
PING

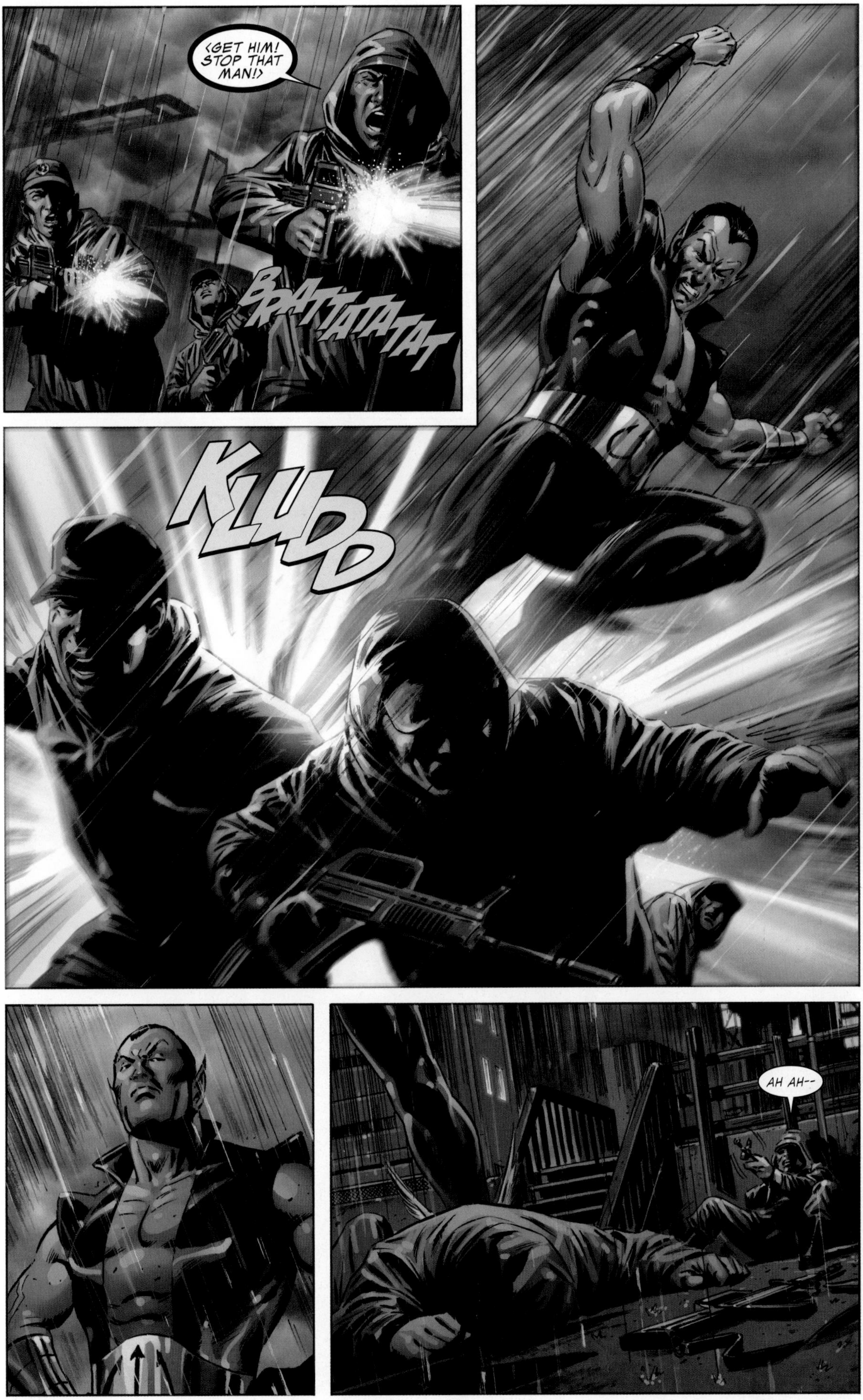
<GET HIM! STOP THAT MAN!>
BRATTATATAT
KLUDD
AH AH--

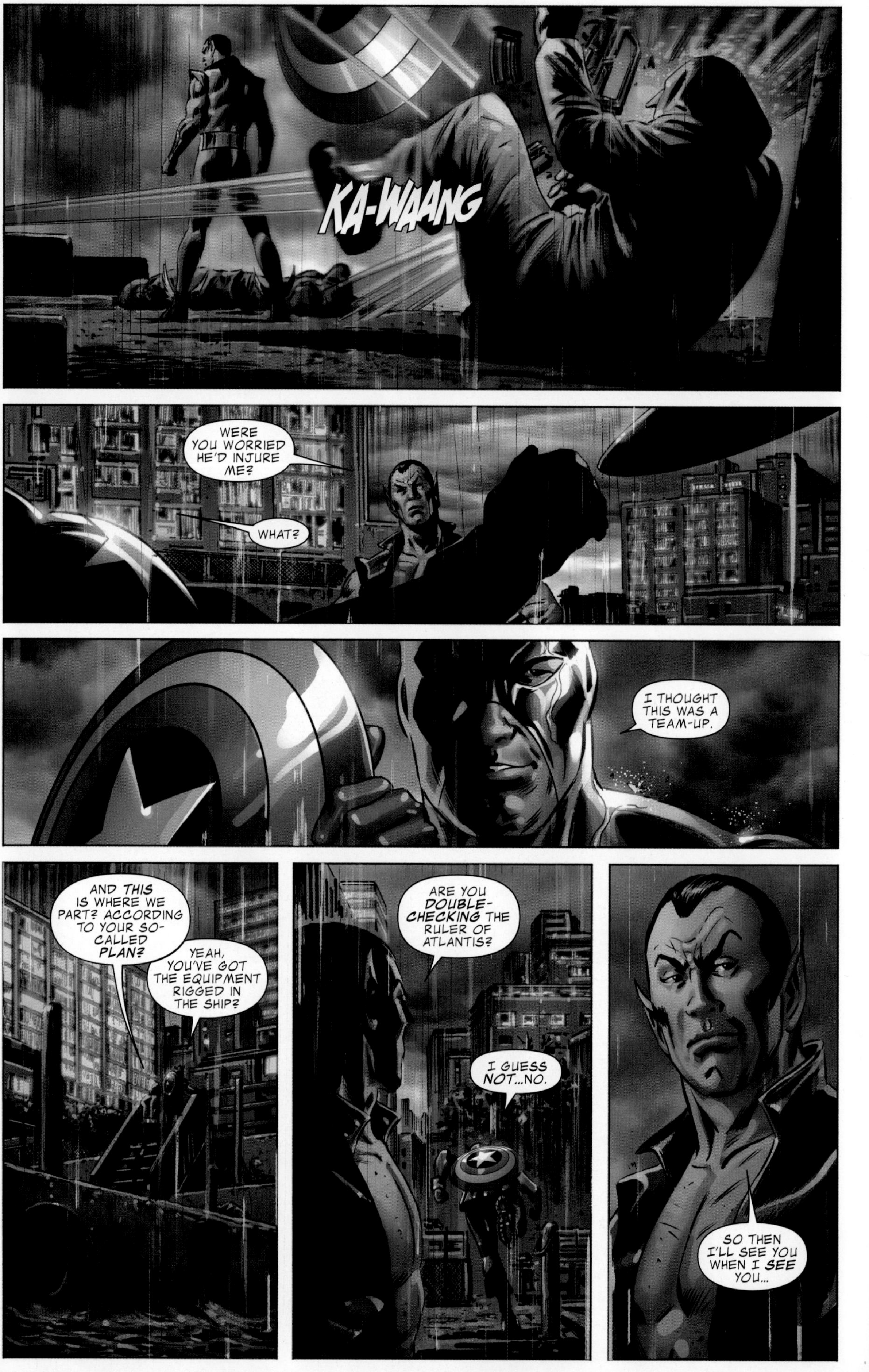
KA-WAANG
WERE YOU WORRIED HE'D INJURE ME?
WHAT?
I THOUGHT THIS WAS A TEAM-UP.
AND THIS IS WHERE WE PART? ACCORDING TO YOUR SO-CALLED PLAN?
YEAH, YOU'VE GOT THE EQUIPMENT RIGGED IN THE SHIP?
ARE YOU DOUBLE-CHECKING THE RULER OF ATLANTIS?
I GUESS NOT...NO.
SO THEN I'LL SEE YOU WHEN I SEE YOU...

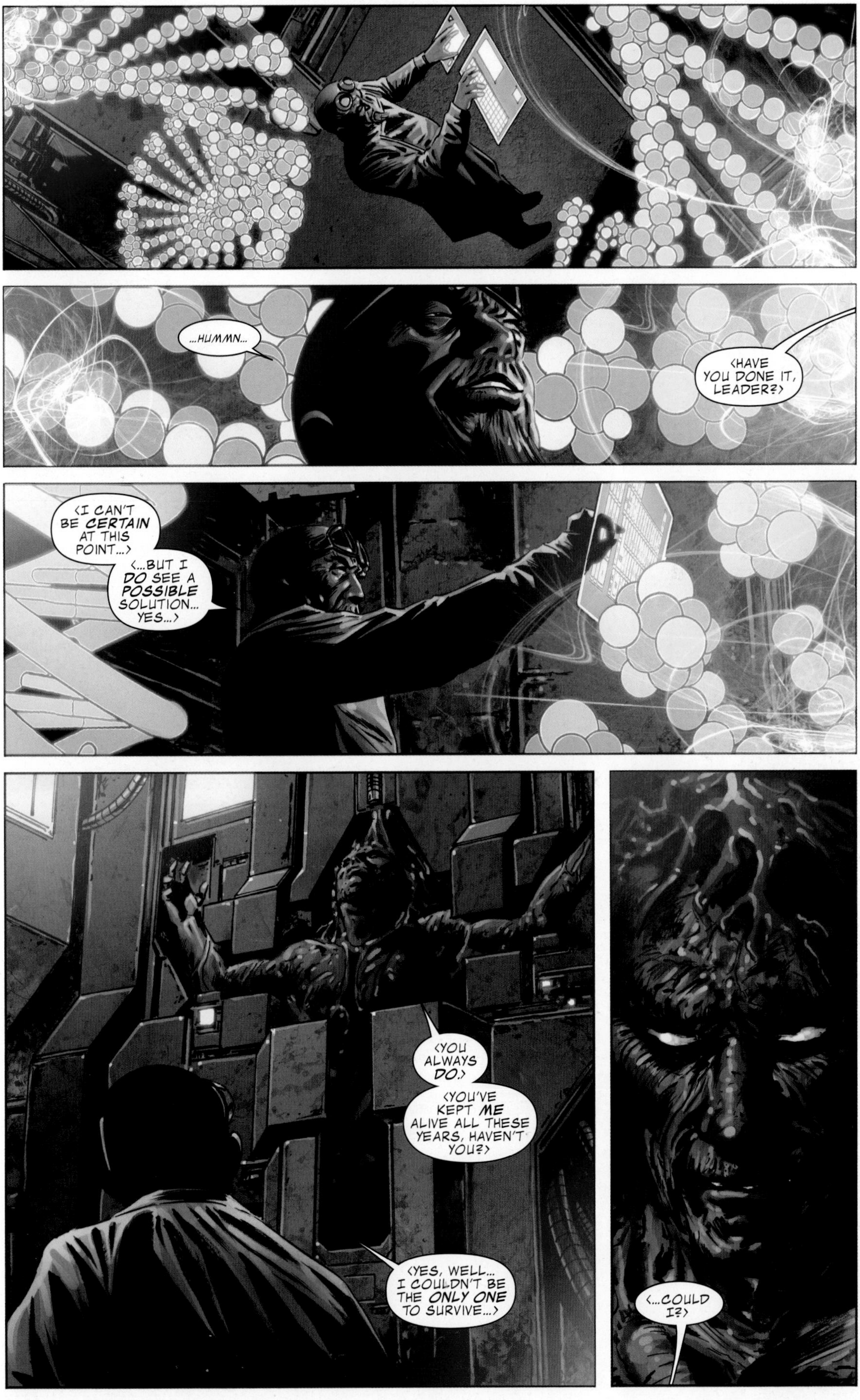
...HUMMN...
<HAVE YOU DONE IT, LEADER?>
<I CAN'T BE CERTAIN AT THIS POINT...>
<...BUT I DO SEE A POSSIBLE SOLUTION... YES...>
<YOU ALWAYS DO.>
<YOU'VE KEPT ME ALIVE ALL THESE YEARS, HAVEN'T YOU?>
<YES, WELL... I COULDN'T BE THE ONLY ONE TO SURVIVE...>
<...COULD I?>

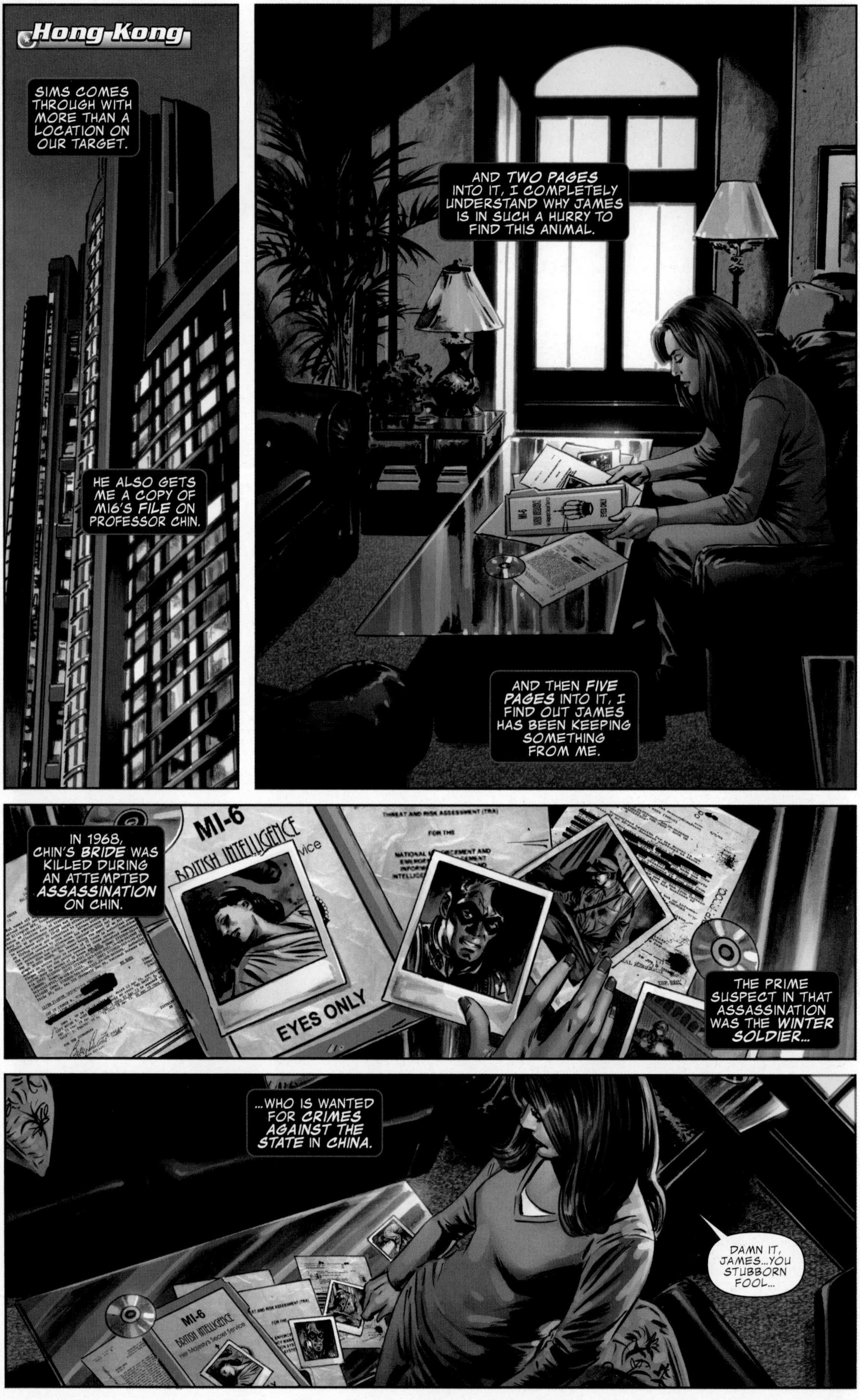
Hong Kong
SIMS COMES THROUGH WITH MORE THAN A LOCATION ON OUR TARGET.
HE ALSO GETS ME A COPY OF MI6'S FILE ON PROFESSOR CHIN.
AND TWO PAGES INTO IT, I COMPLETELY UNDERSTAND WHY JAMES IS IN SUCH A HURRY TO FIND THIS ANIMAL.
AND THEN FIVE PAGES INTO IT, I FIND OUT JAMES HAS BEEN KEEPING SOMETHING FROM ME.
IN 1968, CHIN'S BRIDE WAS KILLED DURING AN ATTEMPTED ASSASSINATION ON CHIN.
MI-6
BRITISH INTELLIGENCE
EYES ONLY
THE PRIME SUSPECT IN THAT ASSASSINATION WAS THE WINTER SOLDIER...
...WHO IS WANTED FOR CRIMES AGAINST THE STATE IN CHINA.
DAMN IT, JAMES...YOU STUBBORN FOOL...
MI-6
BRITISH INTELLIGENCE
Her Majesty's Secret Service

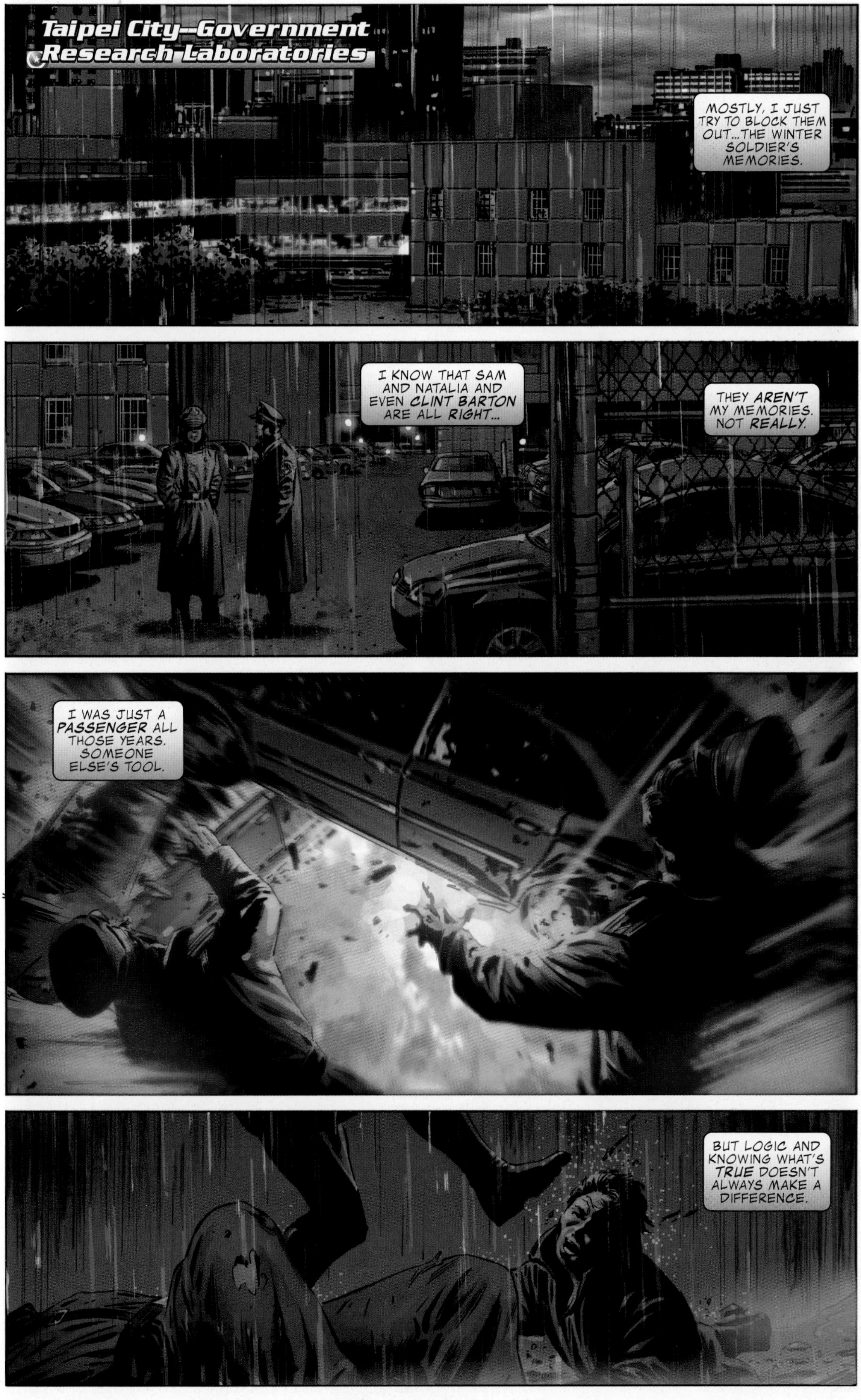
Taipei City--Government Research Laboratories
MOSTLY, I JUST TRY TO BLOCK THEM OUT...THE WINTER SOLDIER'S MEMORIES.
I KNOW THAT SAM AND NATALIA AND EVEN CLINT BARTON ARE ALL RIGHT...
THEY AREN'T MY MEMORIES. NOT REALLY.
I WAS JUST A PASSENGER ALL THOSE YEARS. SOMEONE ELSE'S TOOL.
BUT LOGIC AND KNOWING WHAT'S TRUE DOESN'T ALWAYS MAKE A DIFFERENCE.

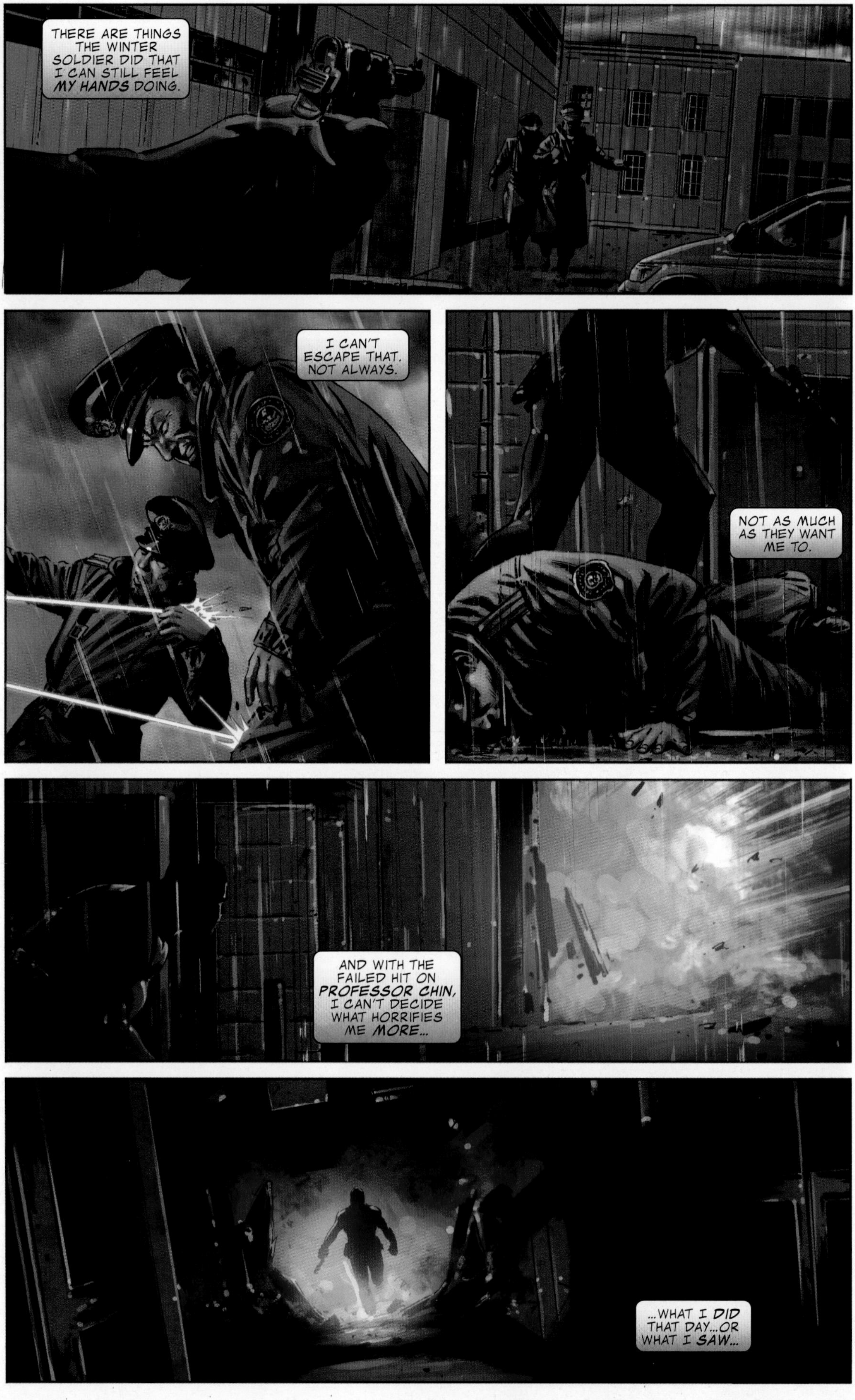
THERE ARE THINGS THE WINTER SOLDIER DID THAT I CAN STILL FEEL MY HANDS DOING.
I CAN'T ESCAPE THAT. NOT ALWAYS.
NOT AS MUCH AS THEY WANT ME TO.
AND WITH THE FAILED HIT ON PROFESSOR CHIN, I CAN'T DECIDE WHAT HORRIFIES ME MORE...
...WHAT I DID THAT DAY...OR WHAT I SAW...

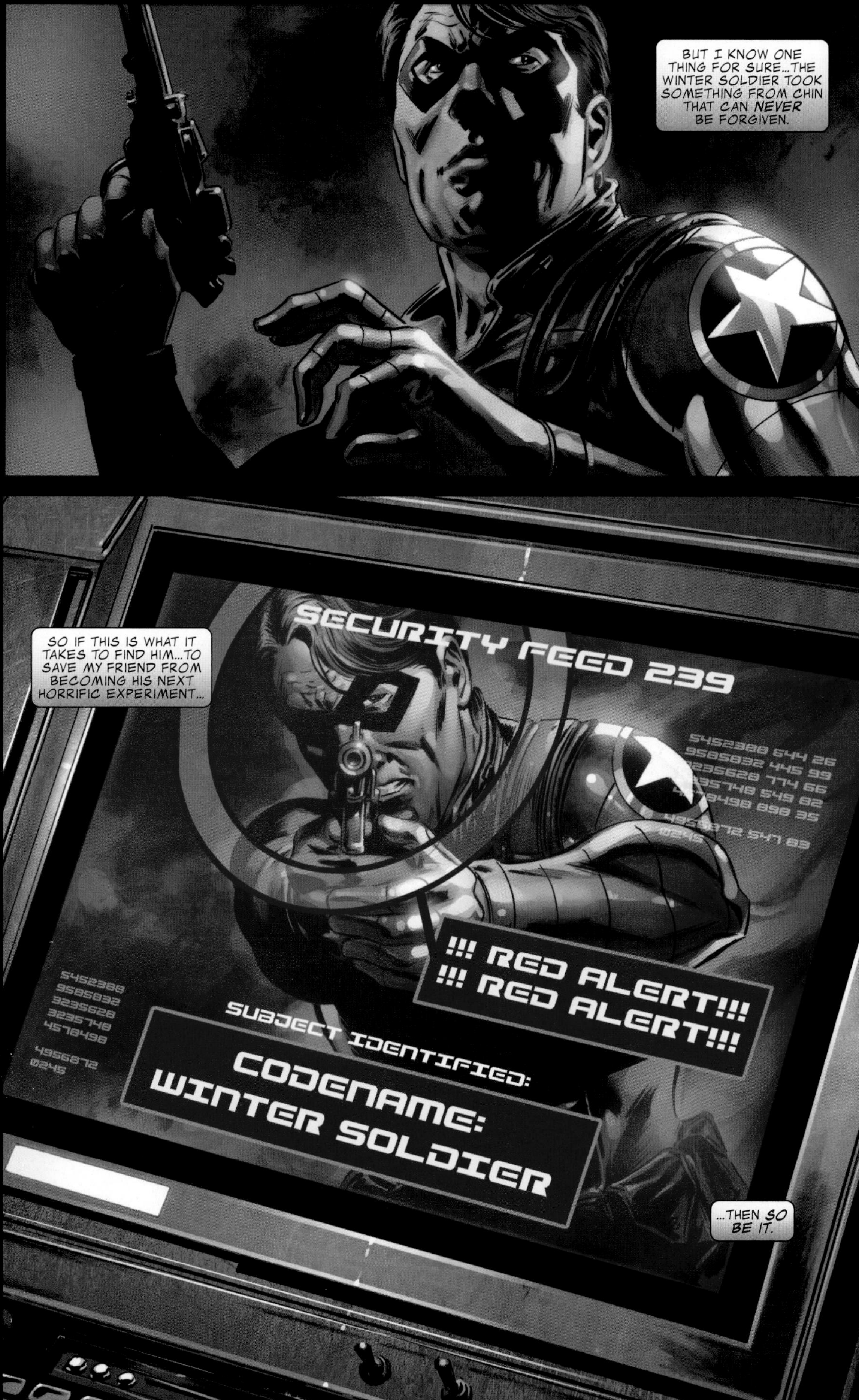

BUT I KNOW ONE THING FOR SURE...THE WINTER SOLDIER TOOK SOMETHING FROM CHIN THAT CAN NEVER BE FORGIVEN.
SO IF THIS IS WHAT IT TAKES TO FIND HIM...TO SAVE MY FRIEND FROM BECOMING HIS NEXT HORRIFIC EXPERIMENT...
SECURITY FEED 239
!!! RED ALERT!!!
!!! RED ALERT!!!
5452388
9585832
3235628
3235748
4578498
4956872
0245
SUBJECT IDENTIFIED:
CODENAME: WINTER SOLDIER
...THEN SO BE IT.

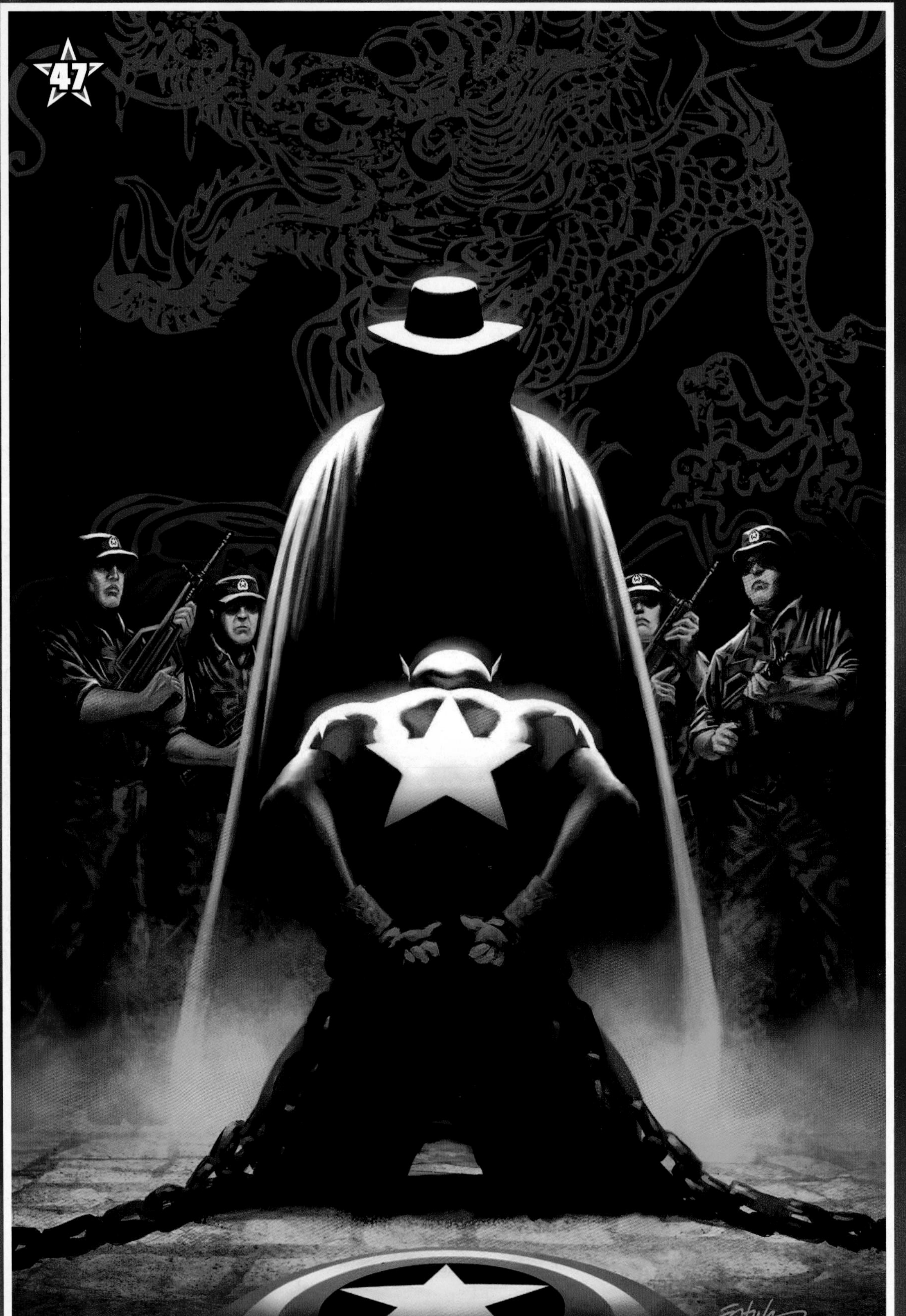

47

OLD FRIENDS AND ENEMIES PART TWO

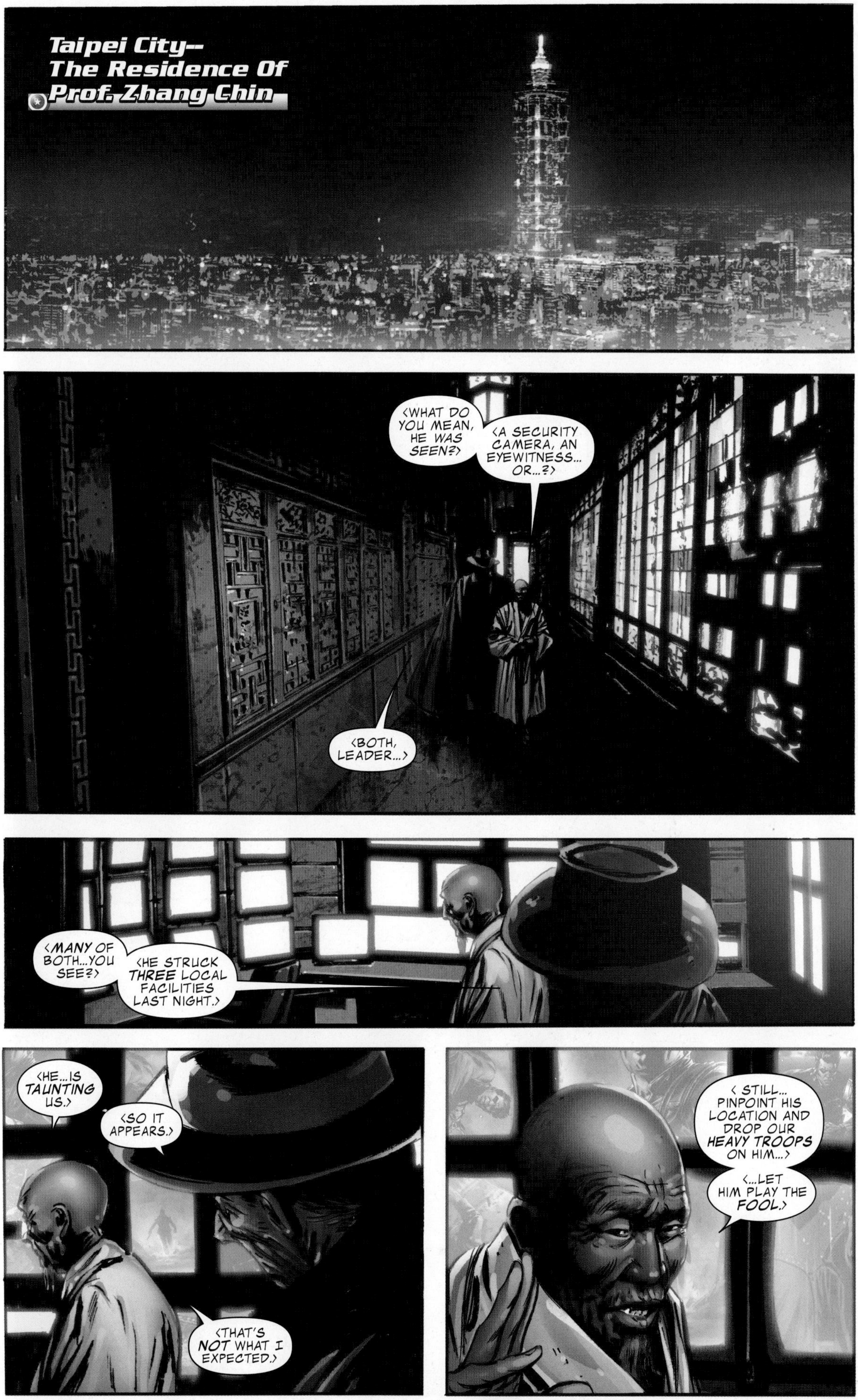
Taipei City--
The Residence Of
Prof. Zhang Chin
‹WHAT DO YOU MEAN, HE WAS SEEN?›
‹A SECURITY CAMERA, AN EYEWITNESS... OR...?›
‹BOTH, LEADER...›
‹MANY OF BOTH...YOU SEE?›
‹HE STRUCK THREE LOCAL FACILITIES LAST NIGHT.›
‹HE...IS TAUNTING US.›
‹SO IT APPEARS.›
‹THAT'S NOT WHAT I EXPECTED.›
‹ STILL... PINPOINT HIS LOCATION AND DROP OUR HEAVY TROOPS ON HIM...›
‹...LET HIM PLAY THE FOOL.›

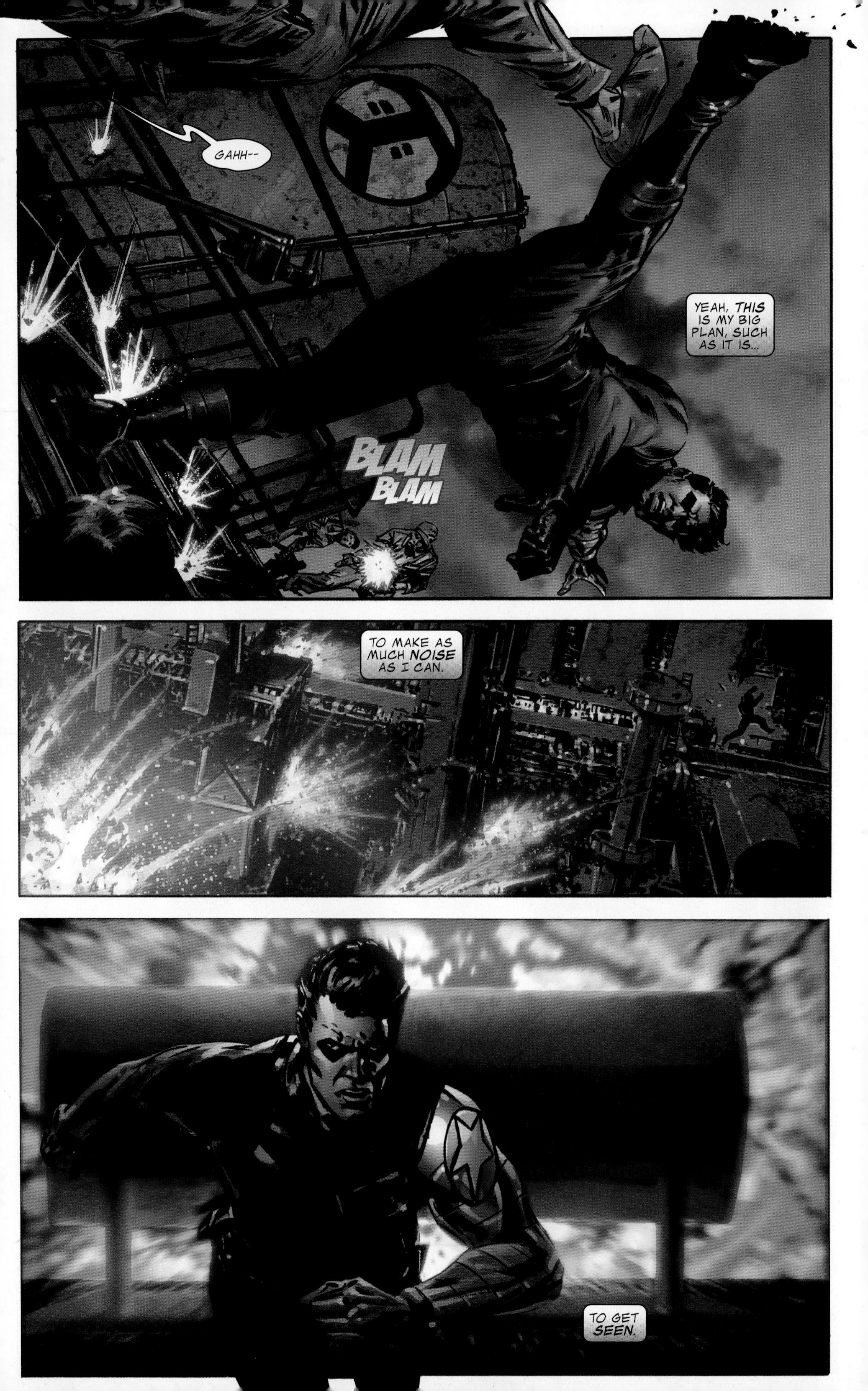
GAHH--
YEAH, THIS IS MY BIG PLAN, SUCH AS IT IS...
BLAM BLAM
TO MAKE AS MUCH NOISE AS I CAN.
TO GET SEEN.

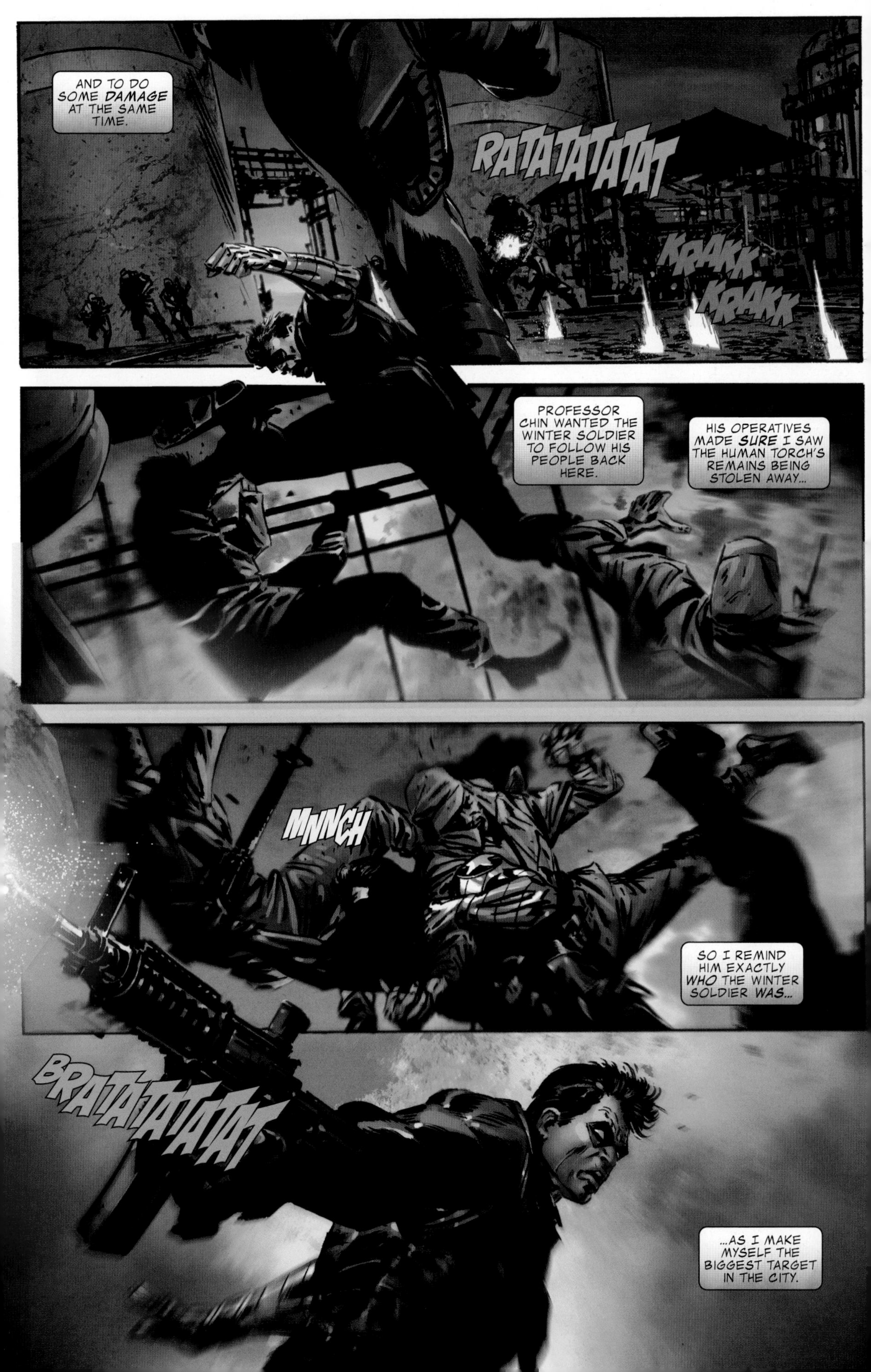
AND TO DO SOME DAMAGE AT THE SAME TIME.
RATATATATAT
KRAKK KRAKK
PROFESSOR CHIN WANTED THE WINTER SOLDIER TO FOLLOW HIS PEOPLE BACK HERE.
HIS OPERATIVES MADE SURE I SAW THE HUMAN TORCH'S REMAINS BEING STOLEN AWAY...
MNNCH
SO I REMIND HIM EXACTLY WHO THE WINTER SOLDIER WAS...
BRATATATATATAT
...AS I MAKE MYSELF THE BIGGEST TARGET IN THE CITY.

BUT EVEN IF CHIN *IS* WATCHING ON SOME MONITOR SOMEWHERE...

TATATATATATAT

...HE ISN'T THE *ONLY* ONE GETTING A REMINDER.

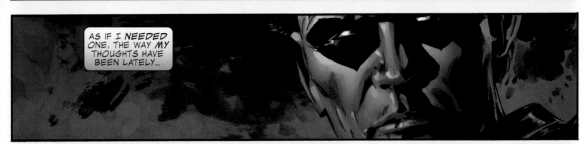

AS IF I *NEEDED* ONE, THE WAY *MY* THOUGHTS HAVE BEEN LATELY...

ALL RIGHT. WHERE *ARE* YOU, JAMES?

KRAKK

ANSWER ME, DAMN YOU.

LITTLE BUSY HERE, NAT.

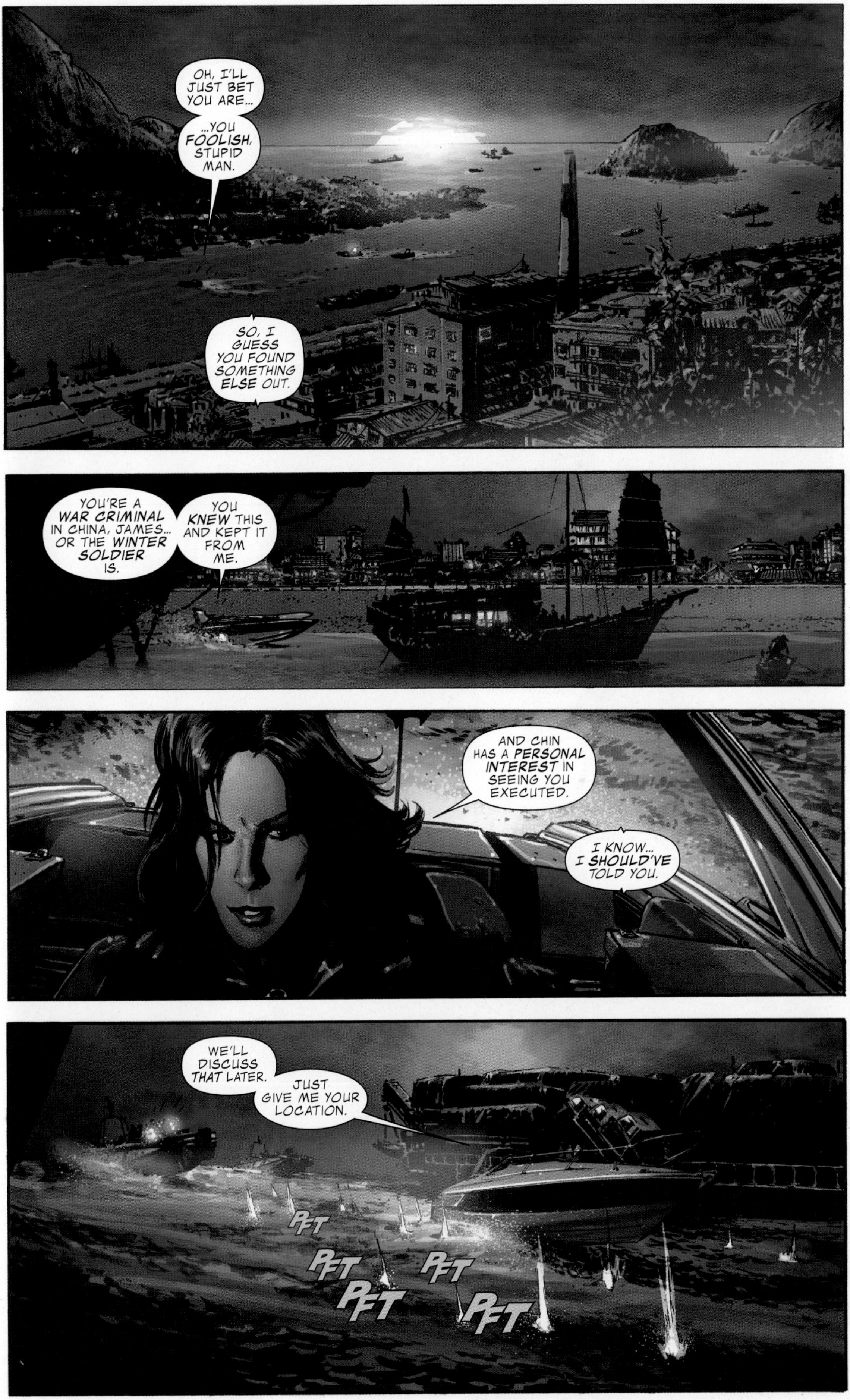
OH, I'LL JUST BET YOU ARE...
...YOU FOOLISH, STUPID MAN.
SO, I GUESS YOU FOUND SOMETHING ELSE OUT.
YOU'RE A WAR CRIMINAL IN CHINA, JAMES... OR THE WINTER SOLDIER IS.
YOU KNEW THIS AND KEPT IT FROM ME.
AND CHIN HAS A PERSONAL INTEREST IN SEEING YOU EXECUTED.
I KNOW... I SHOULD'VE TOLD YOU.
WE'LL DISCUSS THAT LATER.
JUST GIVE ME YOUR LOCATION.
PFT
PFT
PFT
PFT
PFT

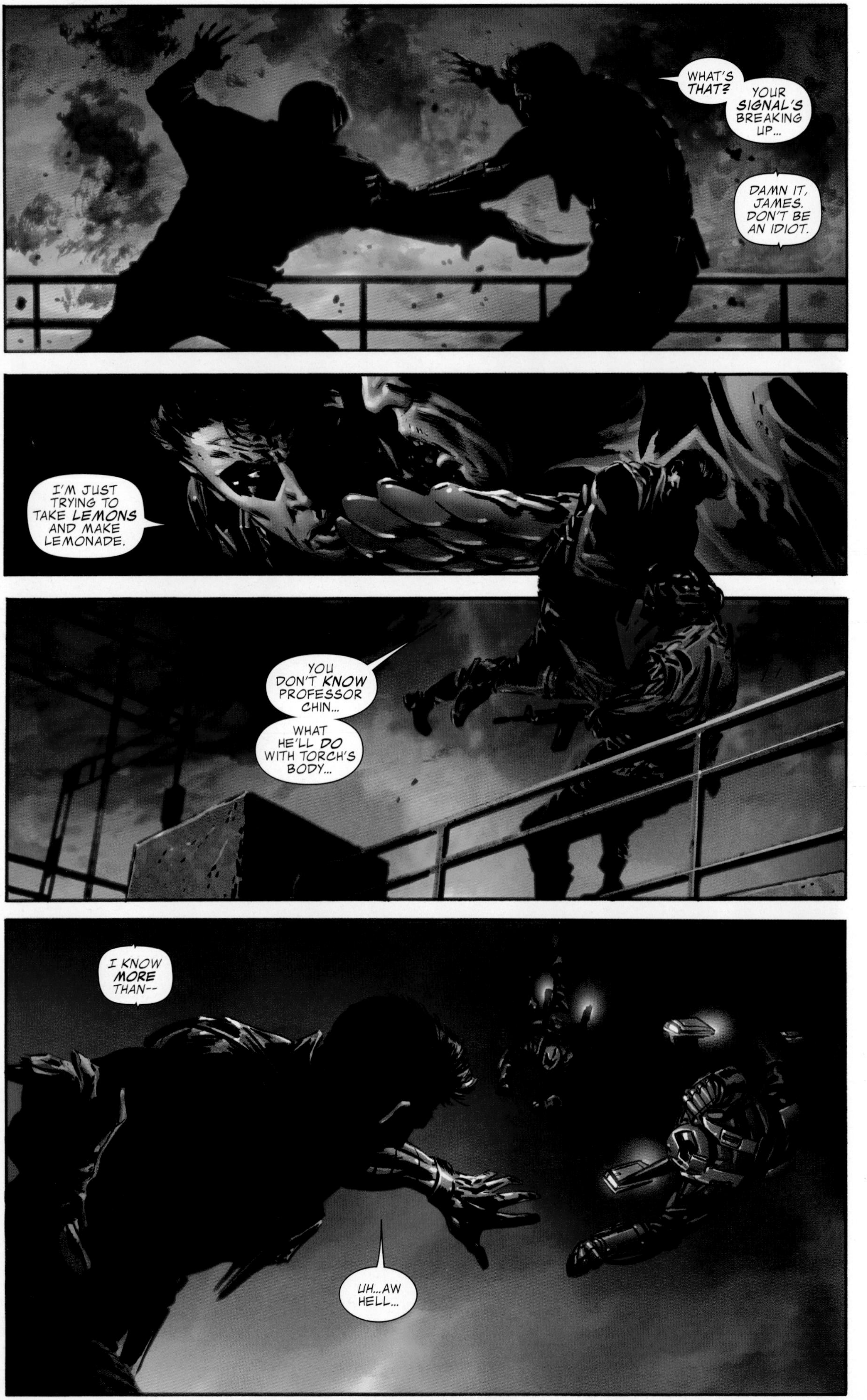
WHAT'S THAT?
YOUR SIGNAL'S BREAKING UP...
DAMN IT, JAMES. DON'T BE AN IDIOT.
I'M JUST TRYING TO TAKE LEMONS AND MAKE LEMONADE.
YOU DON'T KNOW PROFESSOR CHIN...
WHAT HE'LL DO WITH TORCH'S BODY...
I KNOW MORE THAN--
UH...AW HELL...

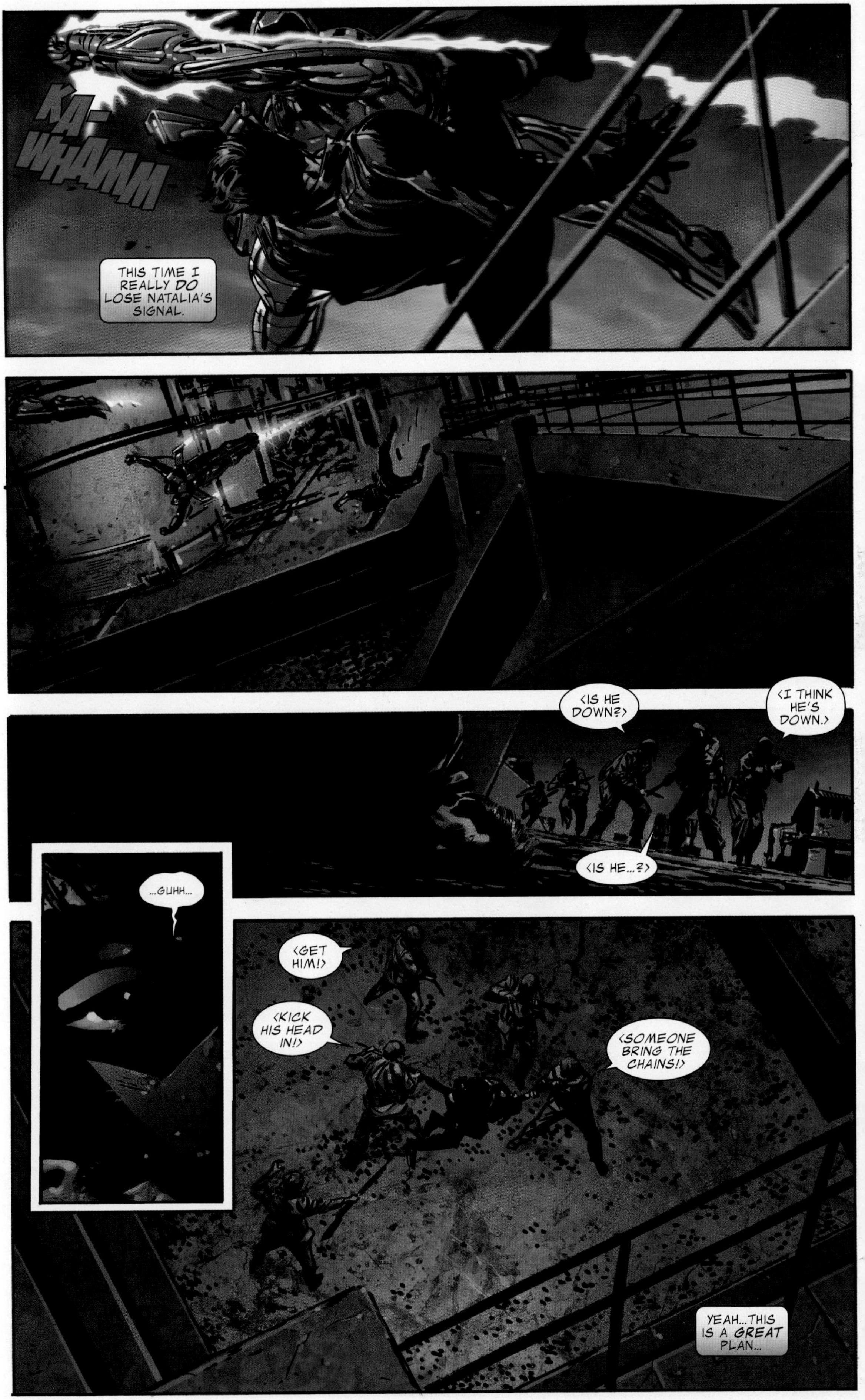
KA-WHAMM
THIS TIME I REALLY DO LOSE NATALIA'S SIGNAL.
<IS HE DOWN?>
<I THINK HE'S DOWN.>
<IS HE...?>
...GUHH...
<GET HIM!>
<KICK HIS HEAD IN!>
<SOMEONE BRING THE CHAINS!>
YEAH...THIS IS A GREAT PLAN...

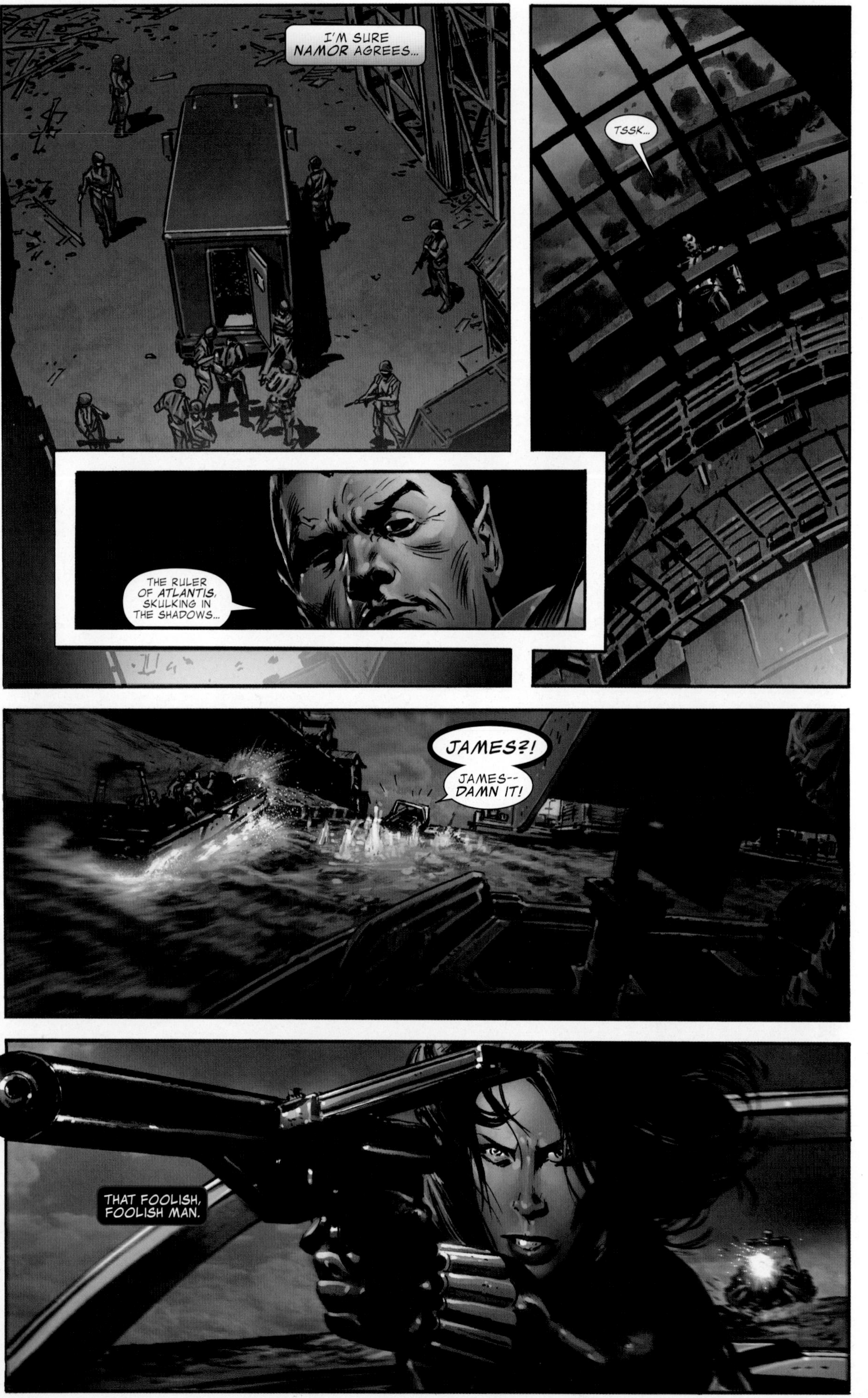
I'M SURE NAMOR AGREES...
TSSK...
THE RULER OF ATLANTIS, SKULKING IN THE SHADOWS...
JAMES?!
JAMES-- DAMN IT!
THAT FOOLISH, FOOLISH MAN.

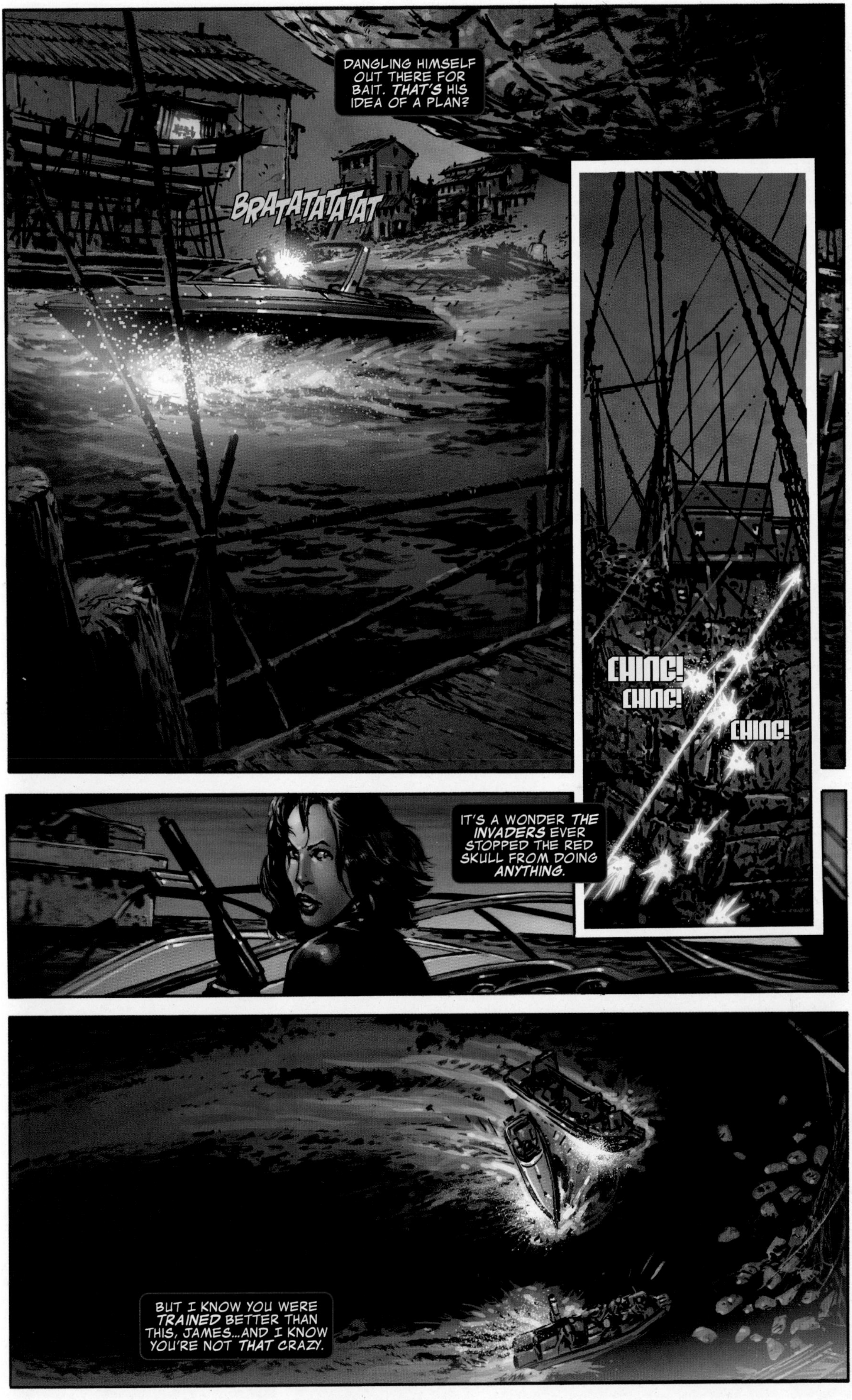
DANGLING HIMSELF OUT THERE FOR BAIT. THAT'S HIS IDEA OF A PLAN?
BRATATATATAT
CHING!
CHING!
CHING!
IT'S A WONDER THE INVADERS EVER STOPPED THE RED SKULL FROM DOING ANYTHING.
BUT I KNOW YOU WERE TRAINED BETTER THAN THIS, JAMES...AND I KNOW YOU'RE NOT THAT CRAZY.

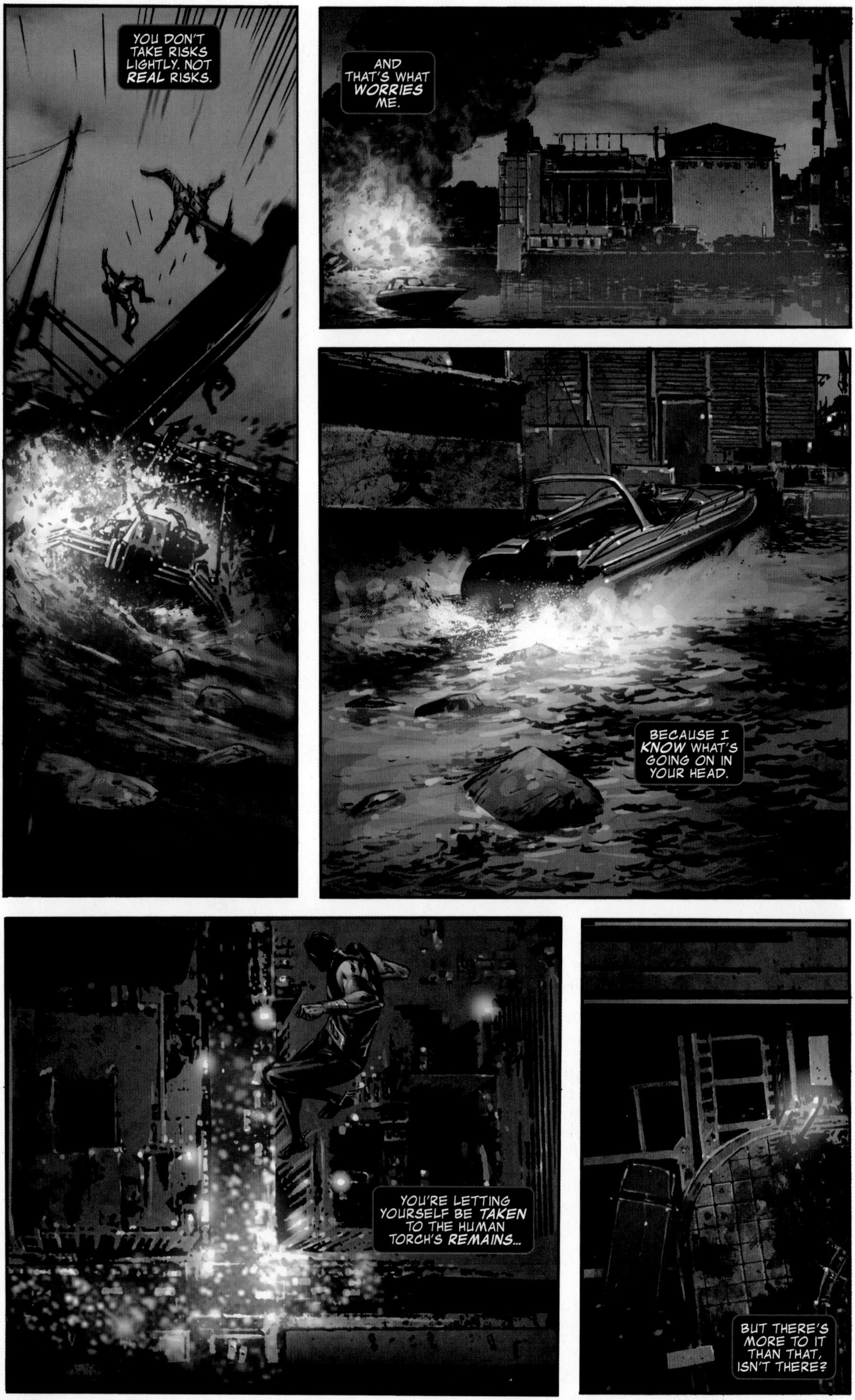
YOU DON'T TAKE RISKS LIGHTLY. NOT REAL RISKS.
AND THAT'S WHAT WORRIES ME.
BECAUSE I KNOW WHAT'S GOING ON IN YOUR HEAD.
YOU'RE LETTING YOURSELF BE TAKEN TO THE HUMAN TORCH'S REMAINS...
BUT THERE'S MORE TO IT THAN THAT, ISN'T THERE?

BECAUSE, ON SOME LEVEL... YOU THINK YOU *DESERVE* IT.

THINK YOU DESERVE TO BE *PUNISHED.*

...UNHH...

...OW...

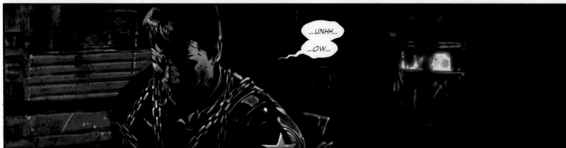

OKAY...BRAIN *SEEMS* TO BE WORKING... MOSTLY...

HAVEN'T BEEN HIT *THAT HARD* IN A LONG TIME. FELT LIKE *WOLVERINE* DECKED ME.

STILL *ALIVE,* THOUGH... *THAT* PART OF THE PLAN WORKED...

ALTHOUGH HIS *JAMMING-FIELD* CLAMP ON MY LEFT ARM IS A BIT MORE TROUBLE THAN I WAS EXPECTING.

BUT THIS SURE *FEELS* LIKE ONE OF PROFESSOR CHIN'S LABS.

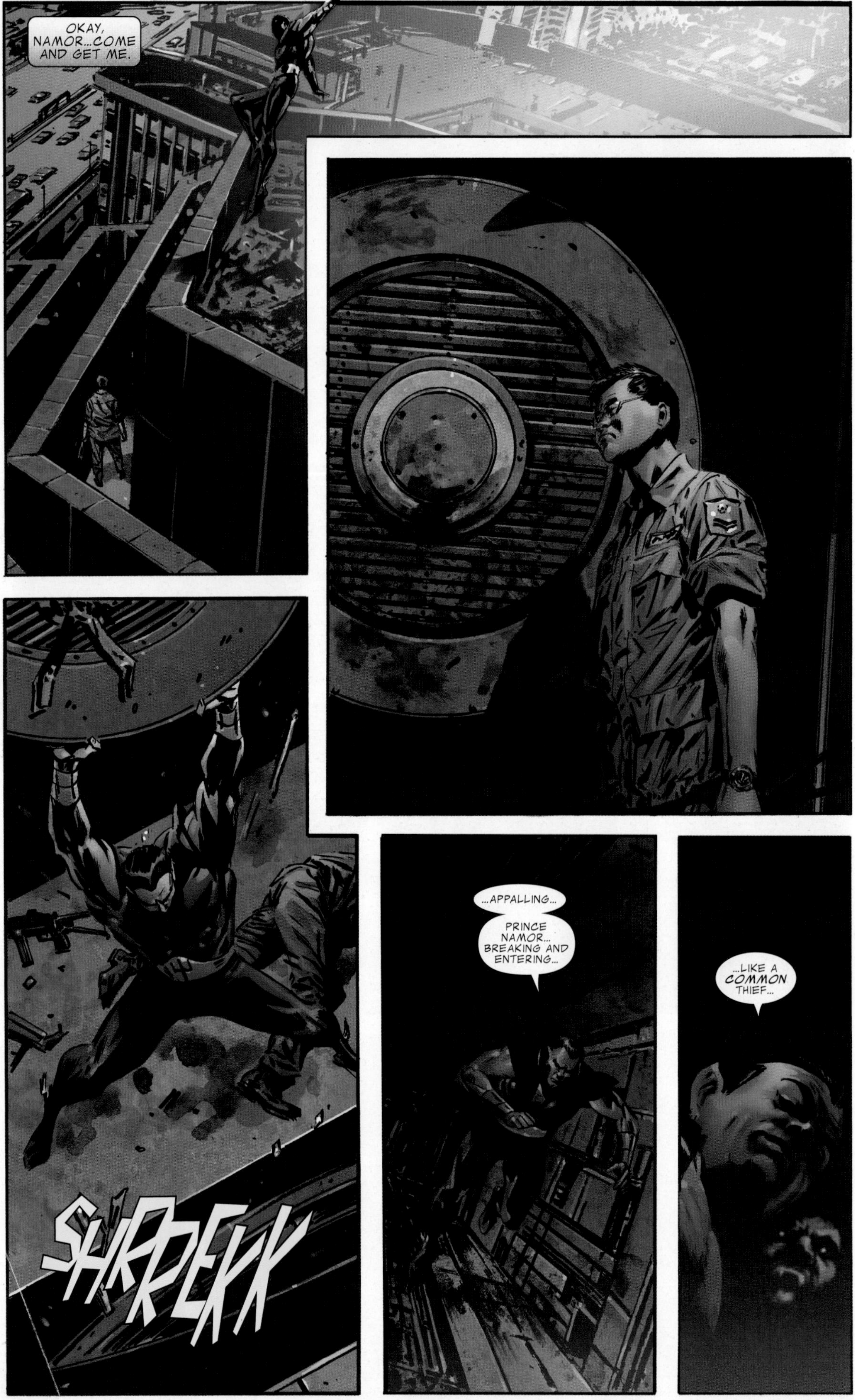
OKAY, NAMOR...COME AND GET ME.
SHRDEKK
...APPALLING...
PRINCE NAMOR... BREAKING AND ENTERING...
...LIKE A COMMON THIEF...

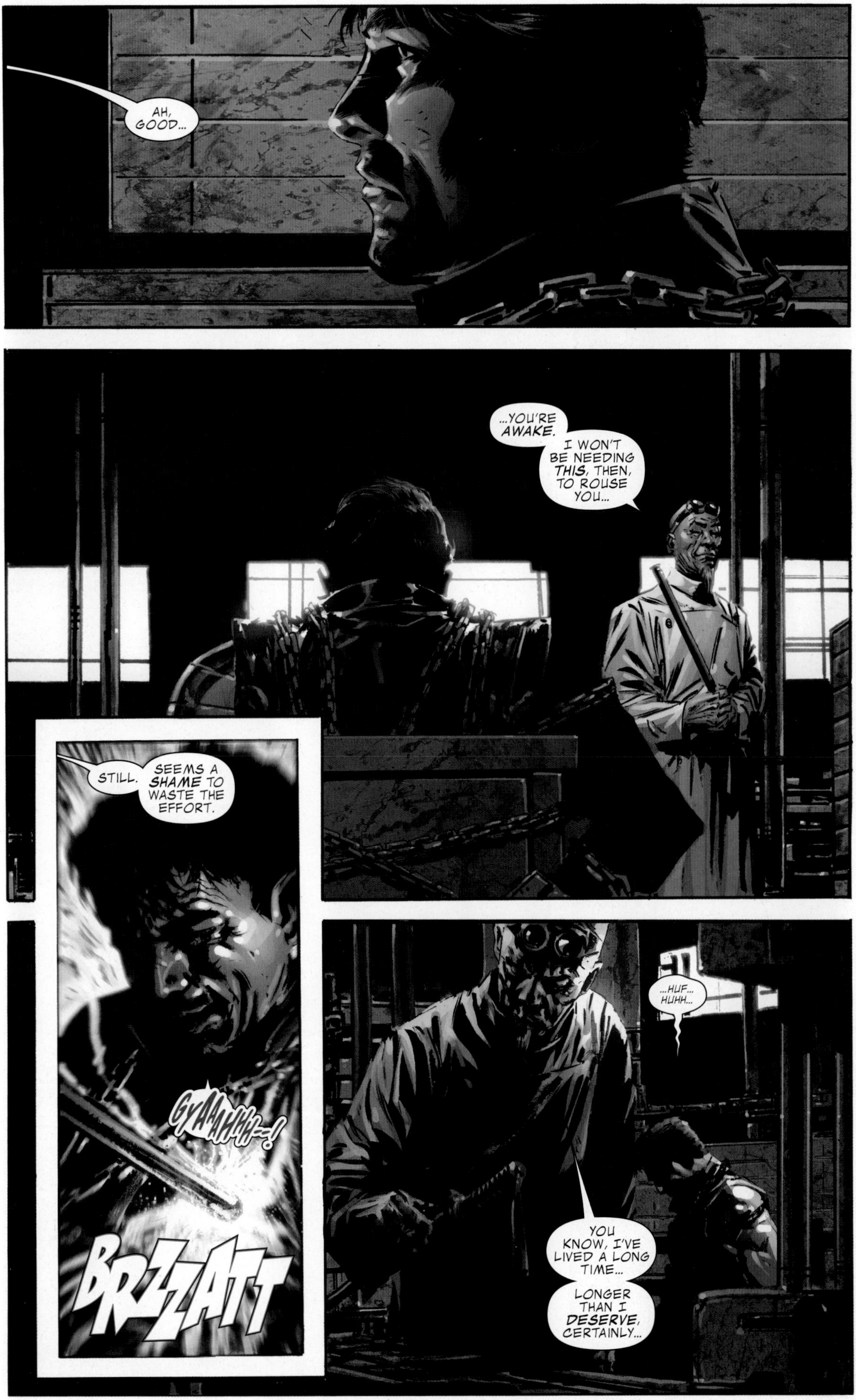
AH, GOOD...
...YOU'RE AWAKE.
I WON'T BE NEEDING THIS, THEN, TO ROUSE YOU...
STILL.
SEEMS A SHAME TO WASTE THE EFFORT.
GYAAAHHH--!
BRZZATT
...HUF... HUHH...
YOU KNOW, I'VE LIVED A LONG TIME...
LONGER THAN I DESERVE, CERTAINLY...

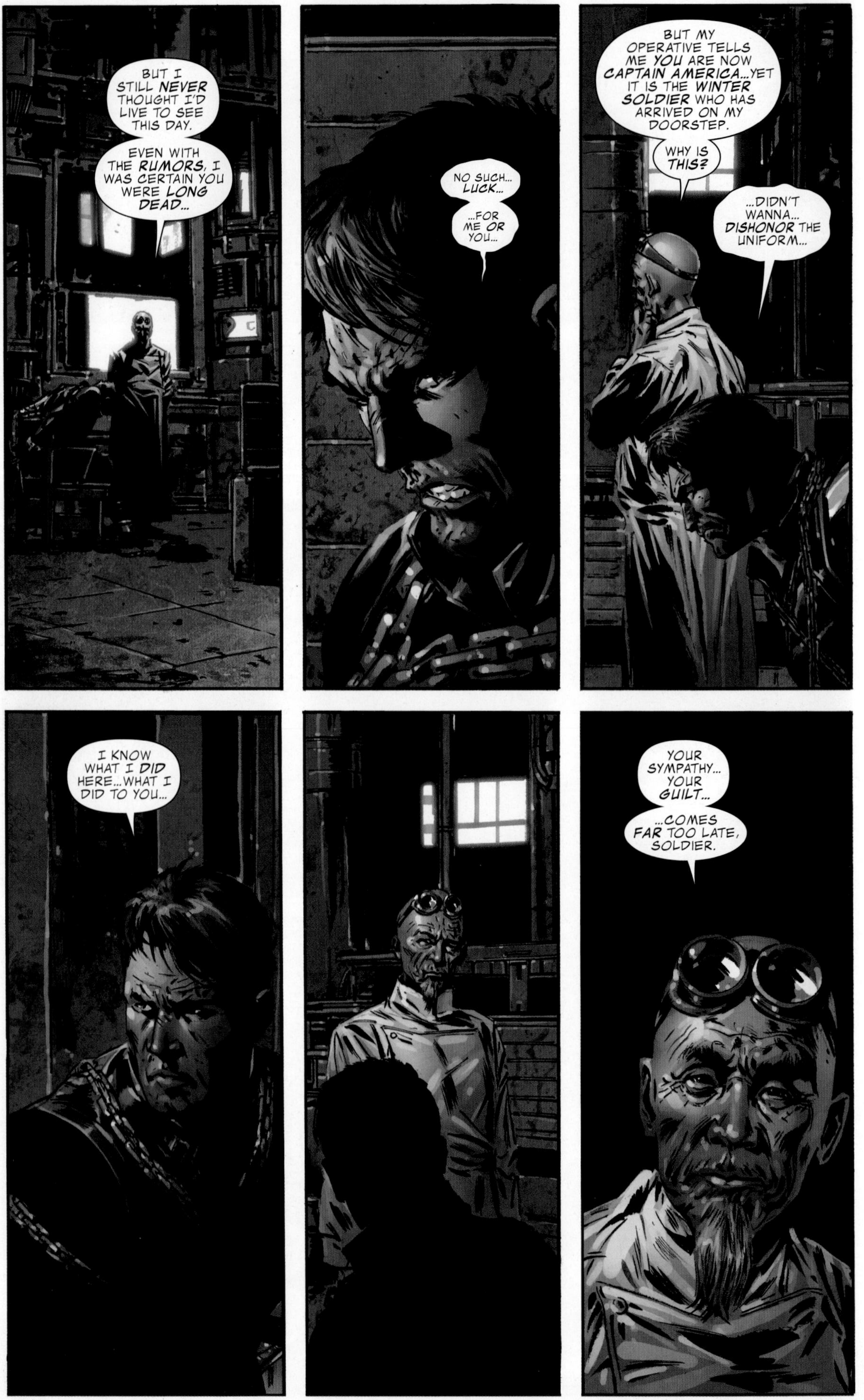

BUT I STILL NEVER THOUGHT I'D LIVE TO SEE THIS DAY.
EVEN WITH THE RUMORS, I WAS CERTAIN YOU WERE LONG DEAD...
NO SUCH... LUCK...
...FOR ME OR YOU...
BUT MY OPERATIVE TELLS ME YOU ARE NOW CAPTAIN AMERICA...YET IT IS THE WINTER SOLDIER WHO HAS ARRIVED ON MY DOORSTEP.
WHY IS THIS?
...DIDN'T WANNA... DISHONOR THE UNIFORM...
I KNOW WHAT I DID HERE...WHAT I DID TO YOU...
YOUR SYMPATHY... YOUR GUILT...
...COMES FAR TOO LATE, SOLDIER.

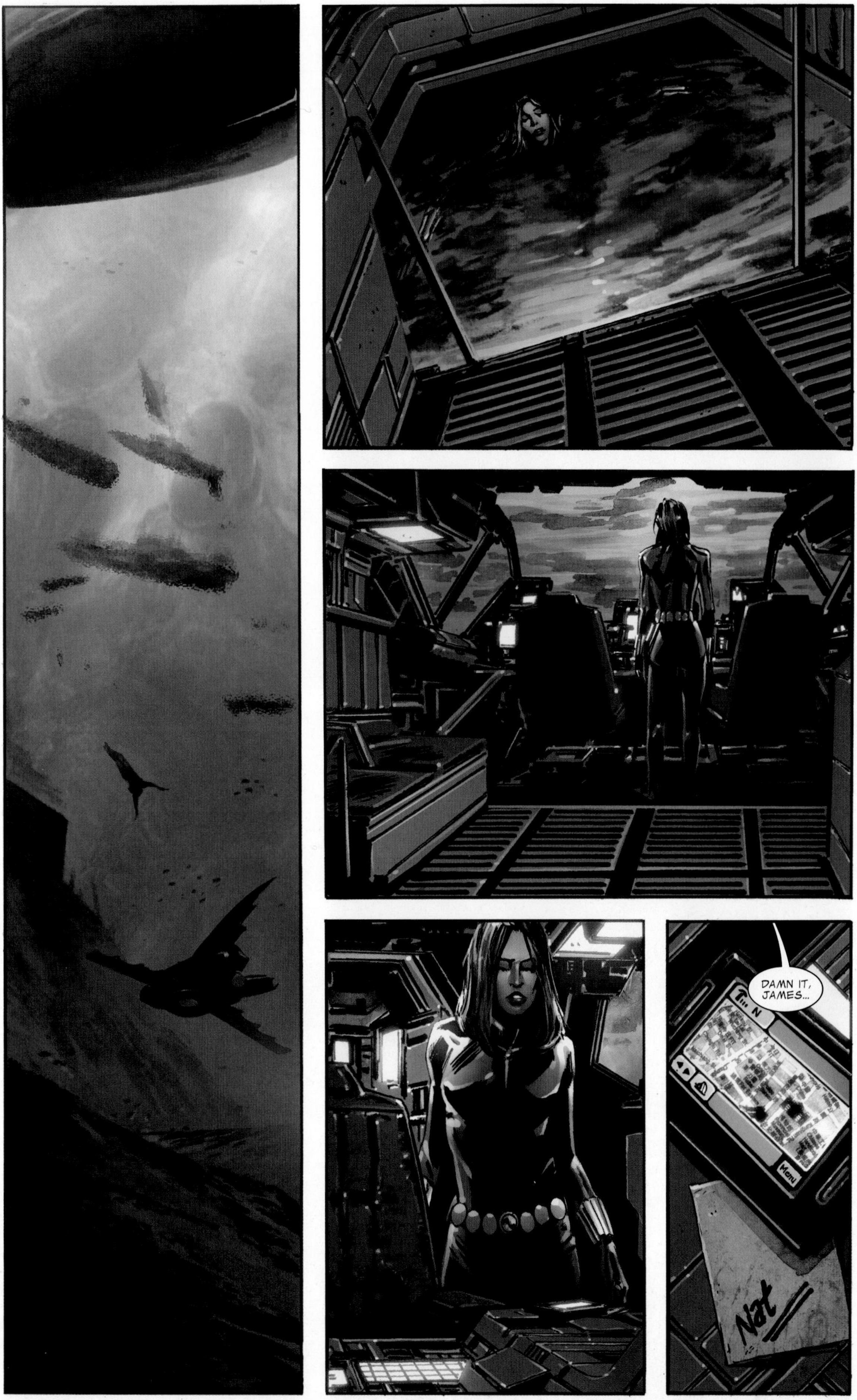
DAMN IT, JAMES...
Menu
Nat

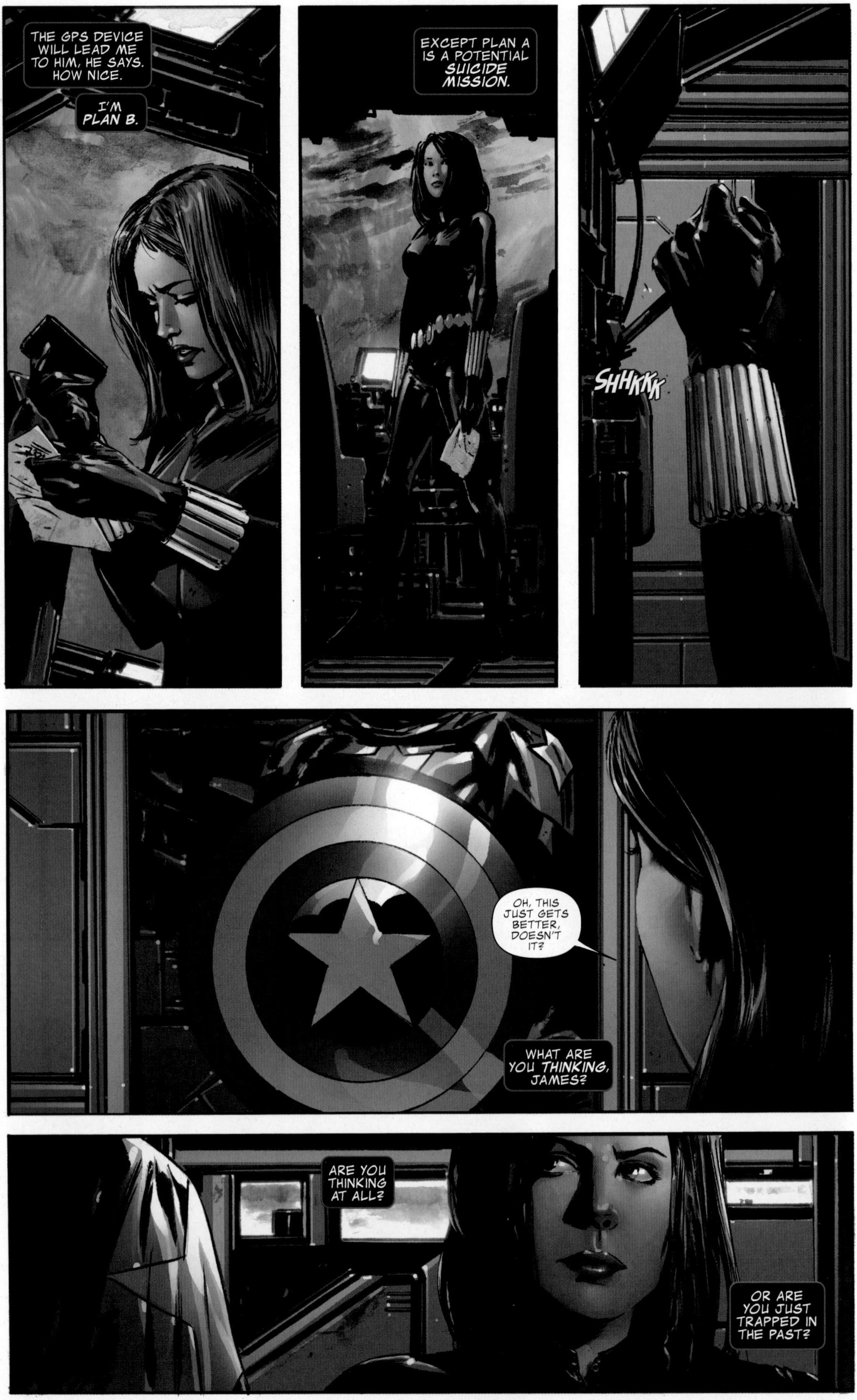
THE GPS DEVICE WILL LEAD ME TO HIM, HE SAYS. HOW NICE.
I'M PLAN B.
EXCEPT PLAN A IS A POTENTIAL SUICIDE MISSION.
SHHKKK
OH, THIS JUST GETS BETTER, DOESN'T IT?
WHAT ARE YOU THINKING, JAMES?
ARE YOU THINKING AT ALL?
OR ARE YOU JUST TRAPPED IN THE PAST?

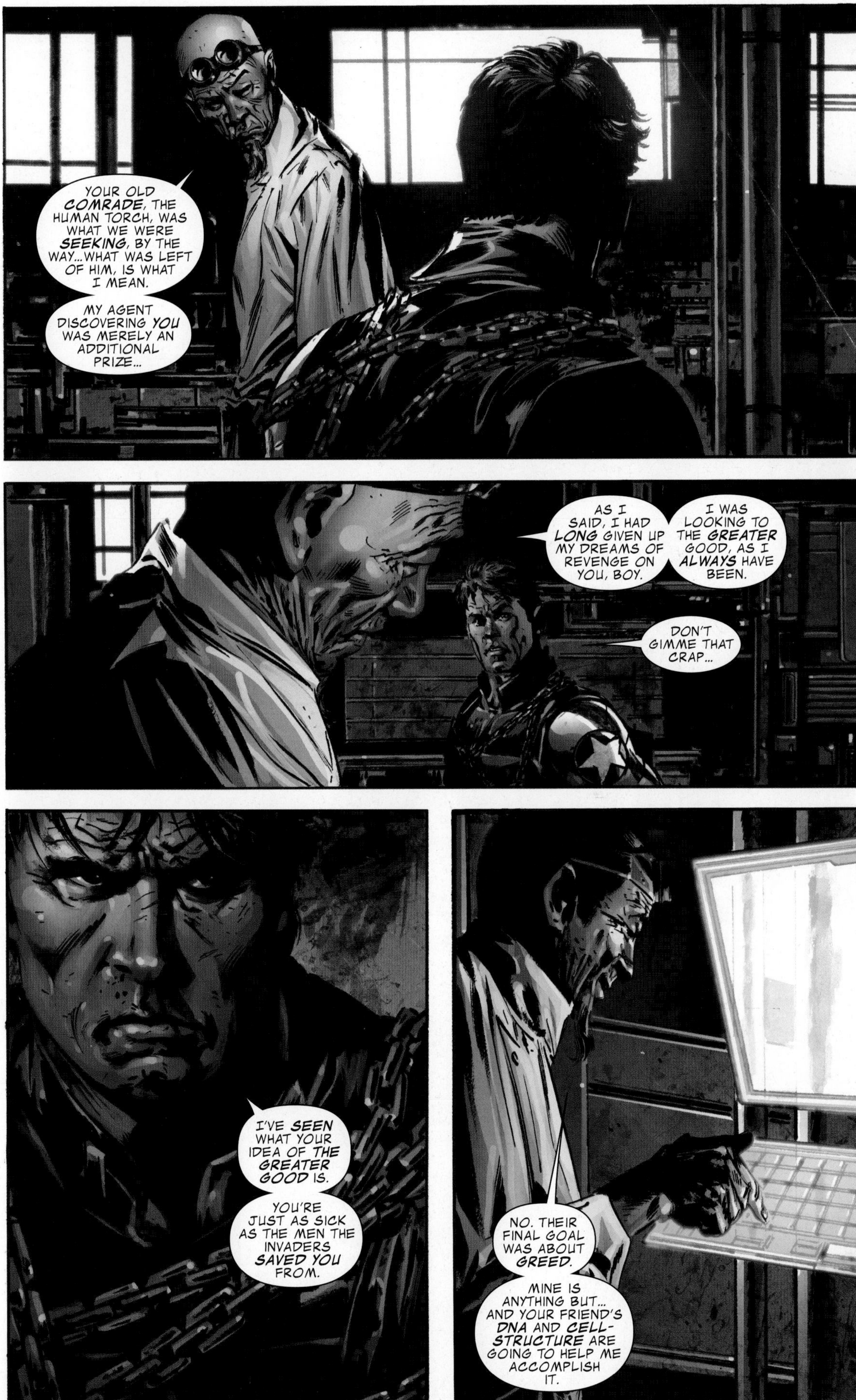
YOUR OLD COMRADE, THE HUMAN TORCH, WAS WHAT WE WERE SEEKING, BY THE WAY...WHAT WAS LEFT OF HIM, IS WHAT I MEAN.
MY AGENT DISCOVERING YOU WAS MERELY AN ADDITIONAL PRIZE...
AS I SAID, I HAD LONG GIVEN UP MY DREAMS OF REVENGE ON YOU, BOY.
I WAS LOOKING TO THE GREATER GOOD, AS I ALWAYS HAVE BEEN.
DON'T GIMME THAT CRAP...
I'VE SEEN WHAT YOUR IDEA OF THE GREATER GOOD IS.
YOU'RE JUST AS SICK AS THE MEN THE INVADERS SAVED YOU FROM.
NO. THEIR FINAL GOAL WAS ABOUT GREED.
MINE IS ANYTHING BUT... AND YOUR FRIEND'S DNA AND CELL-STRUCTURE ARE GOING TO HELP ME ACCOMPLISH IT.

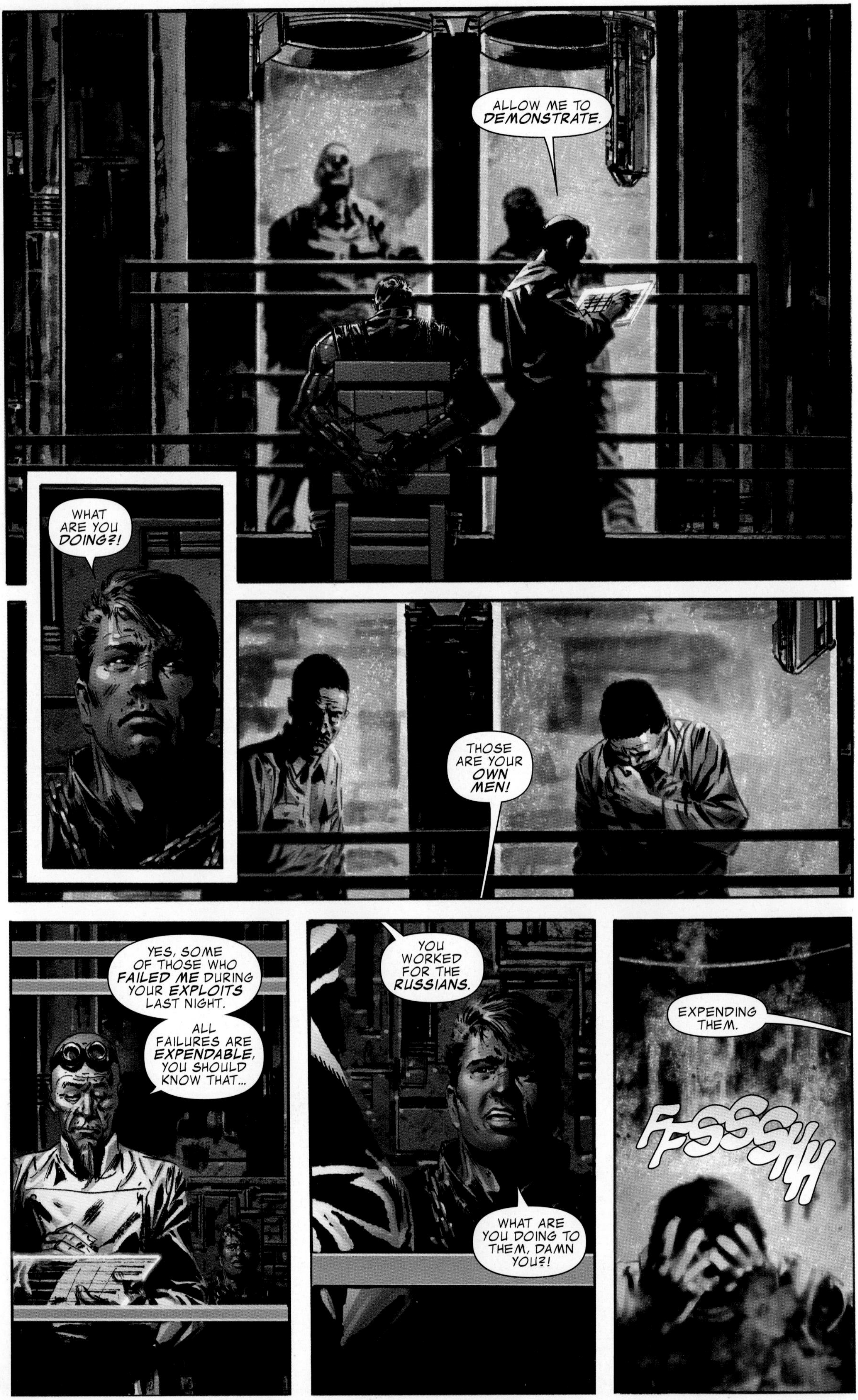
ALLOW ME TO DEMONSTRATE.
WHAT ARE YOU DOING?!
THOSE ARE YOUR OWN MEN!
YES, SOME OF THOSE WHO FAILED ME DURING YOUR EXPLOITS LAST NIGHT.
ALL FAILURES ARE EXPENDABLE, YOU SHOULD KNOW THAT...
YOU WORKED FOR THE RUSSIANS.
WHAT ARE YOU DOING TO THEM, DAMN YOU?!
EXPENDING THEM.
FFSSSHH

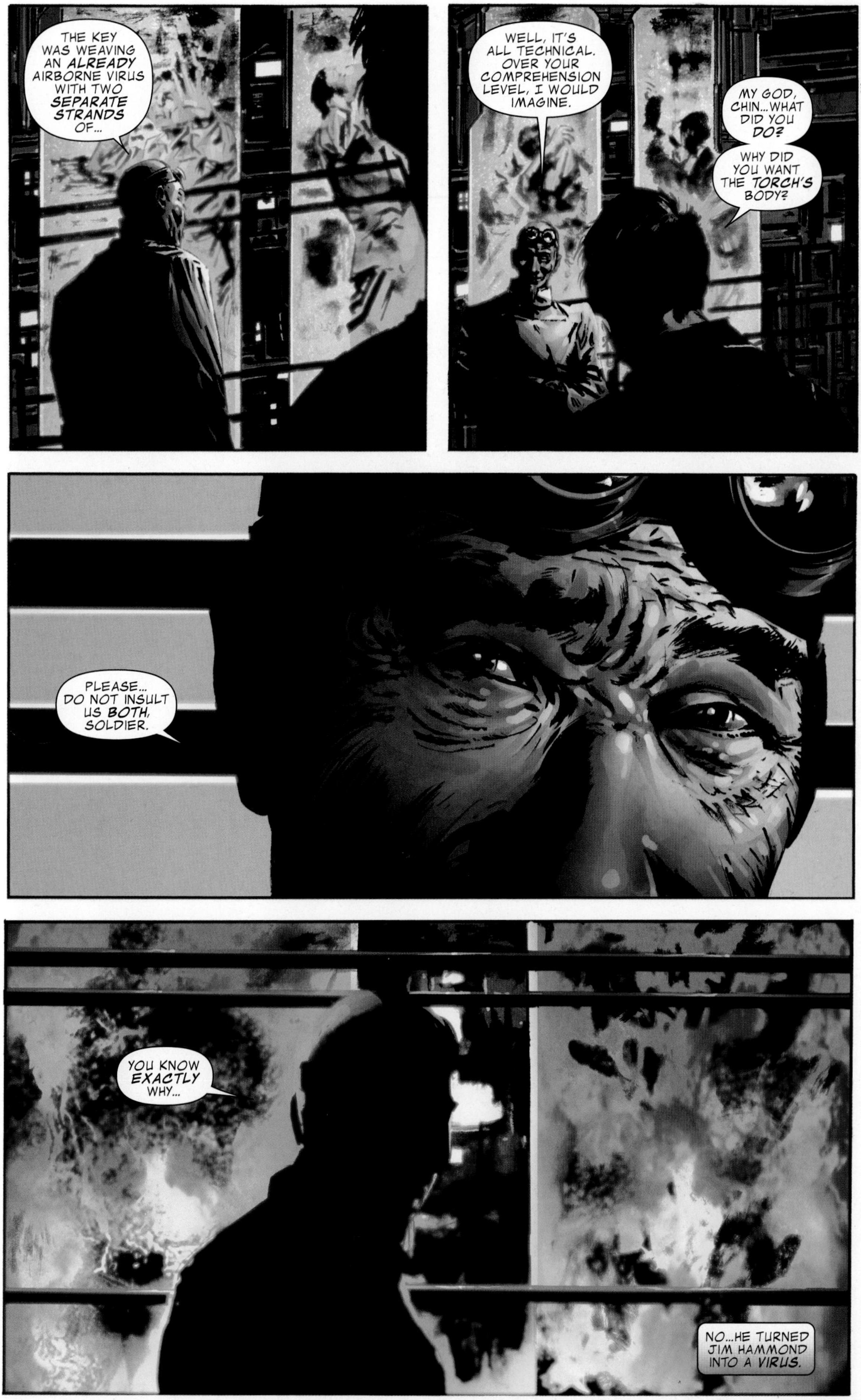

THE KEY WAS WEAVING AN ALREADY AIRBORNE VIRUS WITH TWO SEPARATE STRANDS OF...
WELL, IT'S ALL TECHNICAL. OVER YOUR COMPREHENSION LEVEL, I WOULD IMAGINE.
MY GOD, CHIN...WHAT DID YOU DO?
WHY DID YOU WANT THE TORCH'S BODY?
PLEASE... DO NOT INSULT US BOTH, SOLDIER.
YOU KNOW EXACTLY WHY...
NO...HE TURNED JIM HAMMOND INTO A VIRUS.

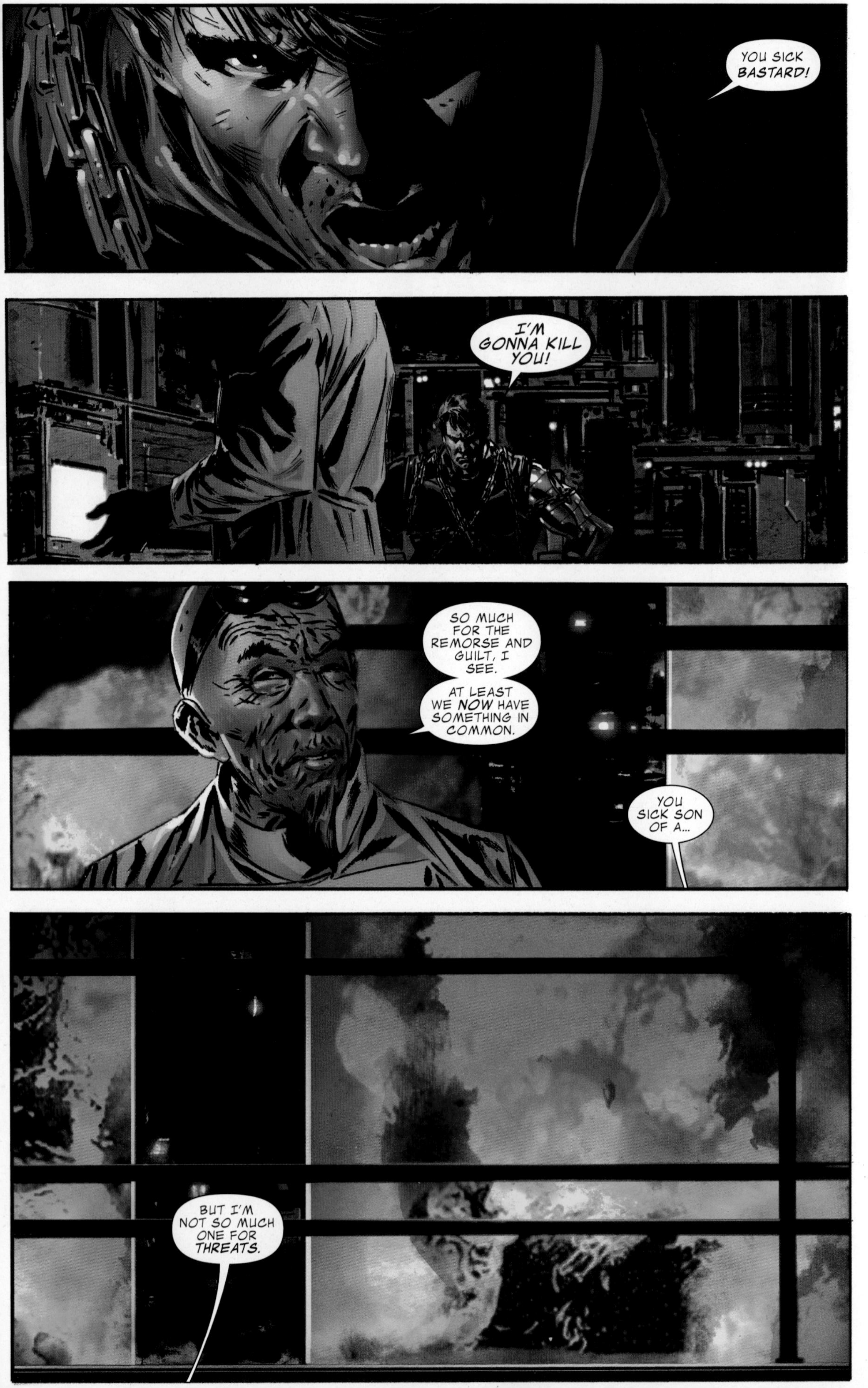
YOU SICK BASTARD!
I'M GONNA KILL YOU!
SO MUCH FOR THE REMORSE AND GUILT, I SEE.
AT LEAST WE NOW HAVE SOMETHING IN COMMON.
YOU SICK SON OF A...
BUT I'M NOT SO MUCH ONE FOR THREATS.

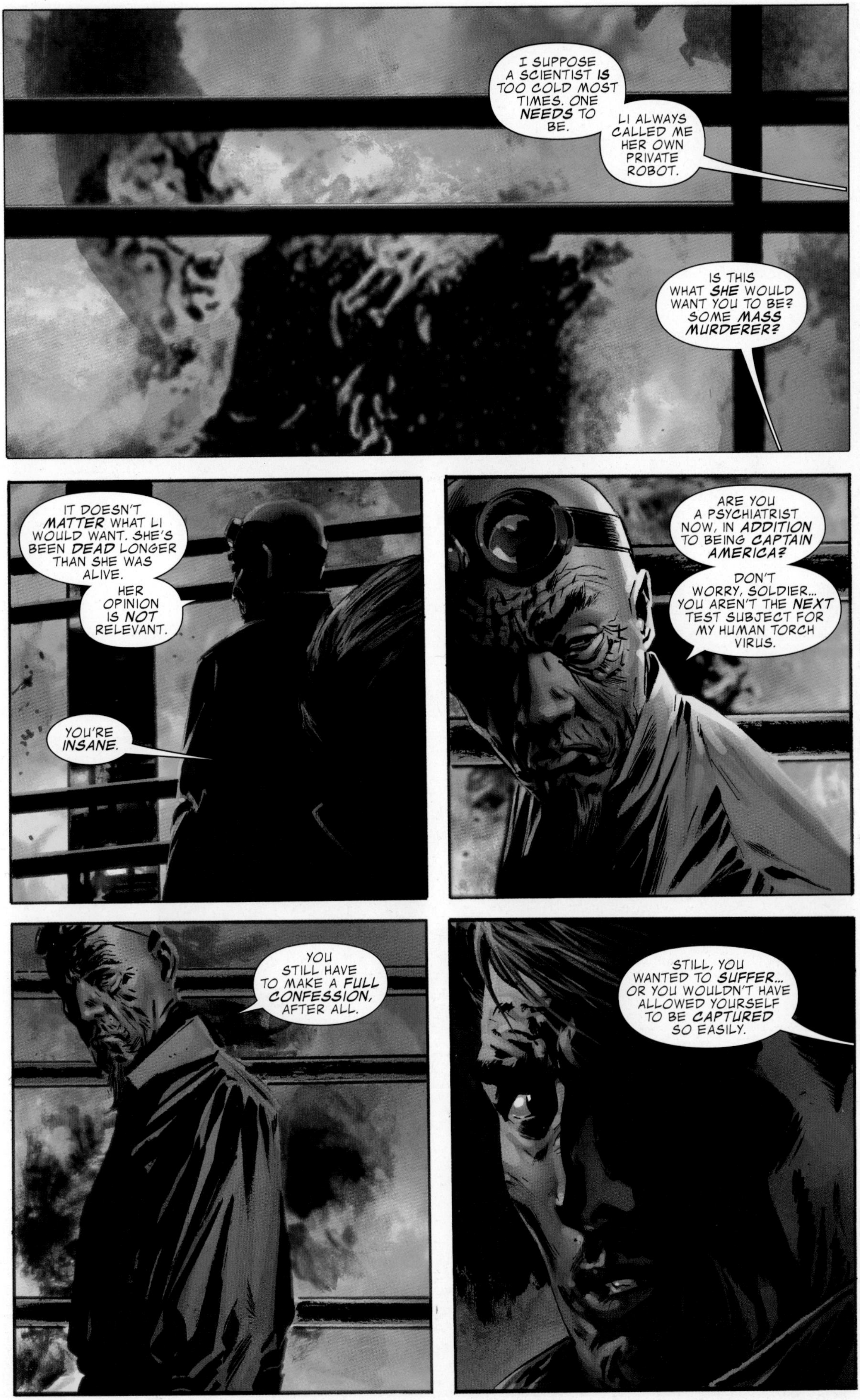
I SUPPOSE A SCIENTIST **IS** TOO COLD MOST TIMES. ONE **NEEDS** TO BE.
LI ALWAYS CALLED ME HER OWN PRIVATE ROBOT.
IS THIS WHAT **SHE** WOULD WANT YOU TO BE? SOME **MASS MURDERER?**
IT DOESN'T **MATTER** WHAT LI WOULD WANT. SHE'S BEEN **DEAD** LONGER THAN SHE WAS ALIVE.
HER OPINION IS **NOT** RELEVANT.
YOU'RE **INSANE.**
ARE YOU A PSYCHIATRIST NOW, IN **ADDITION** TO BEING **CAPTAIN AMERICA?**
DON'T WORRY, SOLDIER... YOU AREN'T THE **NEXT** TEST SUBJECT FOR MY HUMAN TORCH VIRUS.
YOU STILL HAVE TO MAKE A **FULL CONFESSION,** AFTER ALL.
STILL, YOU WANTED TO **SUFFER...** OR YOU WOULDN'T HAVE ALLOWED YOURSELF TO BE **CAPTURED** SO EASILY.

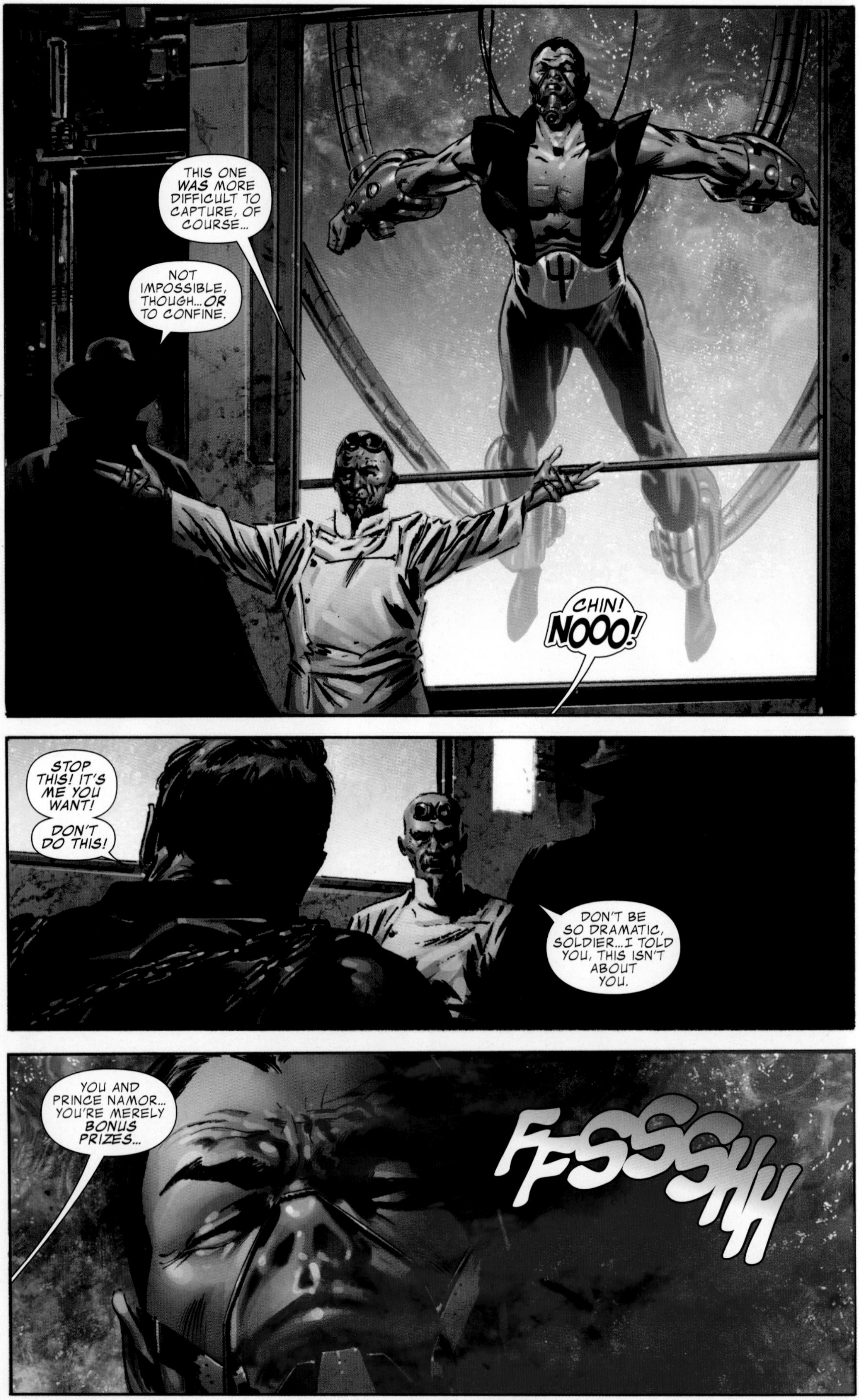
THIS ONE WAS MORE DIFFICULT TO CAPTURE, OF COURSE...
NOT IMPOSSIBLE, THOUGH...OR TO CONFINE.
CHIN! NOOO!
STOP THIS! IT'S ME YOU WANT!
DON'T DO THIS!
DON'T BE SO DRAMATIC, SOLDIER...I TOLD YOU, THIS ISN'T ABOUT YOU.
YOU AND PRINCE NAMOR... YOU'RE MERELY BONUS PRIZES...
FFSSSHH

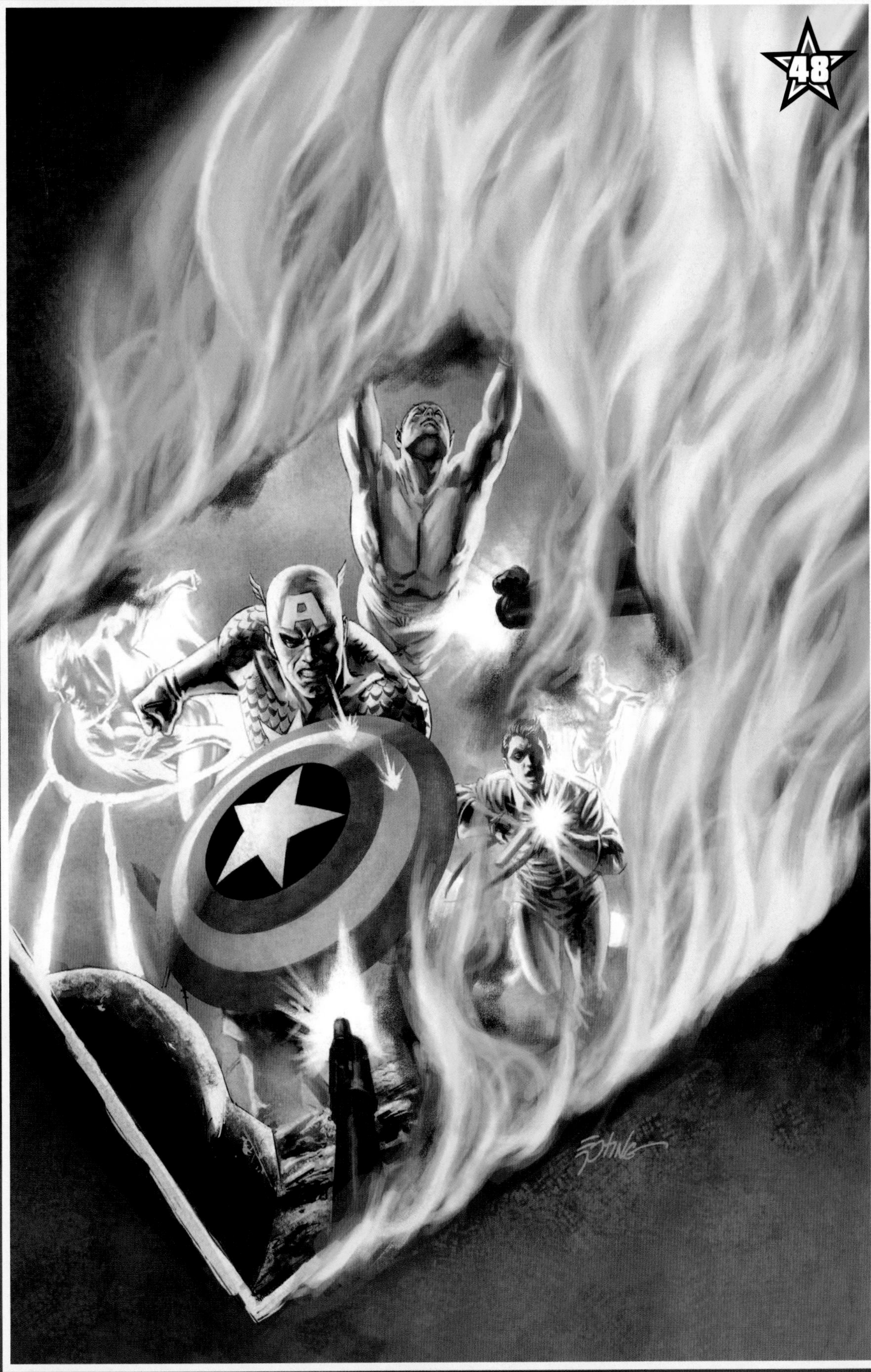
48

OLD FRIENDS AND ENEMIES PART THREE

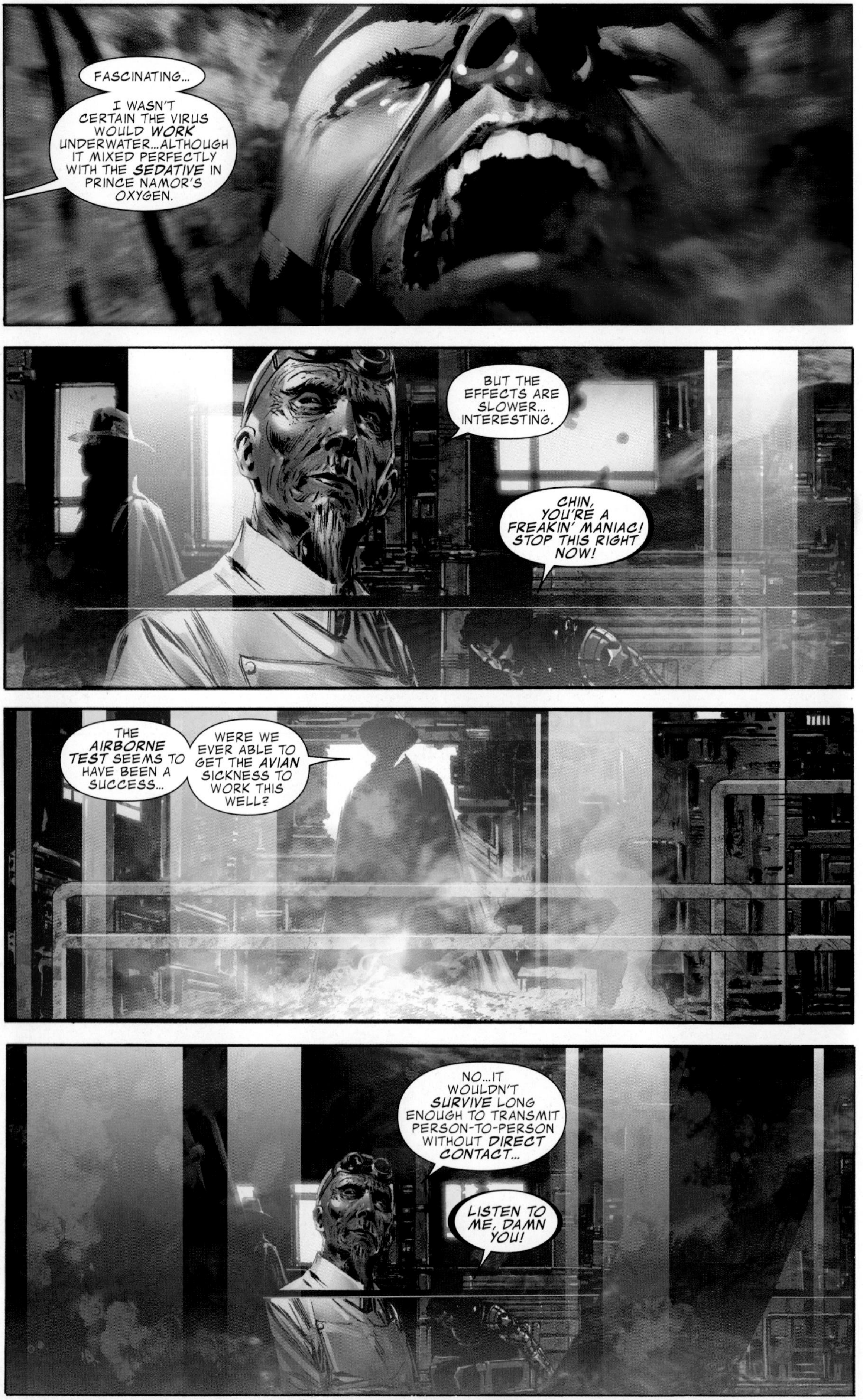
FASCINATING...
I WASN'T CERTAIN THE VIRUS WOULD WORK UNDERWATER...ALTHOUGH IT MIXED PERFECTLY WITH THE SEDATIVE IN PRINCE NAMOR'S OXYGEN.
BUT THE EFFECTS ARE SLOWER... INTERESTING.
CHIN, YOU'RE A FREAKIN' MANIAC! STOP THIS RIGHT NOW!
THE AIRBORNE TEST SEEMS TO HAVE BEEN A SUCCESS...
WERE WE EVER ABLE TO GET THE AVIAN SICKNESS TO WORK THIS WELL?
NO...IT WOULDN'T SURVIVE LONG ENOUGH TO TRANSMIT PERSON-TO-PERSON WITHOUT DIRECT CONTACT...
LISTEN TO ME, DAMN YOU!

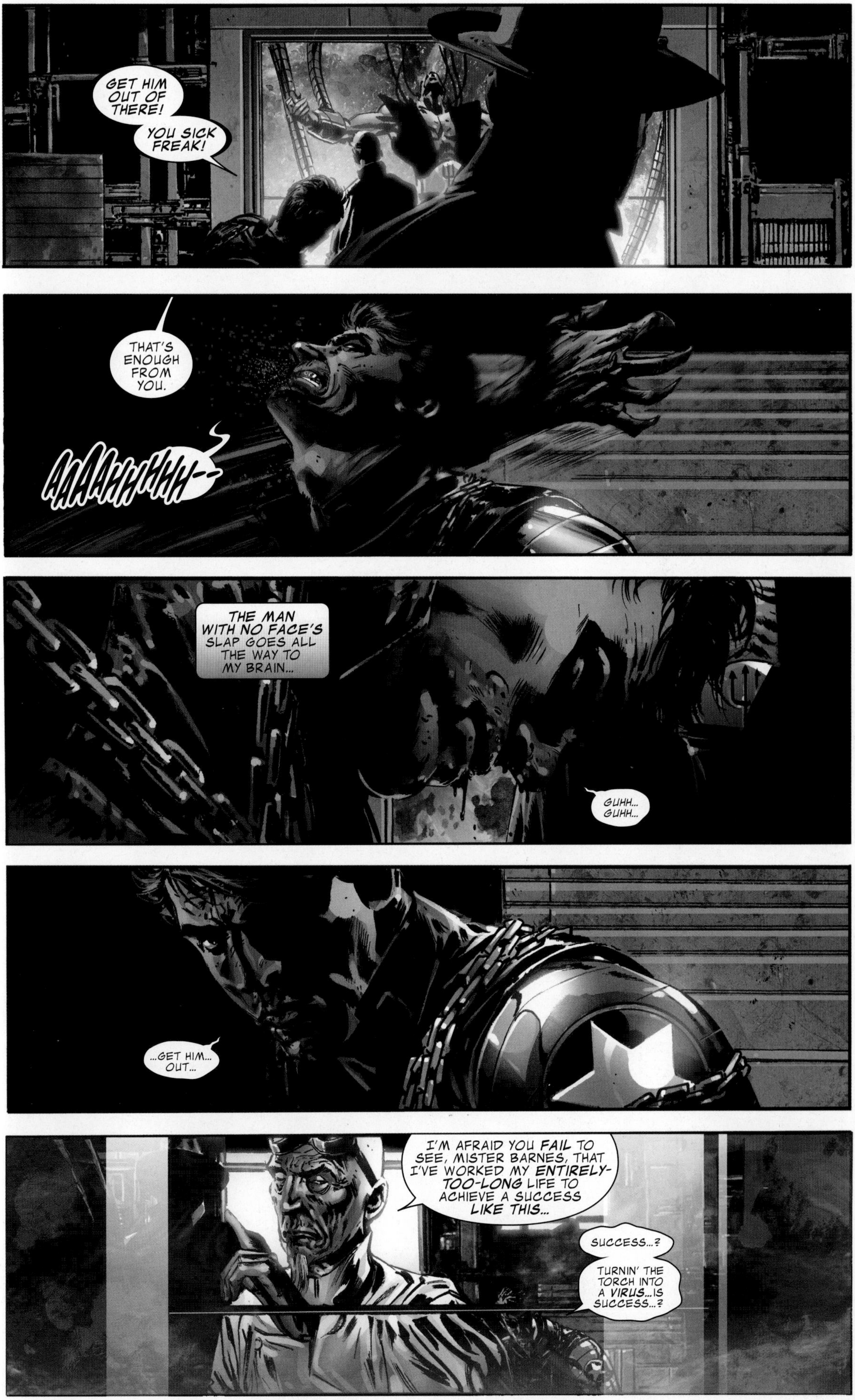
GET HIM OUT OF THERE!
YOU SICK FREAK!
THAT'S ENOUGH FROM YOU.
AAAAHHHHHH--
THE MAN WITH NO FACE'S SLAP GOES ALL THE WAY TO MY BRAIN...
GUHH... GUHH...
...GET HIM... OUT...
I'M AFRAID YOU FAIL TO SEE, MISTER BARNES, THAT I'VE WORKED MY ENTIRELY-TOO-LONG LIFE TO ACHIEVE A SUCCESS LIKE THIS...
SUCCESS...?
TURNIN' THE TORCH INTO A VIRUS...IS SUCCESS...?

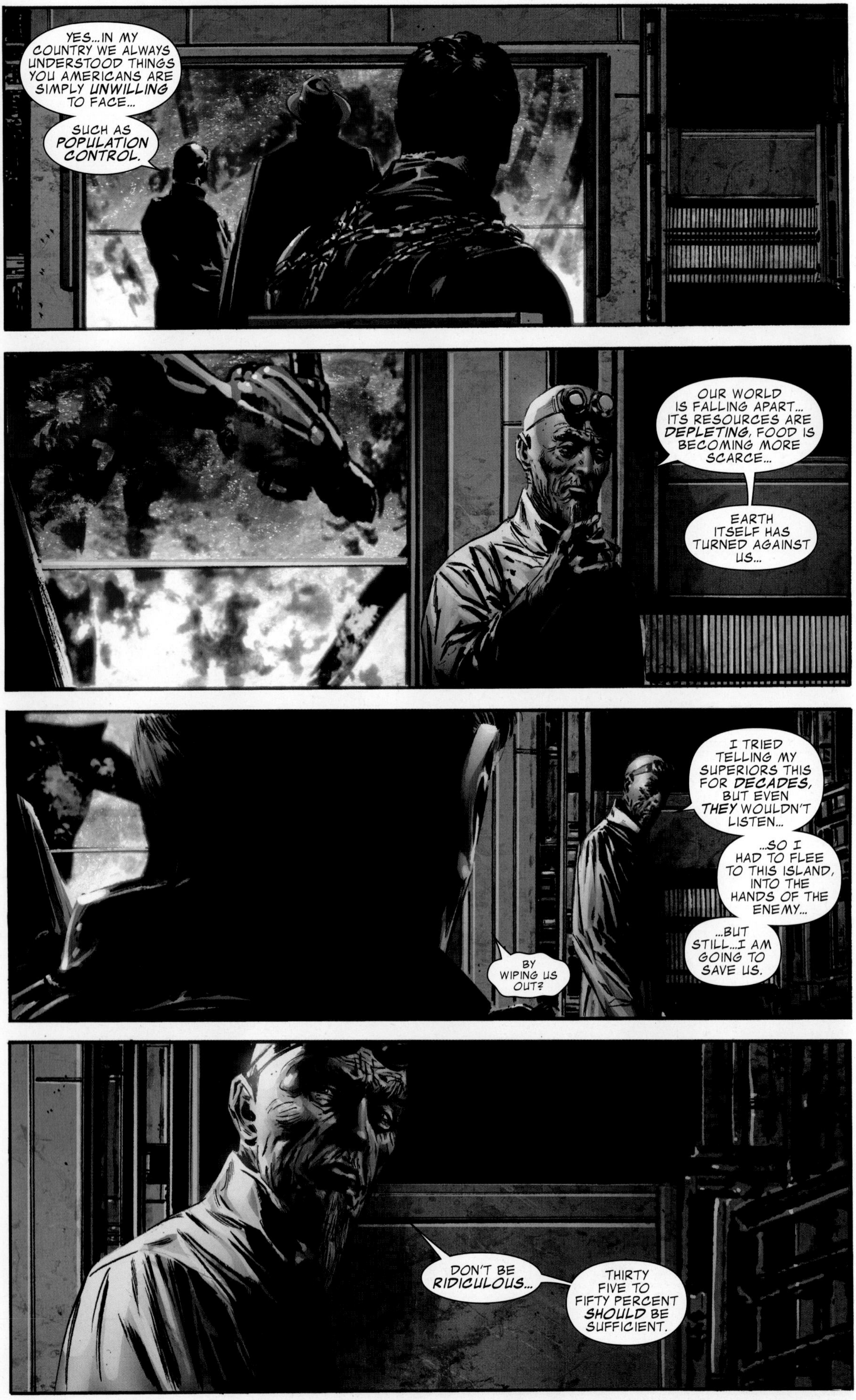
YES...IN MY COUNTRY WE ALWAYS UNDERSTOOD THINGS YOU AMERICANS ARE SIMPLY UNWILLING TO FACE...
SUCH AS POPULATION CONTROL.
OUR WORLD IS FALLING APART... ITS RESOURCES ARE DEPLETING, FOOD IS BECOMING MORE SCARCE...
EARTH ITSELF HAS TURNED AGAINST US...
I TRIED TELLING MY SUPERIORS THIS FOR DECADES, BUT EVEN THEY WOULDN'T LISTEN...
...SO I HAD TO FLEE TO THIS ISLAND, INTO THE HANDS OF THE ENEMY...
...BUT STILL...I AM GOING TO SAVE US.
BY WIPING US OUT?
DON'T BE RIDICULOUS...
THIRTY FIVE TO FIFTY PERCENT SHOULD BE SUFFICIENT.

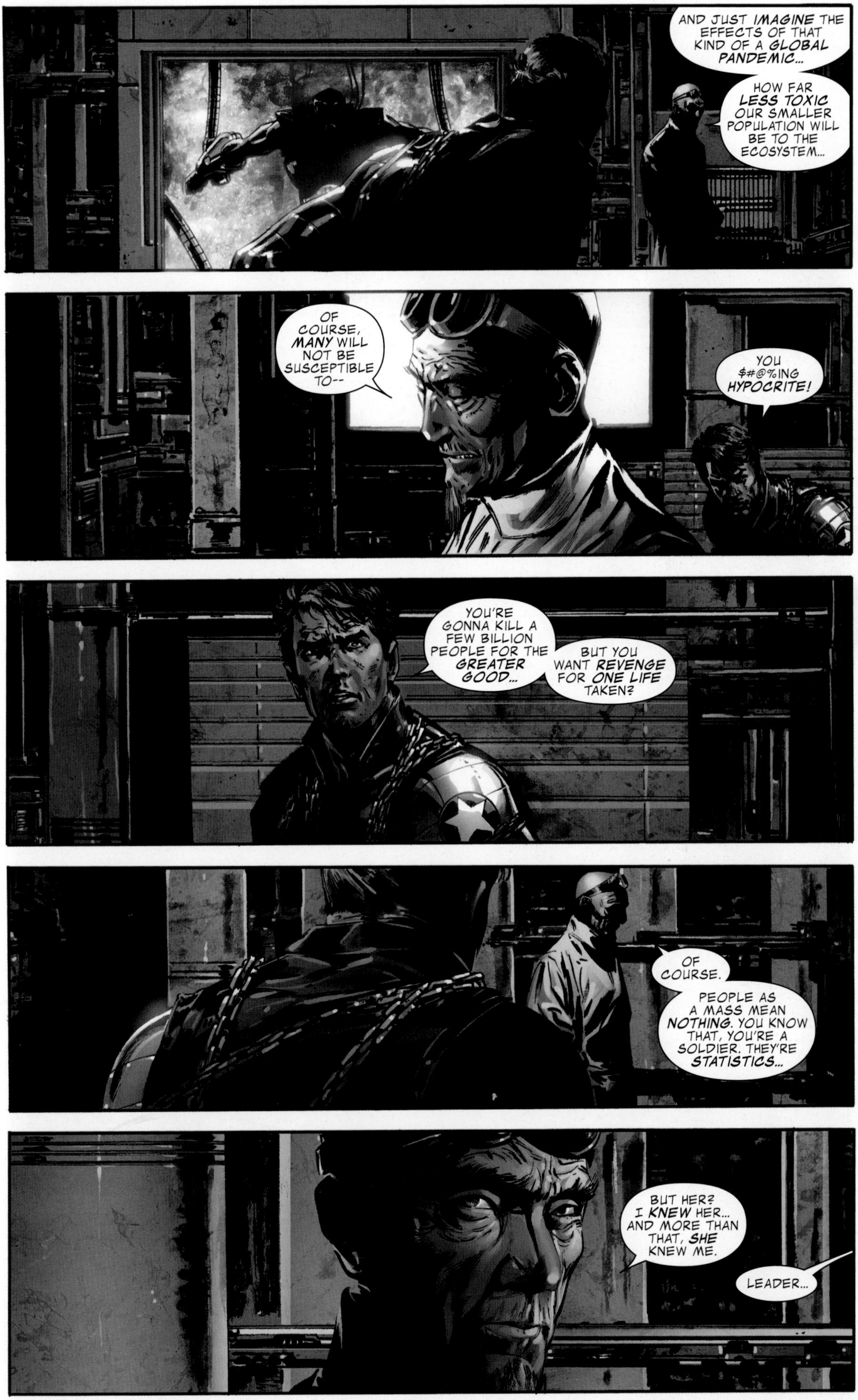
AND JUST IMAGINE THE EFFECTS OF THAT KIND OF A GLOBAL PANDEMIC...
HOW FAR LESS TOXIC OUR SMALLER POPULATION WILL BE TO THE ECOSYSTEM...
OF COURSE, MANY WILL NOT BE SUSCEPTIBLE TO--
YOU $#@%ING HYPOCRITE!
YOU'RE GONNA KILL A FEW BILLION PEOPLE FOR THE GREATER GOOD...
BUT YOU WANT REVENGE FOR ONE LIFE TAKEN?
OF COURSE.
PEOPLE AS A MASS MEAN NOTHING. YOU KNOW THAT, YOU'RE A SOLDIER. THEY'RE STATISTICS...
BUT HER? I KNEW HER... AND MORE THAN THAT, SHE KNEW ME.
LEADER...

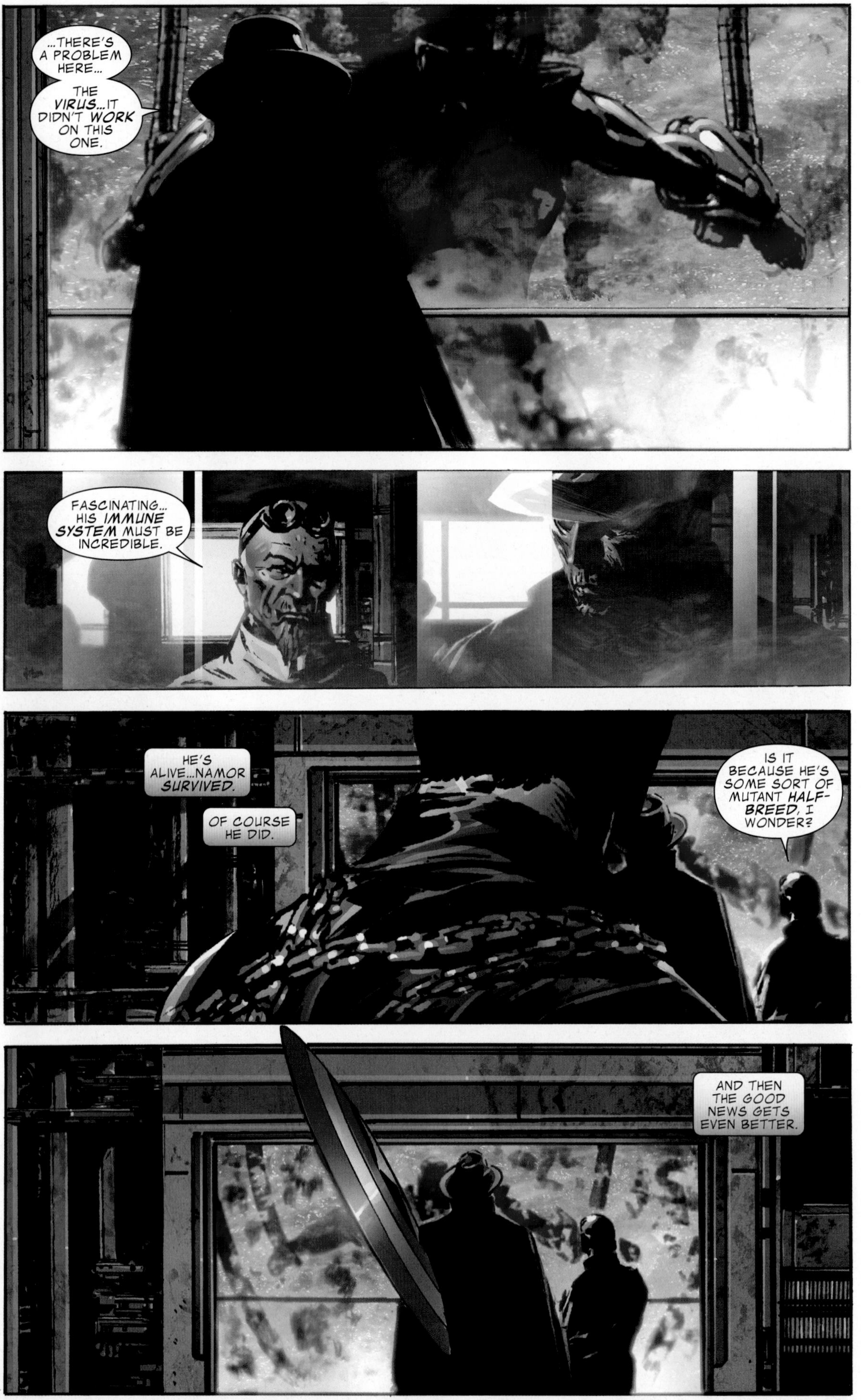
...THERE'S A PROBLEM HERE...
THE VIRUS...IT DIDN'T WORK ON THIS ONE.
FASCINATING... HIS IMMUNE SYSTEM MUST BE INCREDIBLE.
HE'S ALIVE...NAMOR SURVIVED.
OF COURSE HE DID.
IS IT BECAUSE HE'S SOME SORT OF MUTANT HALF-BREED, I WONDER?
AND THEN THE GOOD NEWS GETS EVEN BETTER.

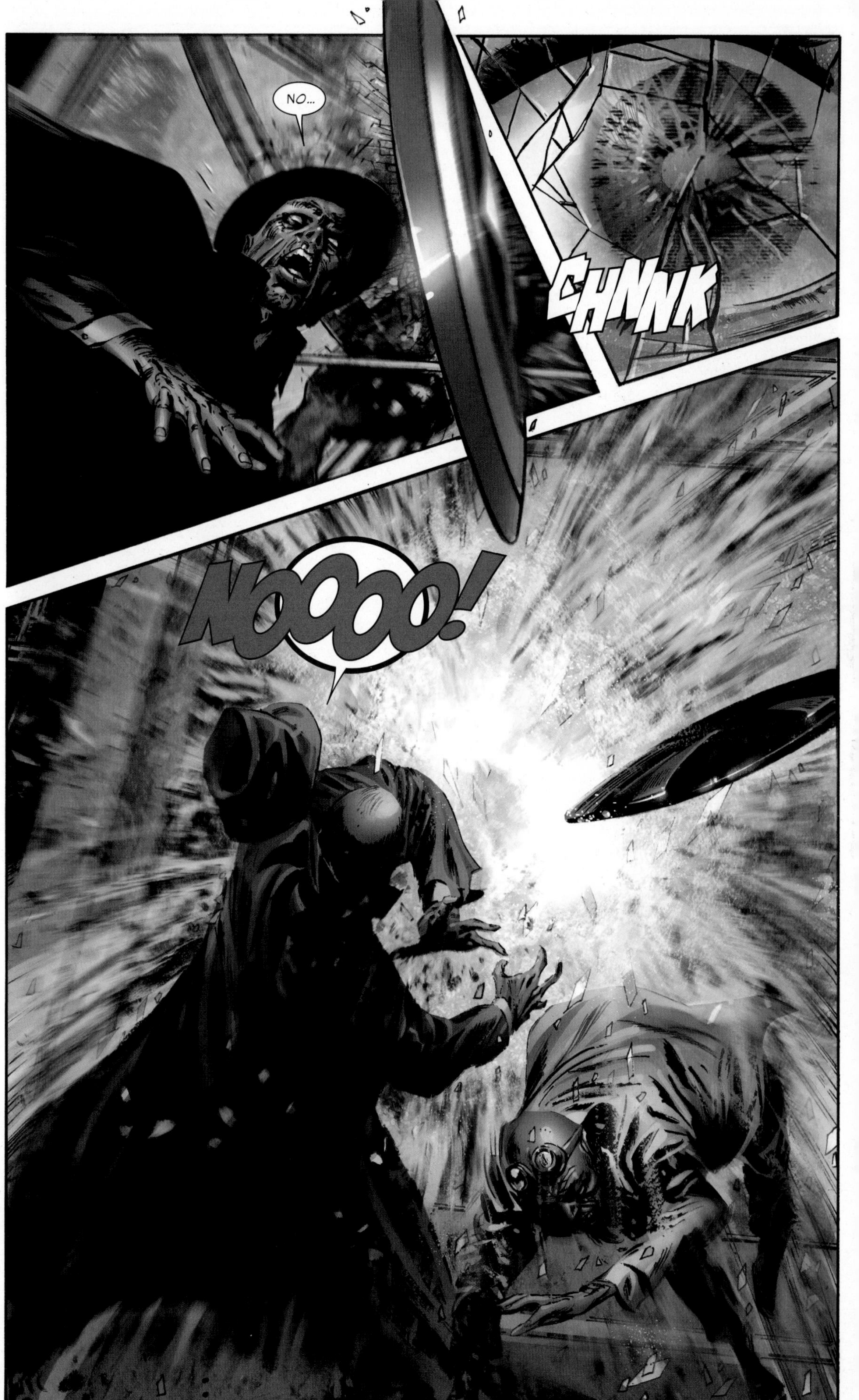
NO...
CHNNK
NOOOO!

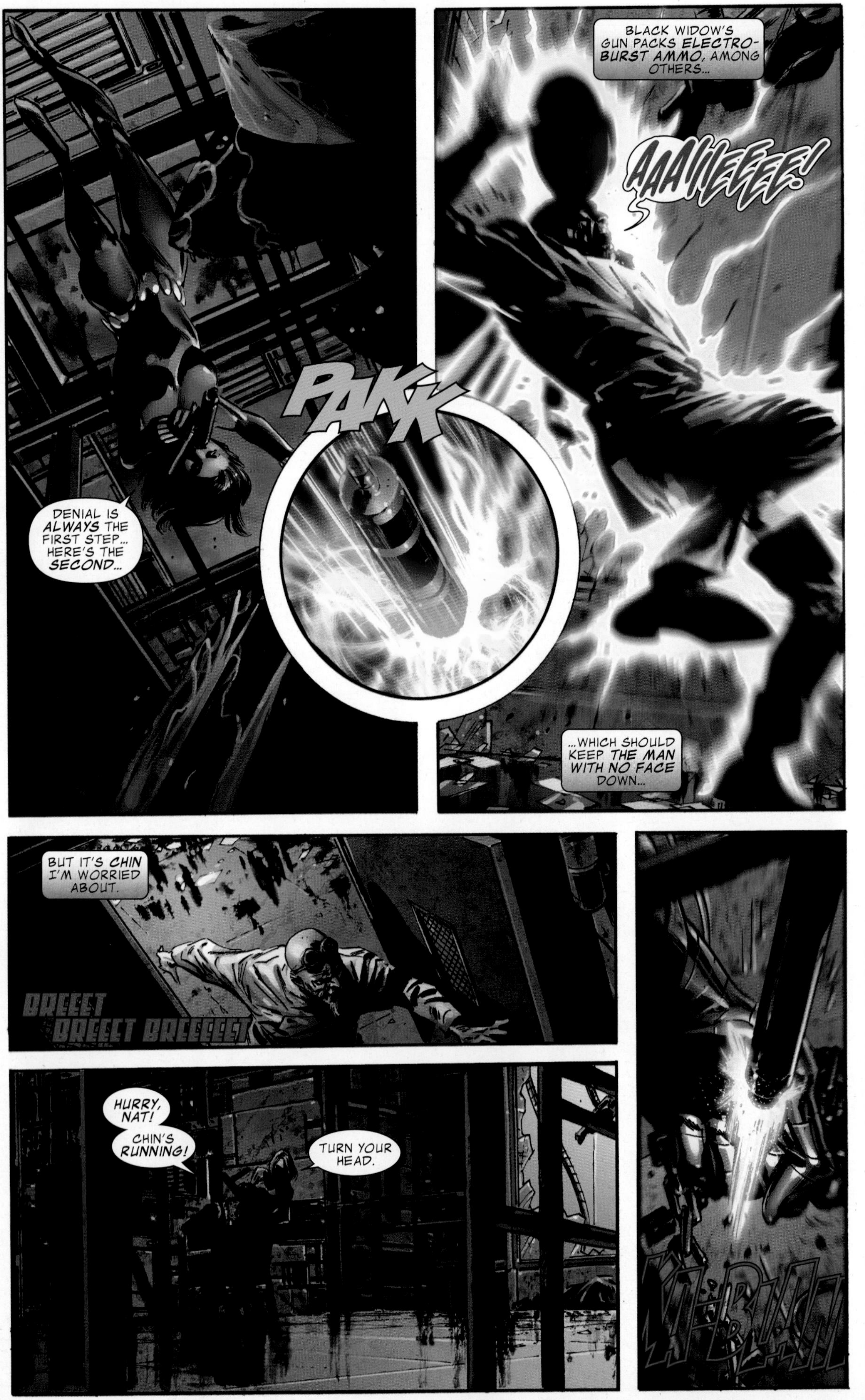
DENIAL IS ALWAYS THE FIRST STEP... HERE'S THE SECOND...
PAKK
BLACK WIDOW'S GUN PACKS ELECTRO-BURST AMMO, AMONG OTHERS...
AAAIIEEEE!
...WHICH SHOULD KEEP THE MAN WITH NO FACE DOWN...
BUT IT'S CHIN I'M WORRIED ABOUT.
BREEET BREEET BREEEEET
HURRY, NAT! CHIN'S RUNNING!
TURN YOUR HEAD.

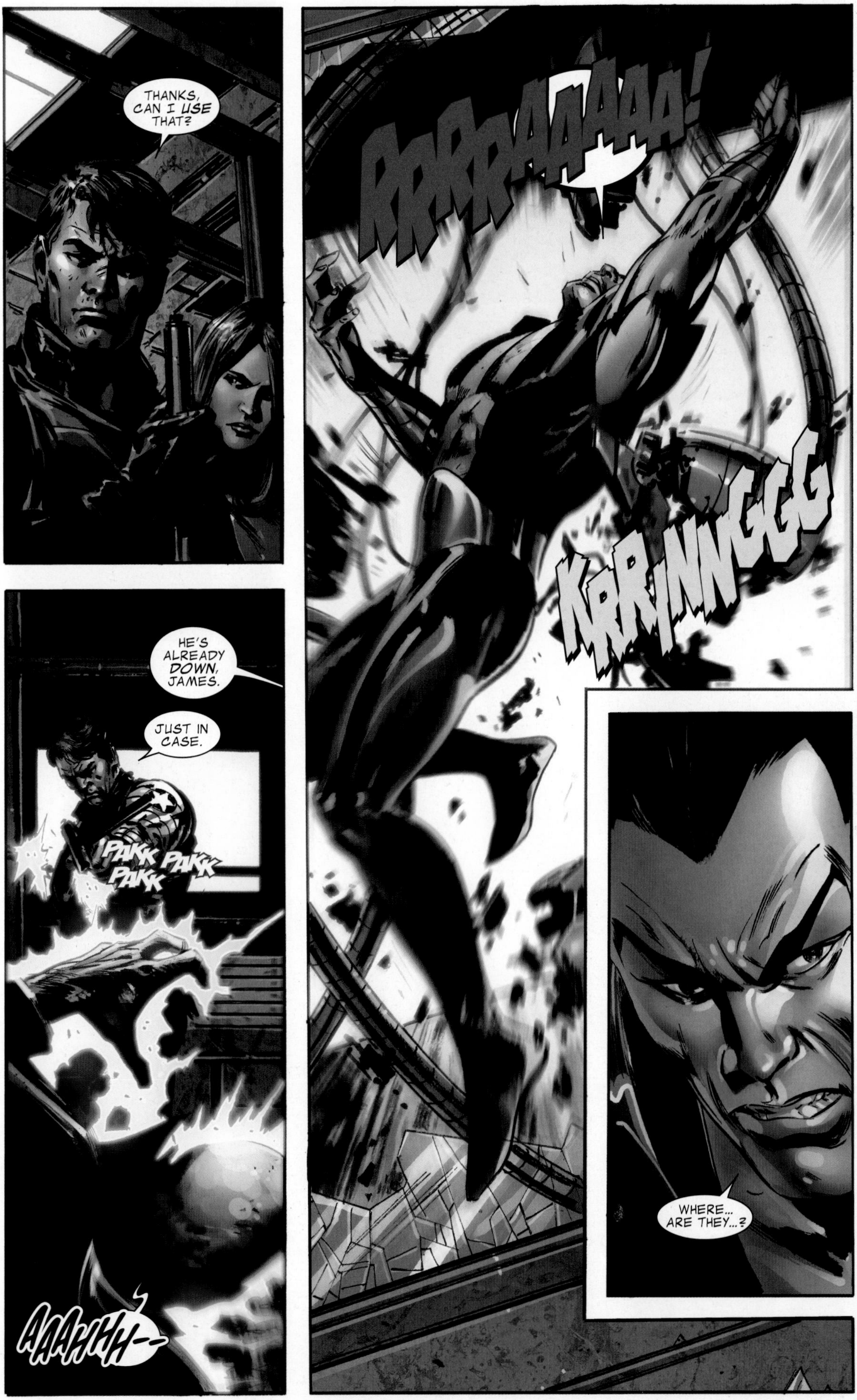

THANKS, CAN I USE THAT?
HE'S ALREADY DOWN, JAMES.
JUST IN CASE.
PAKK PAKK PAKK
AAAHHH--
RRRRAAAAA!
KRRINNGGG
WHERE... ARE THEY...?

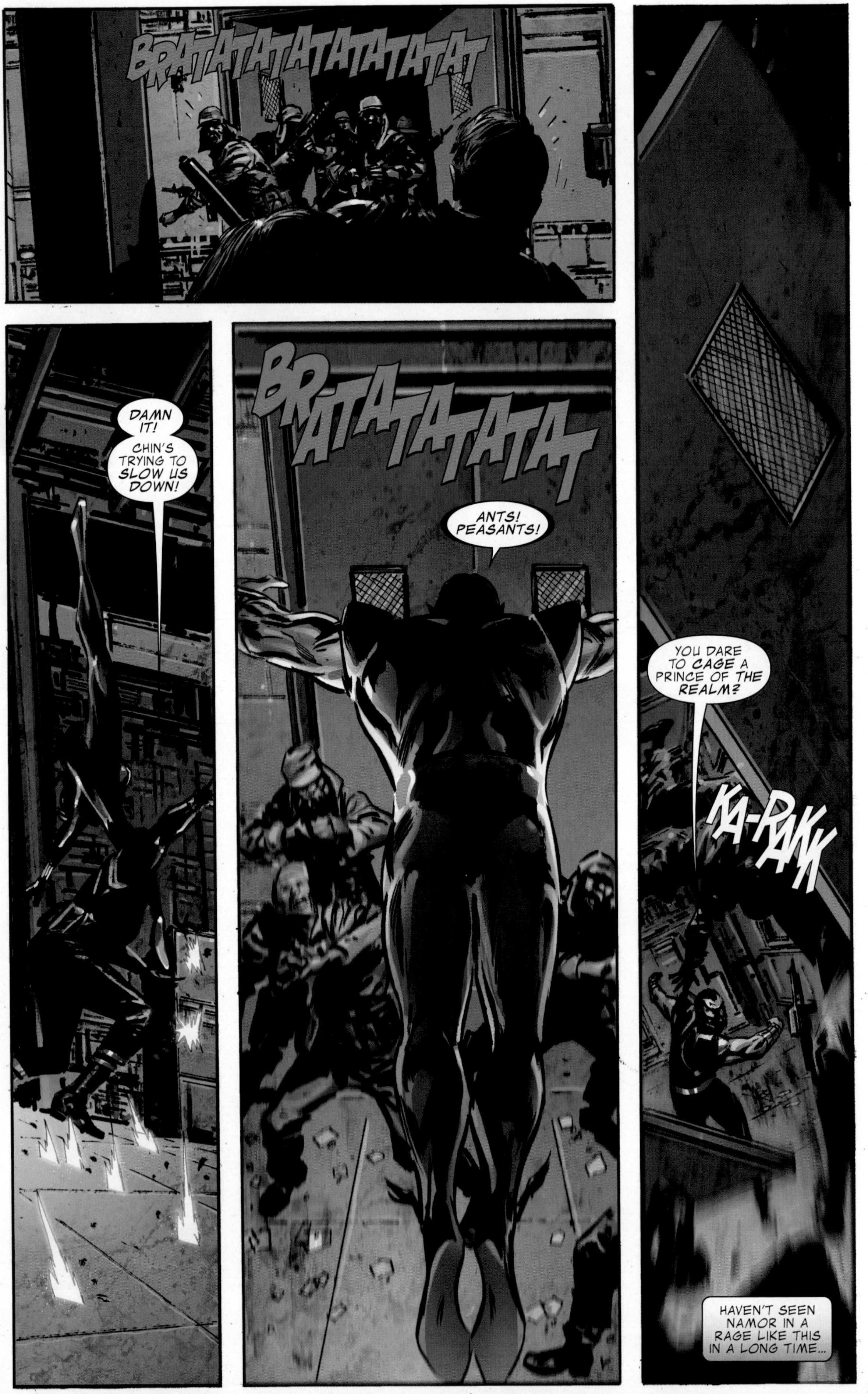
BRATATATATATATATAT
DAMN IT! CHIN'S TRYING TO SLOW US DOWN!
BRATATATATAT
ANTS! PEASANTS!
YOU DARE TO CAGE A PRINCE OF THE REALM?
KA-RAKK
HAVEN'T SEEN NAMOR IN A RAGE LIKE THIS IN A LONG TIME...

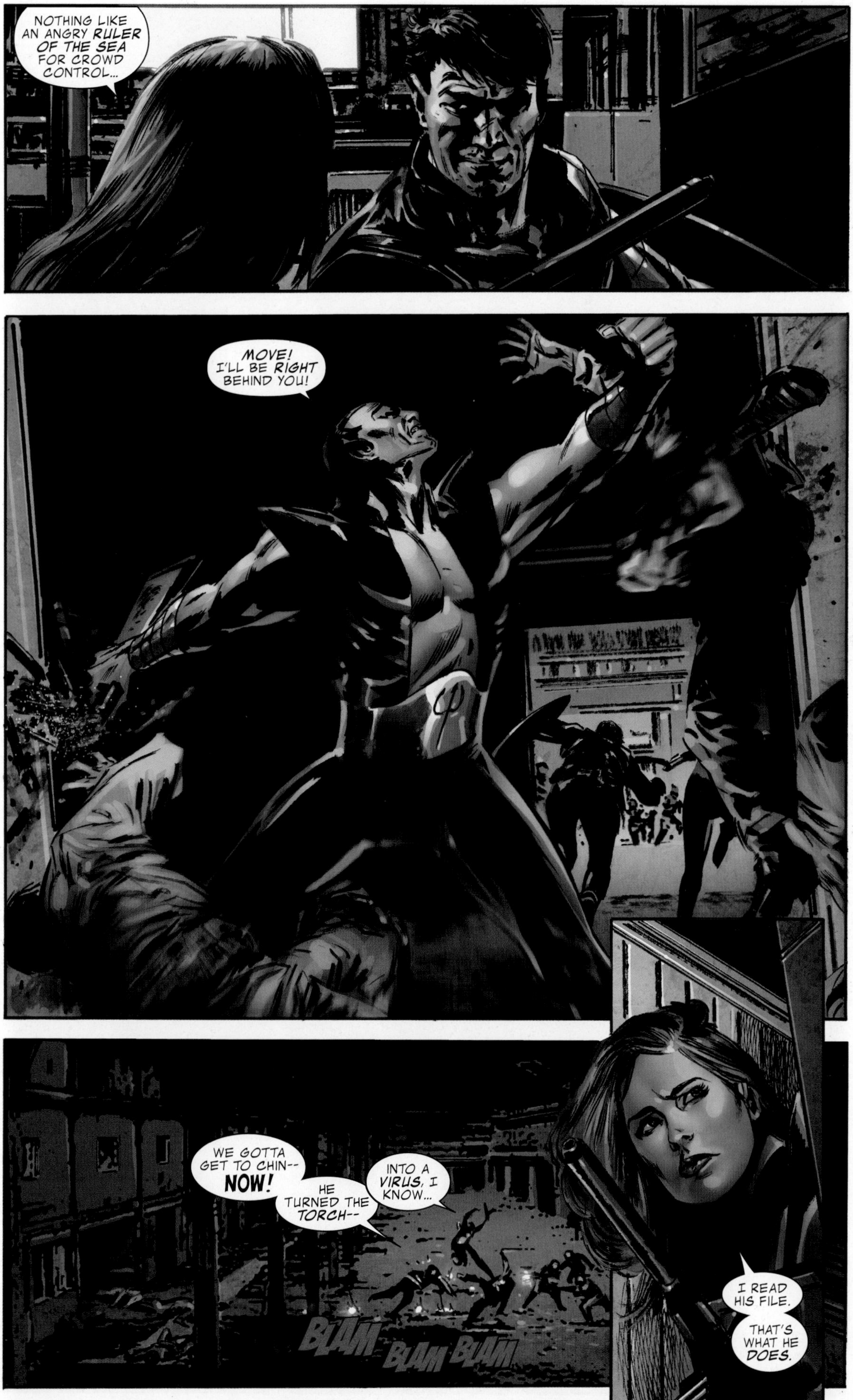
NOTHING LIKE AN ANGRY RULER OF THE SEA FOR CROWD CONTROL...
MOVE! I'LL BE RIGHT BEHIND YOU!
WE GOTTA GET TO CHIN-- NOW!
HE TURNED THE TORCH--
INTO A VIRUS, I KNOW...
I READ HIS FILE.
THAT'S WHAT HE DOES.
BLAM BLAM BLAM

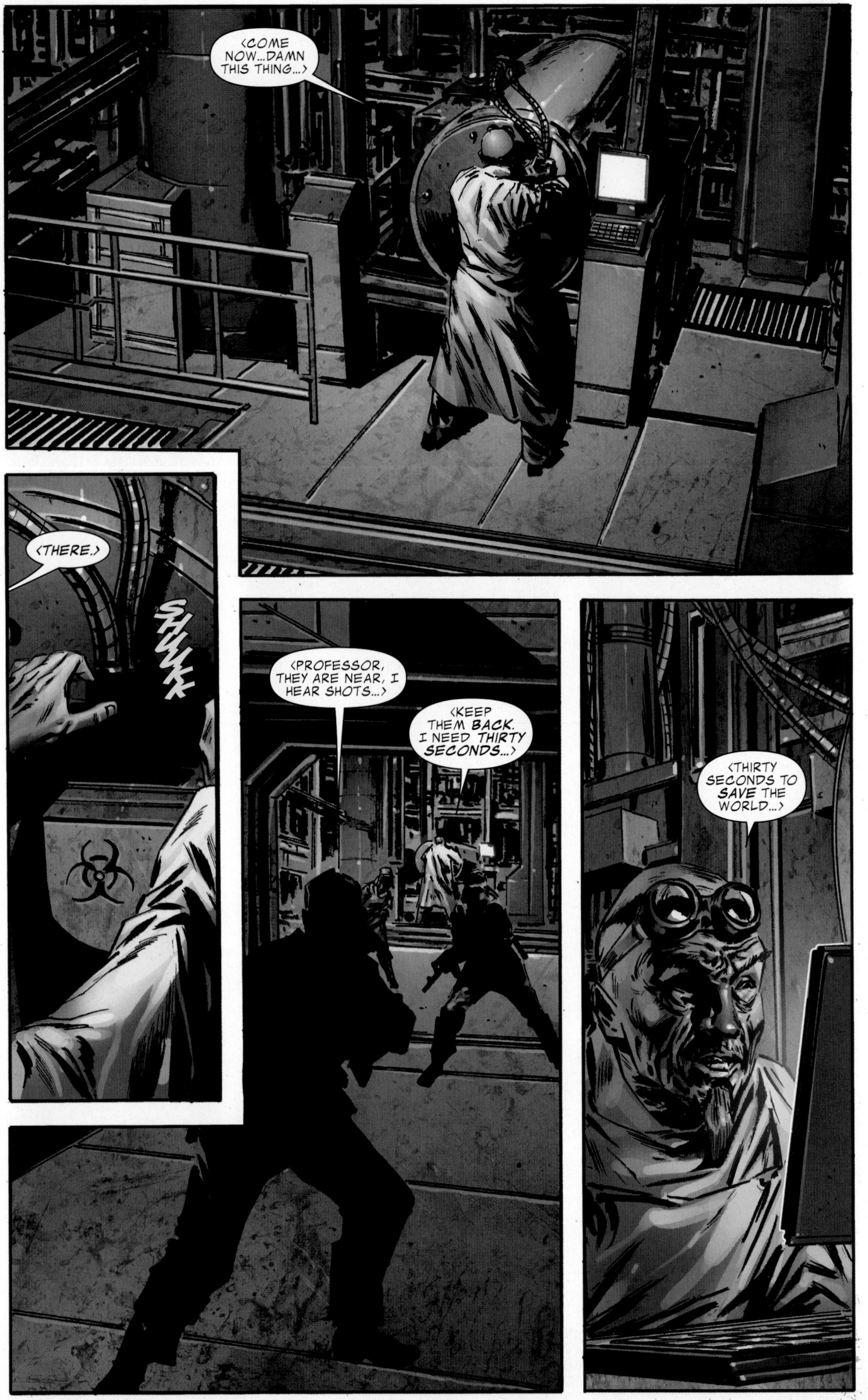
‹COME NOW...DAMN THIS THING...›
‹THERE.›
SHUNK
‹PROFESSOR, THEY ARE NEAR, I HEAR SHOTS...›
‹KEEP THEM **BACK**. I NEED **THIRTY SECONDS**...›
‹THIRTY SECONDS TO **SAVE** THE WORLD...›

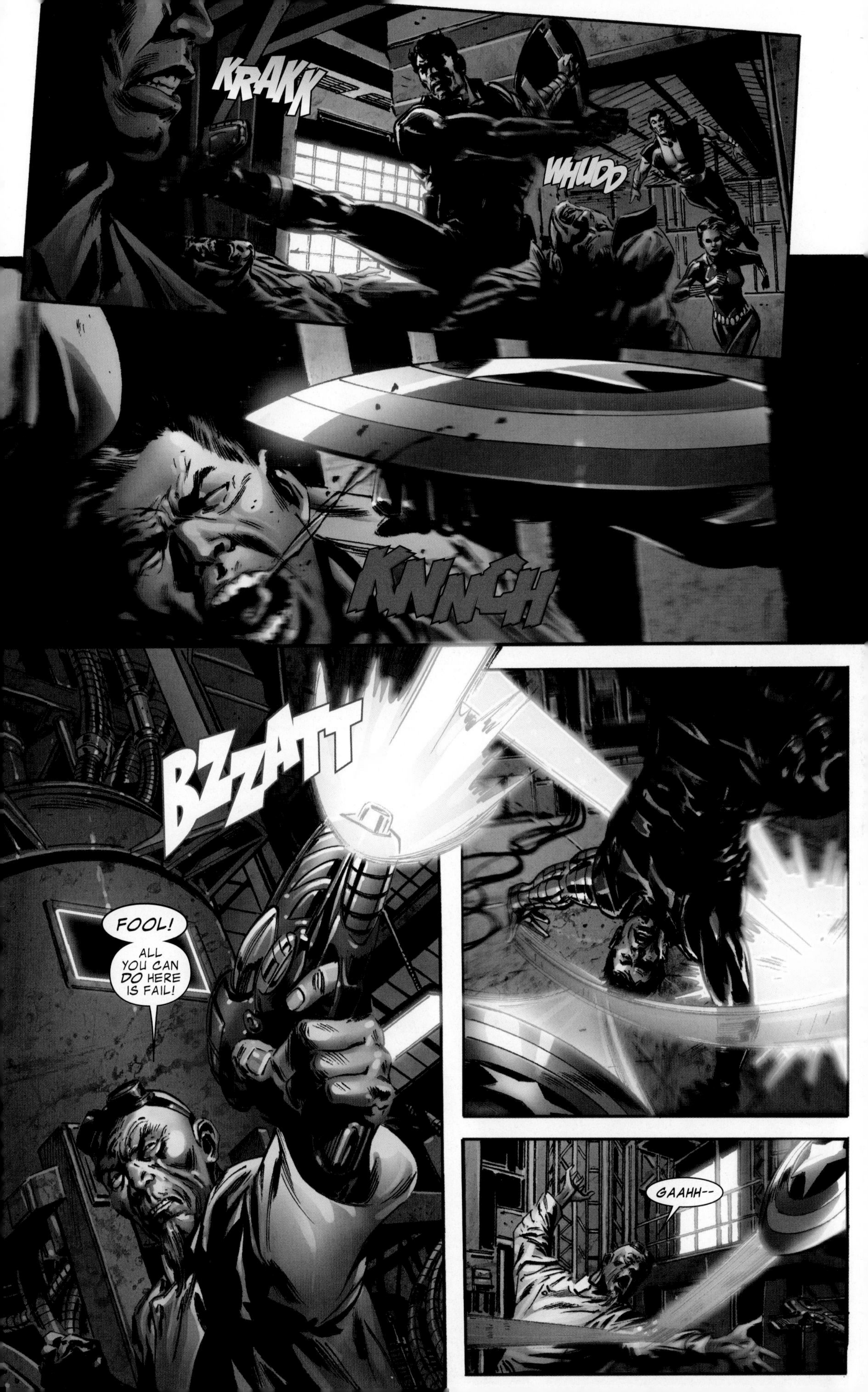
KRAKK
WHUDD
KNNCH
BZZATT
FOOL!
ALL YOU CAN DO HERE IS FAIL!
GAAHH--

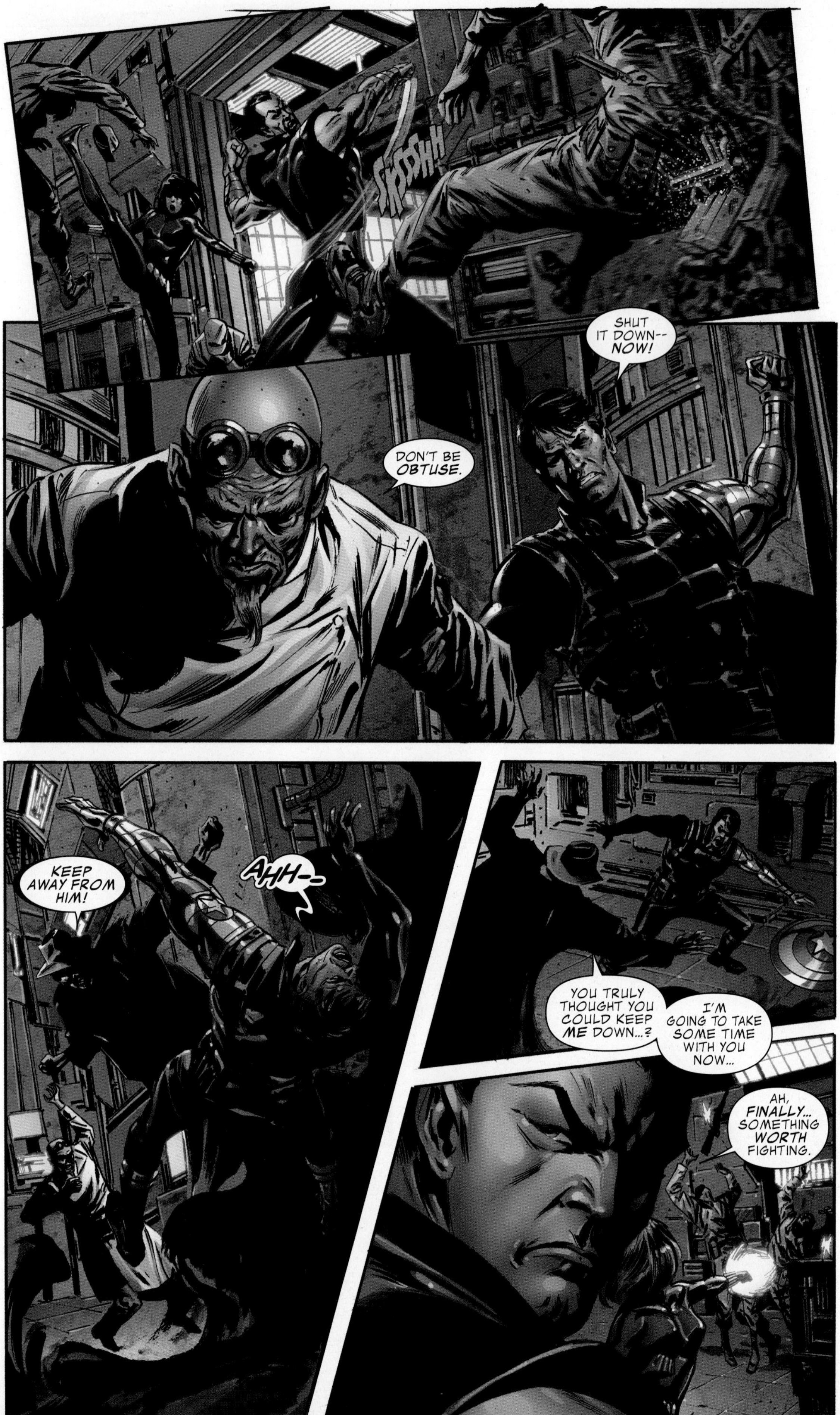
SKSSHH
SHUT IT DOWN-- NOW!
DON'T BE OBTUSE.
KEEP AWAY FROM HIM!
AHH--
YOU TRULY THOUGHT YOU COULD KEEP ME DOWN...?
I'M GOING TO TAKE SOME TIME WITH YOU NOW...
AH, FINALLY... SOMETHING WORTH FIGHTING.

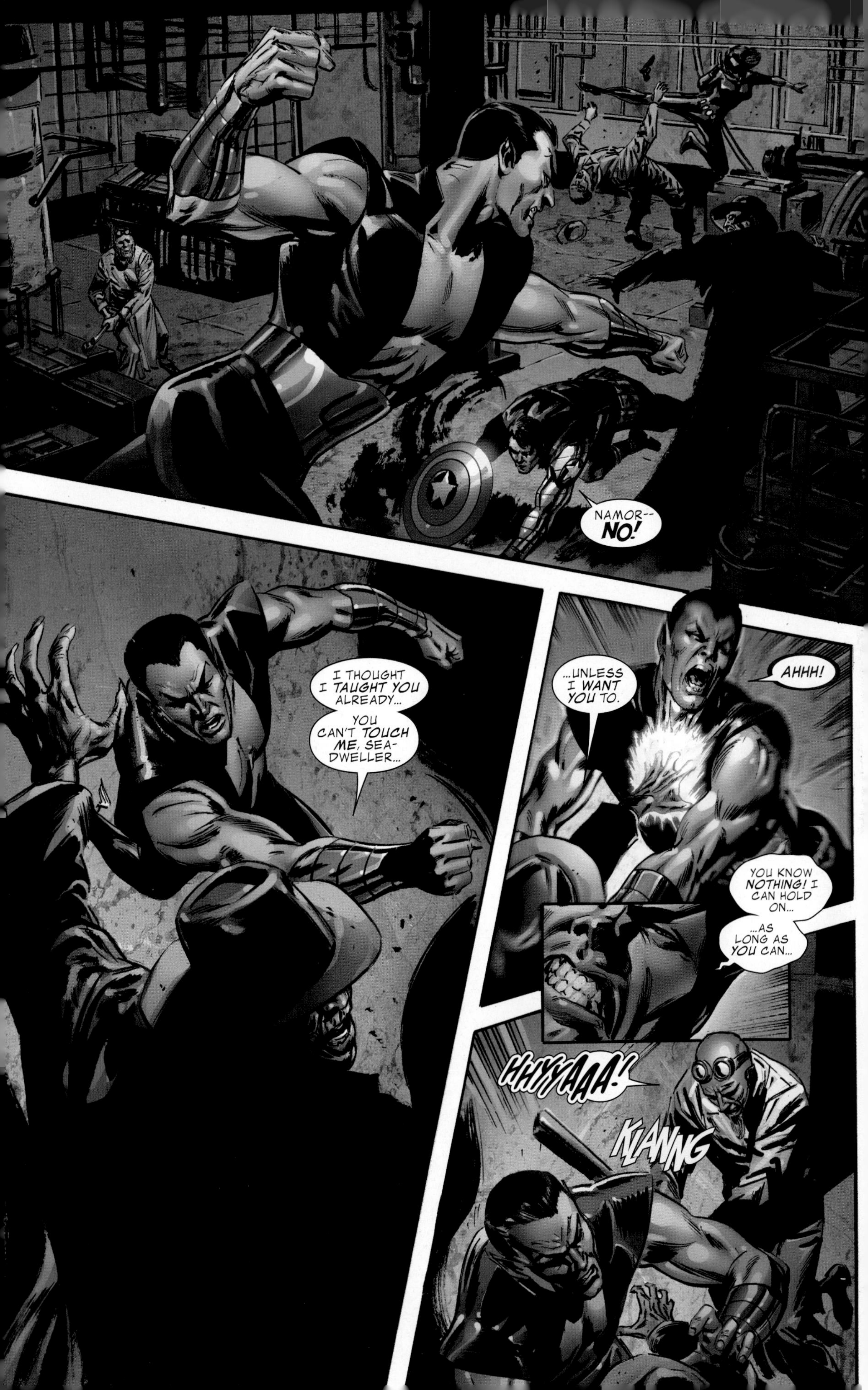
NAMOR-- NO!
I THOUGHT I TAUGHT YOU ALREADY...
YOU CAN'T TOUCH ME, SEA-DWELLER...
...UNLESS I WANT YOU TO.
AHHH!
YOU KNOW NOTHING! I CAN HOLD ON...
...AS LONG AS YOU CAN...
HHYYAAA!
KLANNG

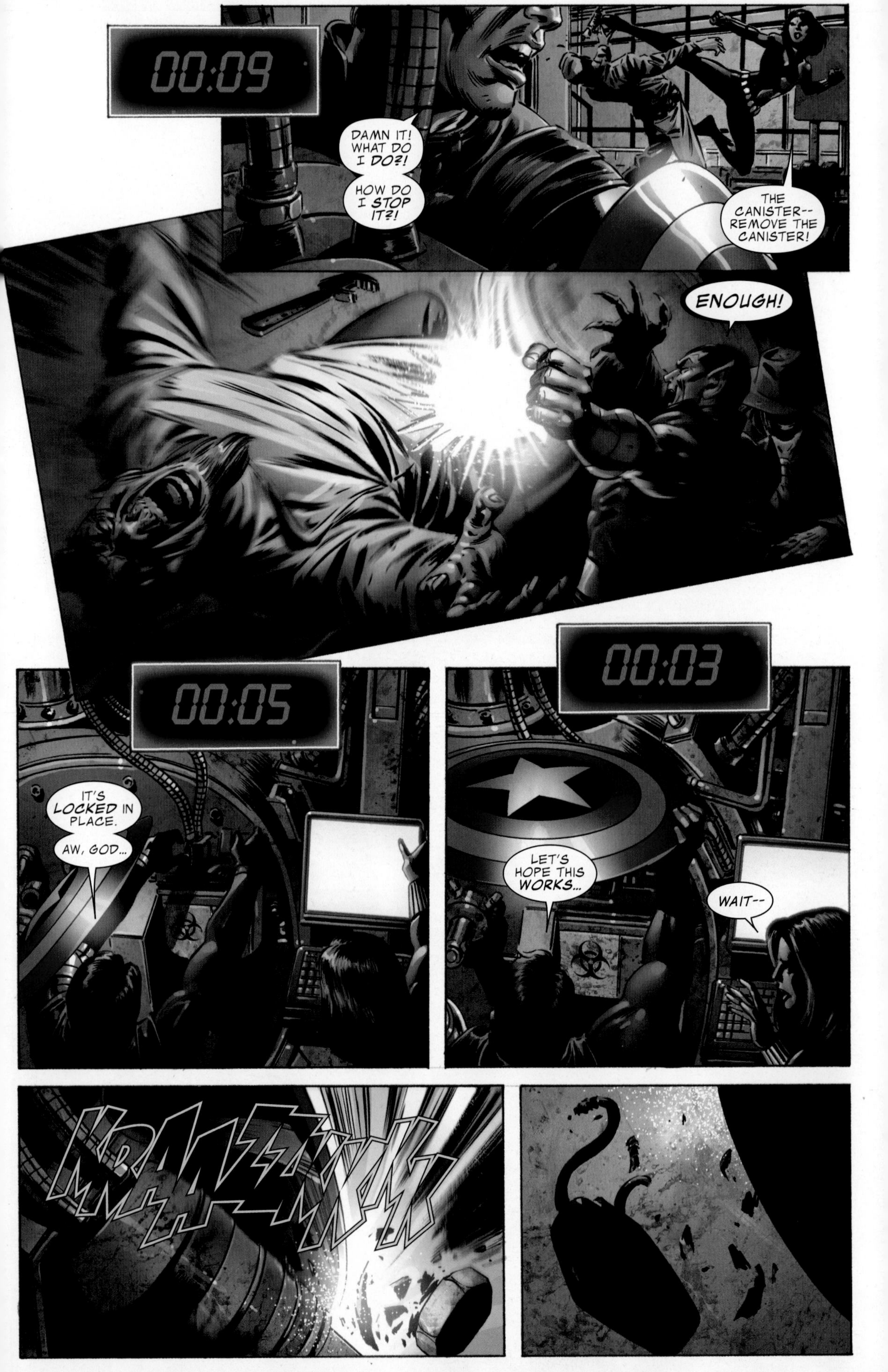
00:09
DAMN IT! WHAT DO I DO?!
HOW DO I STOP IT?!
THE CANISTER-- REMOVE THE CANISTER!
ENOUGH!
00:05
IT'S LOCKED IN PLACE.
AW, GOD...
00:03
LET'S HOPE THIS WORKS...
WAIT--

I CANNOT *BELIEVE* YOU JUST DID THAT... YOU COULD HAVE EXPOSED US ALL.

IN A SECOND IT WOULDN'T HAVE MATTERED...

...ANYWAY...

NO... NO...UT... UT...

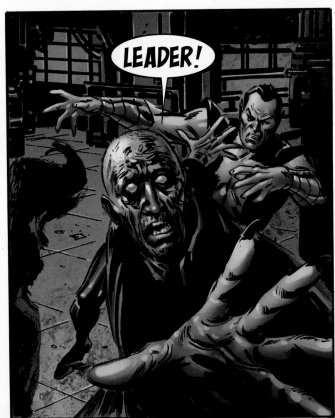

LEADER!

NO...NO...

SHOULD I...?

WAIT.

NO...I CAN'T BE THE ONLY ONE...

...THE ONLY ONE TO SURVIVE...

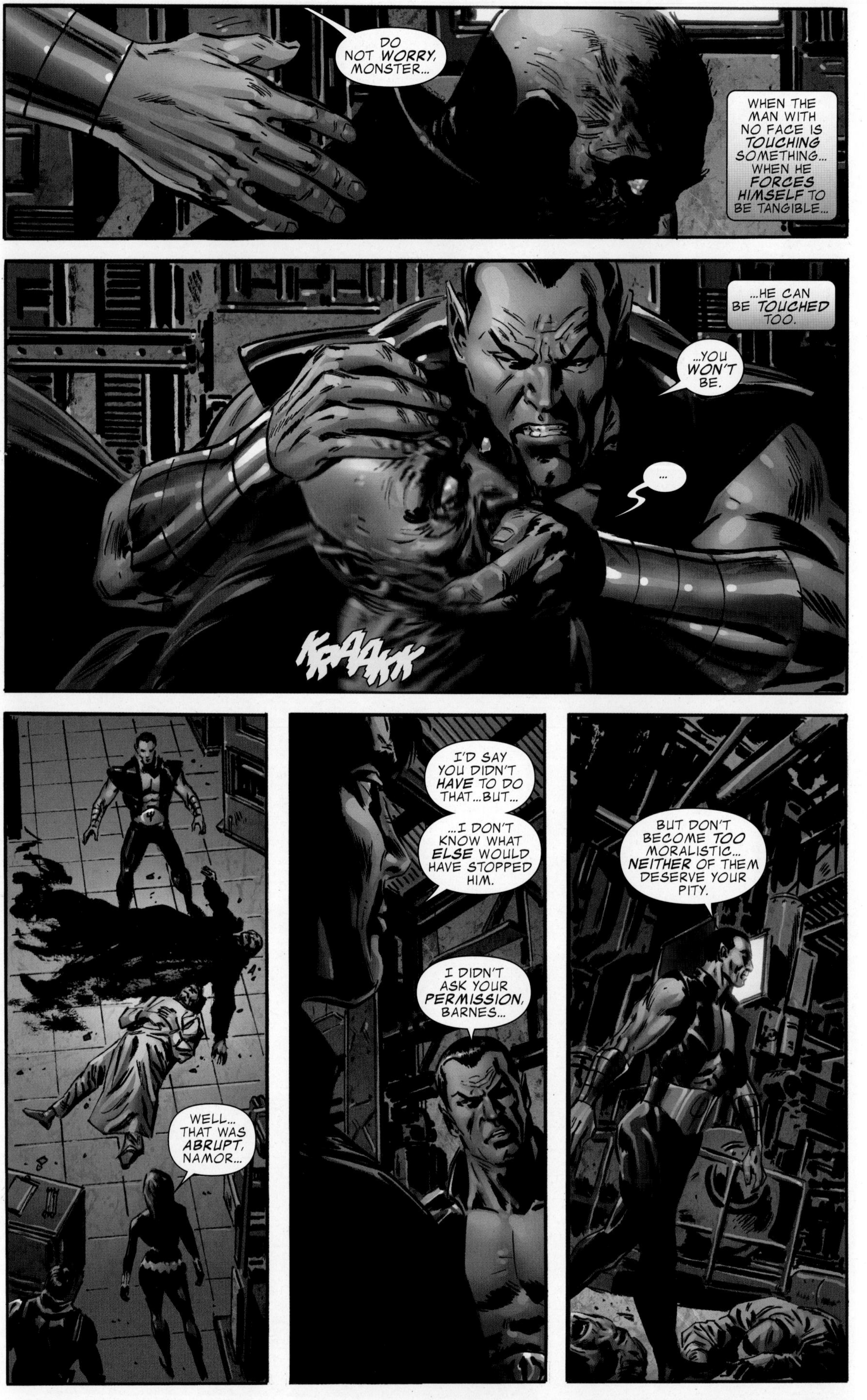
DO NOT WORRY, MONSTER...
WHEN THE MAN WITH NO FACE IS TOUCHING SOMETHING... WHEN HE FORCES HIMSELF TO BE TANGIBLE...
...HE CAN BE TOUCHED TOO.
...YOU WON'T BE.
...
KRAAKK
WELL... THAT WAS ABRUPT, NAMOR...
I'D SAY YOU DIDN'T HAVE TO DO THAT...BUT...
...I DON'T KNOW WHAT ELSE WOULD HAVE STOPPED HIM.
I DIDN'T ASK YOUR PERMISSION, BARNES...
BUT DON'T BECOME TOO MORALISTIC... NEITHER OF THEM DESERVE YOUR PITY.

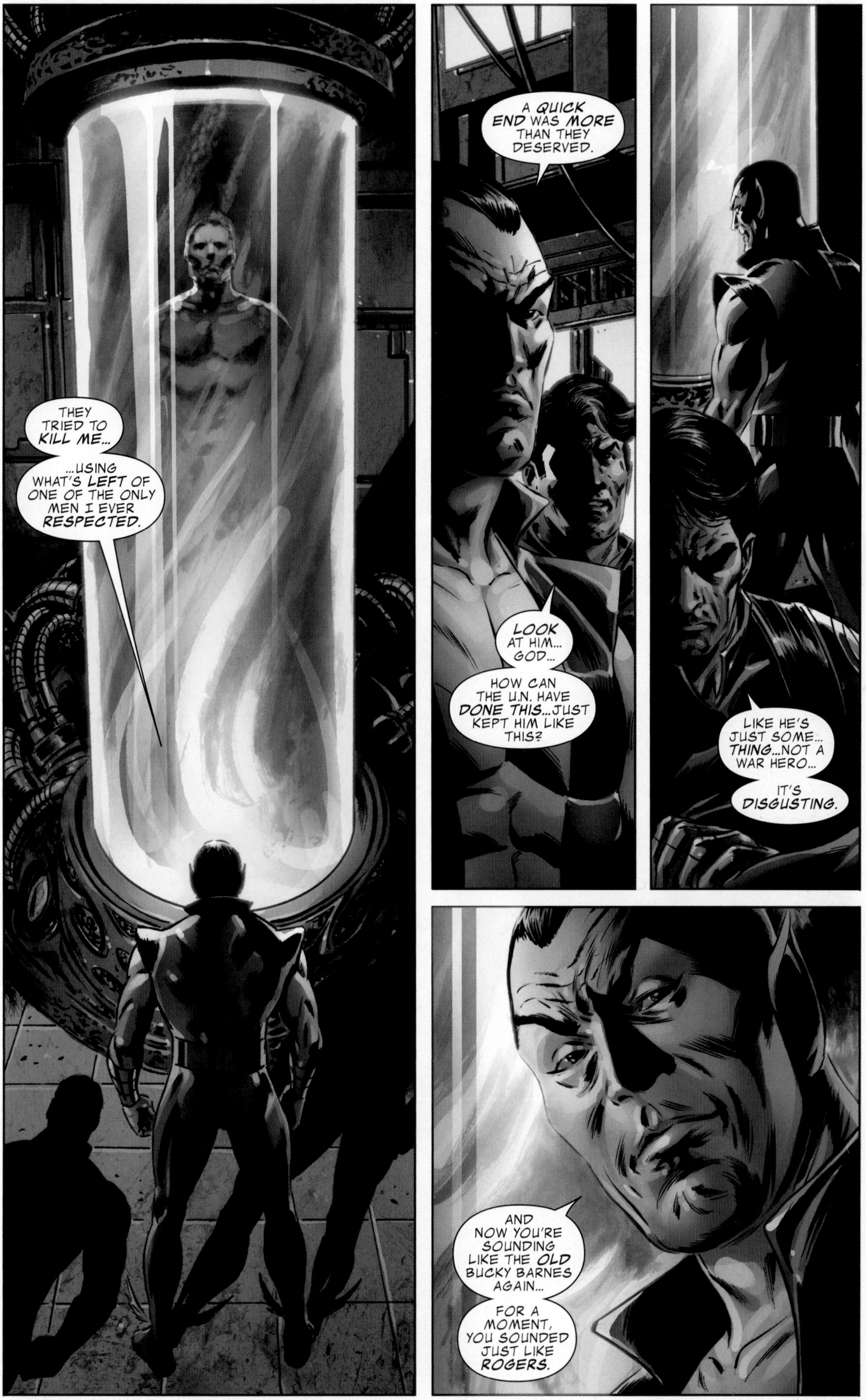
THEY TRIED TO KILL ME...
...USING WHAT'S LEFT OF ONE OF THE ONLY MEN I EVER RESPECTED.
A QUICK END WAS MORE THAN THEY DESERVED.
LOOK AT HIM... GOD...
HOW CAN THE U.N. HAVE DONE THIS...JUST KEPT HIM LIKE THIS?
LIKE HE'S JUST SOME... THING...NOT A WAR HERO...
IT'S DISGUSTING.
AND NOW YOU'RE SOUNDING LIKE THE OLD BUCKY BARNES AGAIN...
FOR A MOMENT, YOU SOUNDED JUST LIKE ROGERS.

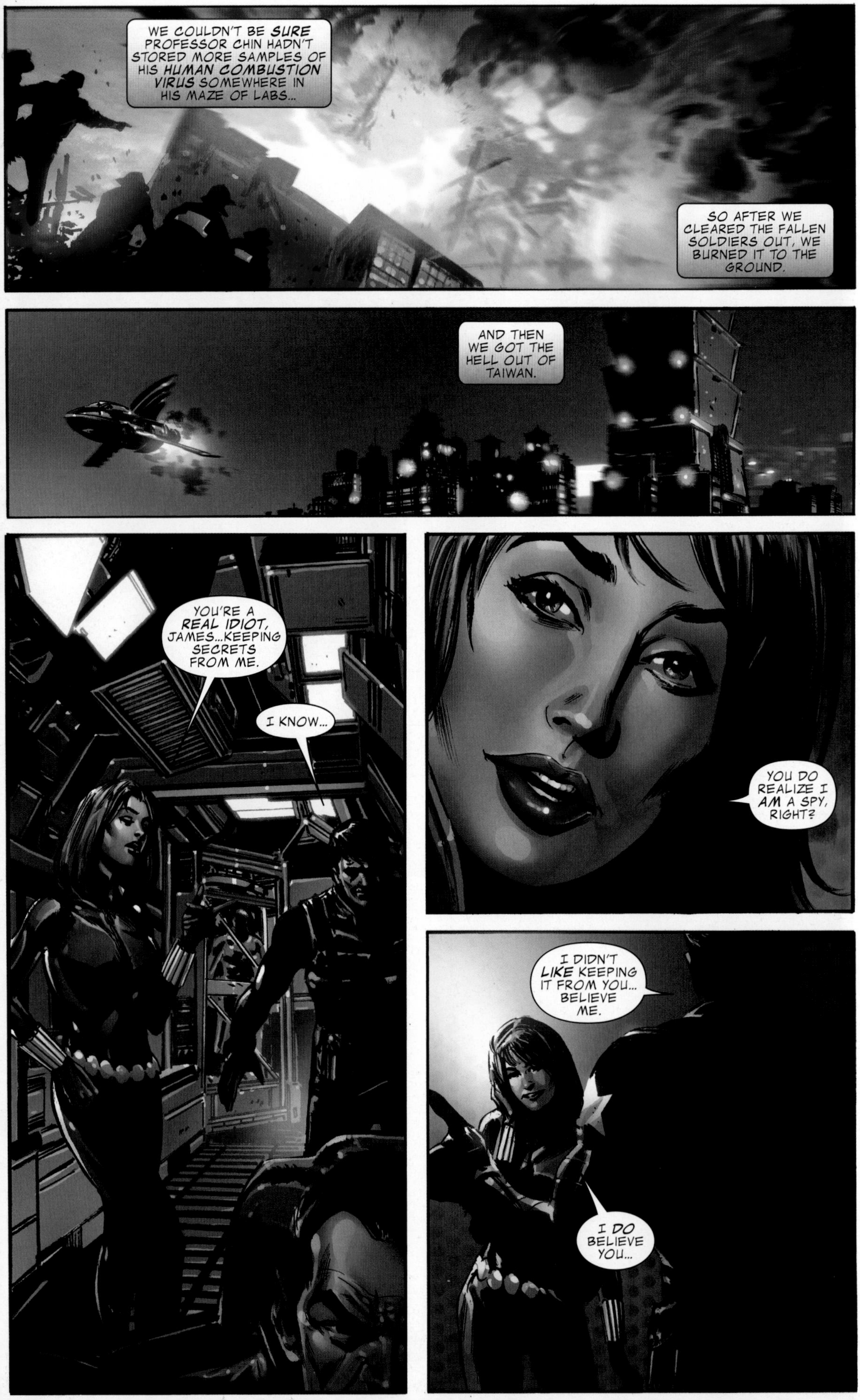
WE COULDN'T BE SURE PROFESSOR CHIN HADN'T STORED MORE SAMPLES OF HIS HUMAN COMBUSTION VIRUS SOMEWHERE IN HIS MAZE OF LABS...
SO AFTER WE CLEARED THE FALLEN SOLDIERS OUT, WE BURNED IT TO THE GROUND.
AND THEN WE GOT THE HELL OUT OF TAIWAN.
YOU'RE A REAL IDIOT, JAMES...KEEPING SECRETS FROM ME.
I KNOW...
YOU DO REALIZE I AM A SPY, RIGHT?
I DIDN'T LIKE KEEPING IT FROM YOU... BELIEVE ME.
I DO BELIEVE YOU...

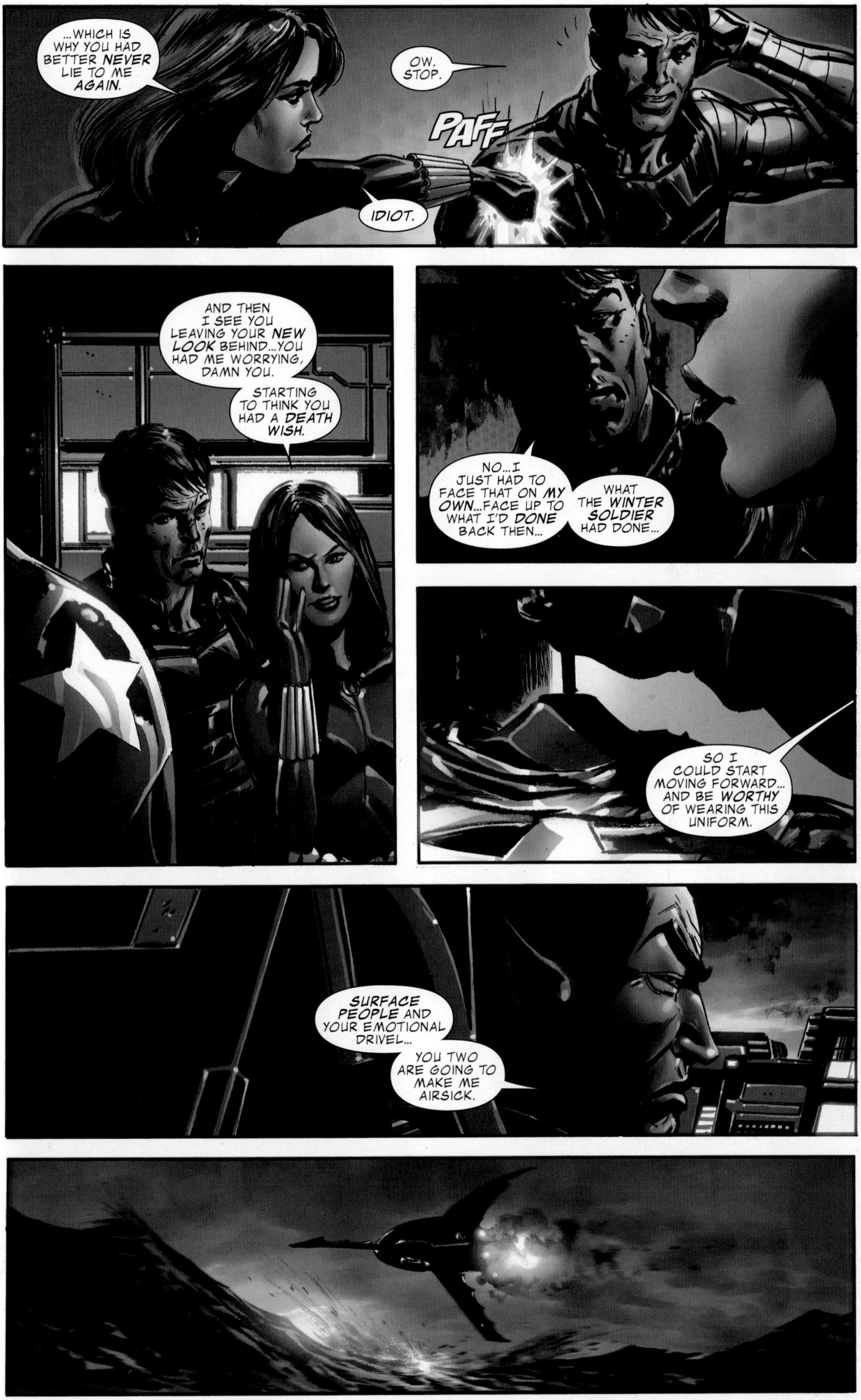
...WHICH IS WHY YOU HAD BETTER NEVER LIE TO ME AGAIN.
OW. STOP.
PAFF
IDIOT.
AND THEN I SEE YOU LEAVING YOUR NEW LOOK BEHIND...YOU HAD ME WORRYING, DAMN YOU.
STARTING TO THINK YOU HAD A DEATH WISH.
NO...I JUST HAD TO FACE THAT ON MY OWN...FACE UP TO WHAT I'D DONE BACK THEN...
WHAT THE WINTER SOLDIER HAD DONE...
SO I COULD START MOVING FORWARD... AND BE WORTHY OF WEARING THIS UNIFORM.
SURFACE PEOPLE AND YOUR EMOTIONAL DRIVEL...
YOU TWO ARE GOING TO MAKE ME AIRSICK.

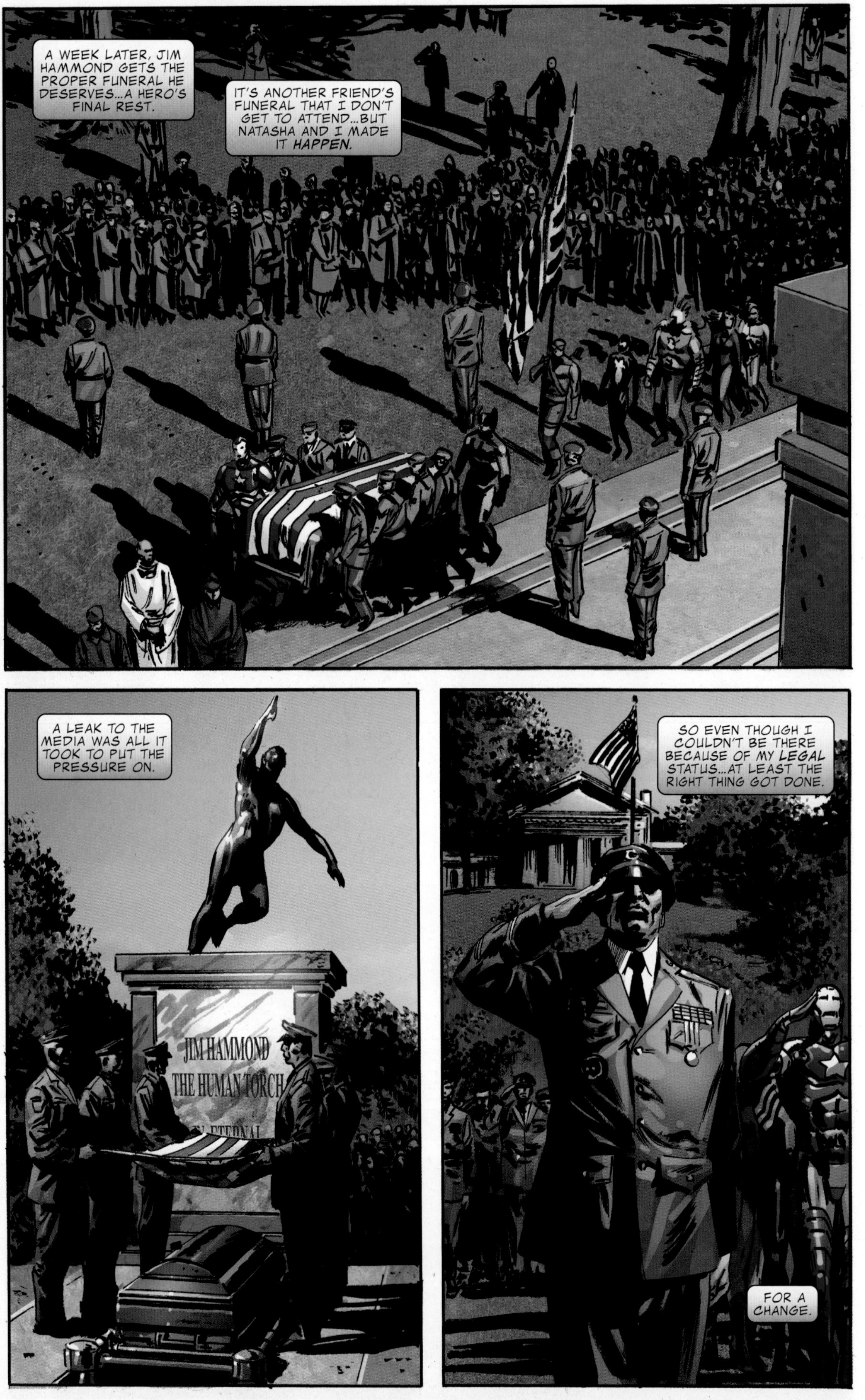
A WEEK LATER, JIM HAMMOND GETS THE PROPER FUNERAL HE DESERVES...A HERO'S FINAL REST.
IT'S ANOTHER FRIEND'S FUNERAL THAT I DON'T GET TO ATTEND...BUT NATASHA AND I MADE IT HAPPEN.
A LEAK TO THE MEDIA WAS ALL IT TOOK TO PUT THE PRESSURE ON.
JIM HAMMOND
THE HUMAN TORCH
SO EVEN THOUGH I COULDN'T BE THERE BECAUSE OF MY LEGAL STATUS...AT LEAST THE RIGHT THING GOT DONE.
FOR A CHANGE.

FUNNY HOW MUCH TIME I'VE SPENT IN GRAVEYARDS SINCE I GOT BACK TO THE WORLD...

I GUESS THAT'S WHAT IT'S LIKE WHEN MOST OF YOUR FRIENDS ARE OLD FRIENDS...

AND STANDING AMONG THE TOMBSTONES...

THE GRAVES OF SOLDIERS LIKE MY DAD...HEROES LIKE STEVE AND TORCH...AND SO MANY OTHERS...

I REALIZE I WASN'T TOTALLY TRUTHFUL WITH NATASHA...I DIDN'T JUST GO BACK TO FACE MY PAST...

I NEEDED, MORE THAN ANYTHING IN THE WORLD, TO SAVE SOMETHING FROM THE PAST...FOR A CHANGE.

REST IN PEACE, OLD SOLDIER.

JIM HAMMOND
- THE HUMAN TORCH -
IN ETERNAL MEMORY

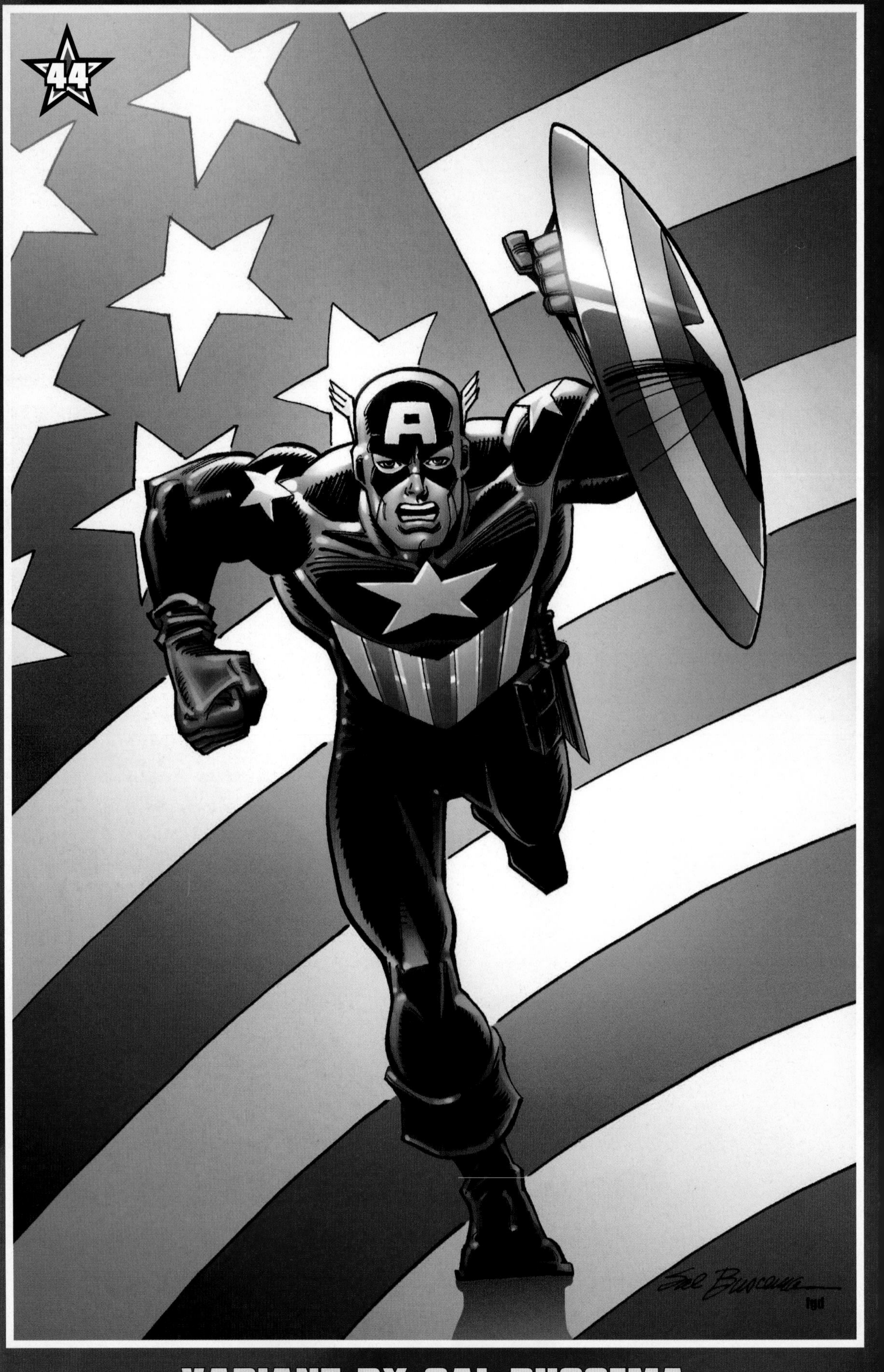
44
Sal Buscema

VARIANT BY SAL BUSCEMA

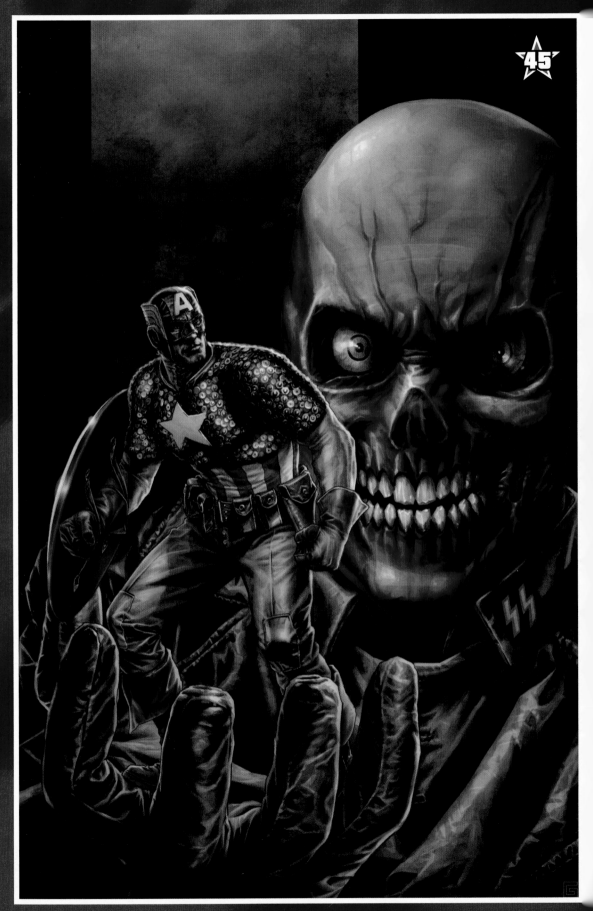

VILLAIN VARIANT BY LEE BERMEJO

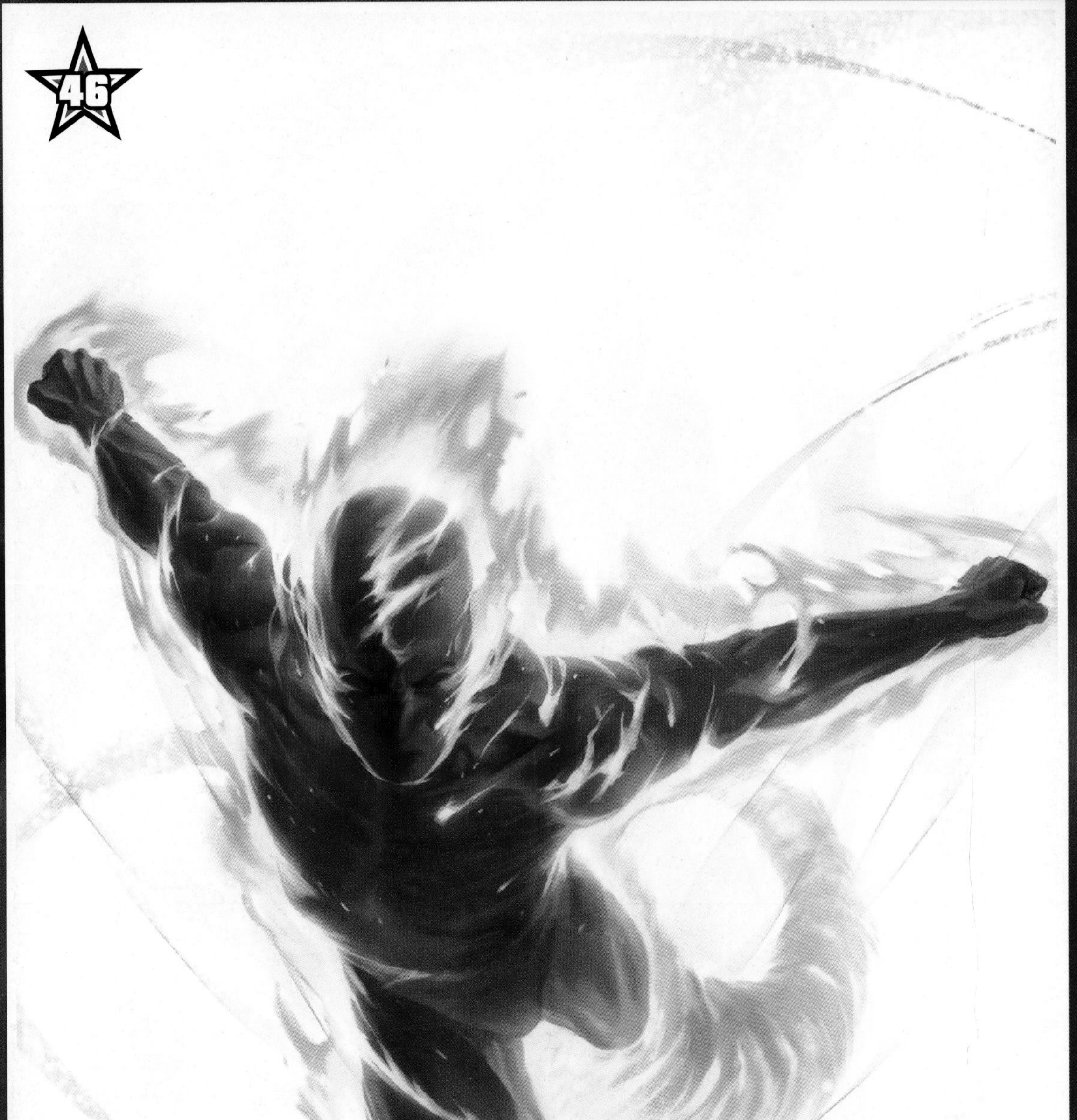
46
HUMAN TORCH
EST. 1939

70TH ANNIVERSARY VARIANT BY MARKO DJURDJEVIC